PRETRIAL STRATEGIES FOR SUCCESS

EDITED BY SAWNIE MCENTIRE

Cover design by Cory Ottenwess/ABA Publishing.

The materials contained herein represent the views of each chapter author in his or her individual capacity and should not be construed as the views of the author's firms, employers, or clients, or of the editors or other chapter authors, or of the American Bar Association or the Solo, Small Firm and General Practice Division, unless adopted pursuant to the bylaws of the Association.

Nothing contained in this book is to be considered as the rendering of legal advice for specific cases, and readers are responsible for obtaining such advice from their own legal counsel. This book is intended for educational and informational purposes only.

Printed in the United States of America

22 21 20 19 18   5 4 3 2 1

Library of Congress Cataloging-in-Publication Data

Names: McEntire, Sawnie A., editor.
Title: From the trenches III : pretrial strategies for success / edited by Sawnie A. McEntire.
Other titles: From the trenches three | From the trenches 3
Description: First edition. | Chicago : American Bar Association, 2018. | Includes index.
Identifiers: LCCN 2018038772 | ISBN 9781641052795 (print) | ISBN
   9781641052801 (epub)
Subjects: LCSH: Pre-trial procedure—United States. | Discovery (Law)—United States. |
   Depositions—United States. | Trial practice—United States.
Classification: LCC KF8900 .F76 2018 | DDC 347.73/72—dc23
LC record available at https://lccn.loc.gov/2018038772

Discounts are available for books ordered in bulk. Special consideration is given to state bars, CLE programs, and other bar-related organizations. Inquire at ABA Publishing, American Bar Association, 321 North Clark Street, Chicago, Illinois 60610-4714.

www.ShopABA.org

TABLE OF CONTENTS

Preface   ix

About the Authors   xi

Chapter 1   **Internal Investigations: Practical Considerations
for Avoiding Pitfalls**   1
W. Scott O'Connell

Overview   1

Threshold Issues   2

Establishing the Privilege: Upjohn *Warnings*   9

Ethical Requirements for Dealing with Witnesses   11

Protecting Notes of Witness Interviews   12

Recording Interviews and Creating Transcripts   12

Compelling Witness Participation   13

Witness Access to Counsel   14

Work Papers and Drafts of the Report   14

Circulation and Control of the Final Report of Investigation   14

Disclosure of Report of Investigation and Privilege Implications   15

Waiver of Privileges   15

Voluntary Waiver of Privilege to Earn Cooperation Credit   15

Joint Defense/Common Interest Agreements   17

Conclusion   17

Chapter 2   **Timing of Mediation: Pre-Litigation, Early Mediation,
or Late Mediation**   19
Andrew R. Kasnetz

Introduction   19

Mediating Pre-Suit   20

Early Mediation   21

	Early(ish) Mediation	22
	Mediating after Completion of Fact Discovery/Investigation	22
	Mediating after Expert Discovery	23
	Mediating Just Prior to Trial	23
	Epilogue	24
	In-House Counsel	24
	Opposing Counsel	24
	Phobias about Giving Away Too Much	25
	False Belief in Summary Judgment	25
	Conclusion	25

Chapter 3   **Picking the Right Place: Venue Selection and Jurisdictional Considerations**   **27**

Tom Waskom

	The Rules Prescribing Where You Can Litigate	27
	The Factors Affecting Where You Want to Litigate Your Case	32
	How Defendants Can Move Cases to Their Own Preferred Forum	37

Chapter 4   **Seeking and Preparing Litigation Holds**   **43**

Howard Merten, Paul M. Kessimian,
and Christopher M. Wildenhain

	Introduction	43
	Litigation Holds, Preservation Obligations, and the Consequences of Spoliation	44
	Preparing to Write a Litigation Hold	50
	Acquiring Information to Communicate, Effectuate, and Monitor the Hold: Who Needs to Preserve Documents and What Do They Need to Preserve?	54
	Writing the Litigation Hold	64
	Obligations after the Hold Goes Out	67
	Conclusion	69
	Appendix A	70

Chapter 5   **Discovery in the Modern Age: Conducting and**
                  Resisting E-Discovery   77

                  J. Michael Showalter

                  Planning, Consistency, and Transparency   78

                  Have Good Information Management Practices   79

                  Build a Plan   80

                  Find a Translator   84

                  Be Proactive, Not Reactive   85

                  Hope for a Good Judge   86

                  Special Points for "Resisting" Discovery   86

                  Conclusion   88

Chapter 6   **Expedited or Pre-Suit Discovery**   89

                  Laurence Kurth

                  Pre-Suit and Expedited Discovery for Litigation   89

                  Rule 27 of the Federal Rules of Civil Procedure   90

                  *Most States Allow Pre-Suit Discovery under State Rules
                  of Civil Procedure*   93

                  Informal Discovery   96

                  Conclusion   98

Chapter 7   **Initial Case Assessment: Preliminary Fact and**
                  Legal Evaluations   99

                  Michael D. Shalhoub and Jill Owens

                  The Initial Interview   101

                  What Next?   103

                  Work-up and Analysis   104

                  For the Plaintiff's Side   107

                  For the Defendant's Side   109

                  Conclusion   110

Chapter 8	**Discovery Themes: Keeping It Simple, but Effective**	**113**
	Sawnie A. McEntire	
	Effective Trial Themes	*113*
	Discovery Plans	*114*
	Every Deposition Is a Trial Deposition	*115*
	Keeping It Simple, Credible, Logical, and Appealing	*116*
	Simplifying Questions during Depositions	*117*
	Action Words: Verbs, Adjectives, and Adverbs	*118*
	Asking "Duty" and "No Lose" Questions	*119*
	Using Demonstrative Exhibits to Simplify Messages	*120*
Chapter 9	**Getting Organized: Preparing Timelines of Important Events and Documents**	**123**
	Robert L. Christie	
Chapter 10	**Motion for Summary Judgment: Strategies and Timing**	**129**
	James Miller	
	Summary Judgment: What It Is and What It Isn't	*130*
	Summary Judgment Standard	*131*
	The Trilogy	*134*
	To File or Not to File	*137*
	Timing	*138*
	Moving for Summary Judgment: Keep It Simple	*139*
	How Judges Decide Summary Judgment Motions	*141*
	Motion for Partial Summary Judgment and Orders Establishing Facts for the Case	*143*
	Opposing Summary Judgment: It's Not So Simple	*144*
	Should You Request a Hearing?	*145*
	Conclusion	*146*
	Appendix A	*147*
Chapter 11	**Shifting Risk with Offers**	**149**
	Alexandra W. Wahl	
	Federal Rules of Civil Procedure Rule 68	*150*

Requisites and Sufficiency of the Offer   151

Are Attorney's Fees Included in "Costs"?   153

Favorability of Offer Compared to the Judgment   154

Using Offers for Judgment Strategically   155

State Rules and Statutes   155

Time Limitations   156

Construction and Interpretation of Terms   157

Allowance and Determination of Attorney's Fees   157

Exemplary Analysis of Texas Rules of Civil Procedure 167   158

Conclusion   159

Chapter 12   Designing and Executing a Critical Witness Deposition   161
Raymond C. Lewis and John Jerry Glas

Demand Definitions from Lay and Expert Witnesses   163

Identify Every Assumption Made by an Expert Witness   167

Collect Factual Admissions from Lay Witnesses   168

Create a Chart Comparing the Qualifications of
Conflicting Experts   169

Think Before You Reveal or Impeach   171

Make Good Television   172

**Chapter 13   Making the Kitchen Hotter: Effective Use of Motions
to Compel   179**
David R. Pruet III

Setting the Table: Developing the Record   180

You Can Dish It Out, but Can You Take It?   185

From the Skillet into the Frying Pan: Creating Win/Win
Scenarios   186

Small Potatoes: Handling Failures to Respond   188

The Proof Is in the Pudding: Briefing and Arguing the Motion
to Compel   188

You Just Laid an Egg: Salvaging Victory from Defeat   191

Chapter 14   **Another Perspective: Jury Consultants, Focus Groups, and Mock Trials**   **193**

Sawnie A. McEntire

Focus Groups   195

Mock Trials   198

Interpreting the Results   198

Timing of Focus Group Studies or Mock Trials   199

Jury Questionnaires   200

Jury Selection   201

Shadow Jurors   202

Variations on a Theme   202

Caveats and Limitations   202

Chapter 15   **The Final Screenplay: Final Trial Preparations, Witness Selection, and Exhibits**   **205**

Lee M. Hollis

Legal Issues   205

Distill Your Case Themes   206

Trial Responsibilities   206

Motions in Limine   207

Prepare Your Opening Well in Advance   208

Voir Dire   208

Witness Selection and Preparation   210

Exhibit Selection   211

Demonstratives   212

Judgments as a Matter of Law   213

Closing   213

Preserving the Record   215

Index   **217**

PREFACE

It is a privilege to serve as the editor and one of several contributing authors for this volume of *From the Trenches*, titled *Pretrial Strategies for Success*. This volume follows two prior successful volumes published by the American Bar Association in 2015 and 2017. Embodied in this current volume are important and invaluable insights from experienced trial lawyers from across the country. Each author volunteered his or her time, skill, and experience in making *From the Trenches Volume 3* a reality.

The topics addressed in Volume 3 are wide ranging, but focus on strategies and techniques to enhance the chances for successful resolution of lawsuits and disputes. The topics begin with discussions of pre-suit tasks and options, including investigations, pre-suit mediation, and pre-suit discovery. The topics also include practice tips for enhancing case organization after the lawsuit is filed, effective advocacy, use of jury consultants, forum selection strategies, and important considerations for witness selection and final trial preparations.

As a result of the editing process, and having reviewed each chapter in this book, it is remarkable that there is a common thread that runs throughout the many diverse topics. It is clear that all of the authors place a premium on effective case management, early planning and preparation, and strategic and creative approaches to issues.

The contributing authors of *From the Trenches Volume 3* come from large, medium size, and small firms from across the country, including Massachusetts, New Hampshire, Missouri, Illinois, Virginia, Rhode Island, Texas, New York, Washington, Florida, Alabama, and Louisiana. Many of these authors contributed to past volumes of *From the Trenches*, and their credentials are well known. Many are leaders within their respective firms and bar organizations, and many enjoy national reputations and trial practices going far beyond their home states. Their collective trial experience is vast. Consistent with the goals of both Volume 1 and Volume 2, this current volume, *Pretrial Strategies for Success*, is prepared as a general reference tool for both beginning lawyers and seasoned trial veterans. As a group, we hope the practice tips and insights are well received.

Many of the contributing authors of this book are affiliated with either the Network of Trial Law Firms or the Federation of Defense & Corporate Counsel (FDCC)—both of which are equally distinguished organizations. I want to thank both organizations for providing me with an opportunity to meet such distinguished trial lawyers. I also want to thank each of the authors for their substantial efforts and insights reflected in this book.

Sawnie A. McEntire

ABOUT THE AUTHORS

Chapter 1: W. Scott O'Connell; Nixon Peabody, Boston & Manchester

W. Scott O'Connell is the chair of Nixon Peabody's Litigation Department and a member of the firm's Management Committee. He is a trial attorney who has appeared as lead counsel in 20 states. He focuses on class action and aggregate litigation, corporate control contests, and unfair and deceptive trade practices claims. He is currently representing financial services, health care, manufacturing, and energy companies in high-exposure disputes with associated significant reputational harm in parallel civil, criminal, and regulatory proceedings. Scott regularly performs internal investigations for clients. He is a former chair of the Network of Trial Law Firms. He earned his JD from the Cornell Law School, where he was an editor of the *Cornell Law Review* and the chancellor of the Moot Court Board. He received his BA from St. Lawrence University.

Chapter 2: Andrew Kasnetz; Sandberg Phoenix & von Gontard, P.C., St. Louis

Andrew R. Kasnetz is a shareholder in the law firm Sandberg Phoenix & von Gontard P.C., a firm with offices in St. Louis, Kansas City, and southern Illinois. He has been a trial lawyer for over 35 years and has significant trial and appellate experience in both state and federal courts. He has tried over 50 cases to conclusion and briefed and argued over 20 appeals. He litigates primarily complex commercial cases, including class actions. He is listed in *Best Lawyers of America* for commercial litigation. In addition to his trial and appellate work, he has completed comprehensive mediation training and has begun his practice in this area. He presently serves as General Counsel at Sandberg Phoenix.

Chapter 3: Thomas R. Waskom; Hunton Andrews Kurth, LLP, Richmond

As a partner in Hunton Andrews Kurth LLP's nationally recognized Retail and Consumer Products Litigation practice, **Thomas R. Waskom** has handled numerous complex matters, including class actions and mass torts. He works closely with his clients—leaders in the financial services, manufacturing, consumer products, and energy industries—to develop novel solutions to significant litigation challenges. His approach to litigation has earned him numerous accolades, including his selection as a "Rising Star" by Virginia *Super Lawyers* magazine for the last four years. Tom earned his JD from the University of Virginia School of Law, and he is admitted to practice throughout the United States, including before the U.S. Supreme Court; the U.S. Court of Appeals for the Third, Fourth, Sixth, Seventh, and Federal Circuits; and numerous state and U.S. district courts. Prior to joining Hunton Andrews Kurth he served as special assistant to the Secretary of Education of Virginia and acting assistant secretary of education for the commonwealth.

Chapter 4: Howard Merten, Paul M. Kessimian, Christopher M. Wildenhain; Partridge Snow & Hahn LLP, Providence

Howard Merten, Paul Kessimian, and Christopher Wildenhain are complex civil litigators in the Providence, Rhode Island, office of Partridge Snow & Hahn LLP. They each have significant experience working with clients to preserve potentially relevant evidence in anticipation of future litigation. They have witnessed the costly and time-consuming litigation detours caused by motions filed in an effort to seek discovery sanctions for spoliation of evidence.

Howard has been a trial lawyer for 34 years, and now also serves as the firm's managing partner. His practice focuses on commercial litigation, products liability, insurance, and intellectual property matters. Howard is a frequent speaker and writer on topics ranging from trial practice to insurance coverage, intellectual property, and legal ethics and professionalism. He is past president of Defense Counsel of Rhode Island and past board member of the Federation of Defense & Corporate Counsel. His achievements have earned him recognition by all the usual peer-reviewed rating entities, including *Best Lawyers in America*, lawyer of the year in Rhode Island for litigation, banking, and finance in 2017 and for litigation and intellectual property in 2016.

Paul is a partner and chair of the firm's Litigation Department. He represents clients at the trial and appellate levels, in cases involving intellectual property; insurance; and commercial, environmental, and real estate disputes. Paul is secretary of the Defense Counsel of Rhode Island, and on the Executive Committee of the Rhode Island chapter of the Federal Bar Association. He serves as co-chair of the Practice Point and E-Discovery Subcommittees of the American Bar Association's Committee on Business and Commercial Litigation. Paul writes and presents frequently on topics including discovery, pre-trial practice, and legal ethics. He has been recognized by *Best Lawyers in America*, *SuperLawyers*, and *Benchmark Litigation*.

Christopher is a senior litigation associate with the firm, and represents publicly traded companies and private businesses before state and federal courts and regulatory agencies in complex commercial, banking, and employment disputes. He plays a critical role in the firm's e-Discovery practice, and manages complicated discovery projects inherent to large litigations. Chris has been named a "Rising Star" by Rhode Island *SuperLawyers* for three years running. Prior to joining Partridge Snow & Hahn, Chris served as a law clerk to the Honorable Alice B. Gibney and the Honorable Sarah Taft-Carter of the Rhode Island Superior Court, and as an intern to the Honorable William P. Robinson III of the Rhode Island Supreme Court. Chris is a graduate of Brown University and Boston College Law School.

Chapter 5: J. Michael Showalter; Schiff Hardin LLP, Chicago

J. Michael Showalter is a member of Schiff Hardin LLP's litigation and environmental groups. Mike's practice focuses on dispute resolution in cases involving businesses, individuals, and the government. In the past year, Mike has represented clients in the manufacturing, energy, health care, and pharmaceutical industries in trial, appellate, and administrative litigation nationwide. Mike began his career as a law clerk for U.S. Magistrate (now District) Judge Michael F. Urbanski in the Western District of Virginia and U.S. District Judge David A. Faber in the Southern District of West Virginia. Mike is a graduate of Columbia University and Vanderbilt Law School.

Chapter 6: Laurence S. "Larry" Kurth; Akerman LLP, San Antonio

Laurence S. "Larry" Kurth, the managing partner at Akerman's San Antonio office, is a Texas board certified civil litigator with more than 36 years of experience. He is a seasoned commercial litigation defense lawyer. He has concentrated in first-party insurance litigation, with significant experience handling policy drafting, interpretation, fraud, arson, and coverage issues. His commercial litigation practice includes products liability, personal injury, property damage, contracts, and general business disputes. His clients include both multinational corporations and top 50 insurance companies. Larry graduated from St. Mary's University School of Law and received his BA from the College of Wooster. He has been listed in *The Best Lawyers in America* for commercial litigation, as a Texas Super Lawyer by *Thomson Reuters*, recognized as a *San Antonio Outstanding Lawyer* by the *San Antonio Business Journal*, and was voted one of San Antonio's best lawyers as rated by peers in *S.A. Scene.* He is licensed in Texas, Colorado, and Oklahoma.

Chapter 7: Mike Shalhoub and Jill C. Owens; Goldberg Segalla, LLP, New York City and White Plains

Michael Shalhoub is a proven trial lawyer and nationally recognized authority on product liability defense, medical device litigation, and trial technique. As co-chair of Goldberg Segalla's Life Sciences Practice Group, Mike counsels and defends numerous leaders of the medical device and pharmaceutical industries. His experience includes cases involving product liability as well as medical malpractice, business and commercial disputes, insurance coverage, construction accidents, and general liability. In over 30 years of practice, he has resolved more than 100 cases at the trial stage and achieved numerous defense verdicts. Mike is the former chair of the International Federation of Defense and Corporate Counsel's Product Liability Section and its Drug, Medical Device, and Biotechnology Section, and is also a past member of the board of directors of the Defense Research Institute and a past chair of DRI's Medical Liability and Health Care Law Committee. He has written and lectured for national audiences on emerging trends in drug and medical device litigation, *Daubert* preclusion of scientific expert testimony, and other topics, and is co-editor of *Life Science Matters*, Goldberg Segalla's blog covering the latest legal developments involving medical devices and pharmaceuticals.

Jill C. Owens is a partner and seasoned litigator in the New York City and White Plains offices of Goldberg Segalla, LLP. In her nearly three decades of practice, Jill has handled complex commercial litigation in federal and state courts nationwide. Jill specializes in the areas of class action defense, products liability and mass tort, FINRA arbitration, directors and officers liability, insurance coverage litigation, and defense of transportation clients. Jill has a range of clients, including Fortune 500 companies, small businesses, and individuals. Jill is a graduate of Dartmouth College and Harvard Law School. Following law school, Jill was law clerk to the Honorable Anne E. Thompson of the U.S. District Court for the District of New Jersey for two years.

Chapter 8 and Chapter 14: Sawnie A. McEntire; Parsons McEntire McCleary PLLC, Dallas

Sawnie A. McEntire is a founding shareholder in and director of the law firm of Parsons McEntire McCleary PLLC, a law firm with offices in Dallas and Houston, Texas, and he serves as the managing partner of the firm's Dallas office. He has been practicing trial law for over 36 years, and has substantial jury trial experience in both state and federal courts in Texas and throughout the country. He has served as regional, statewide, and national counsel for various clients. He is a frequent speaker and author. He specializes in products liability litigation and complex commercial tort litigation. Sawnie previously authored chapters in both Volume 1 and Volume 2 of *From the Trenches*. In 2016, the American Bar Association published his book, entitled *Mastering the Art of Depositions*. Sawnie was identified as a leading product liability lawyer in the United States in 2013 by *Law 360*. He graduated magna cum laude from Dartmouth College and Southern Methodist University School of Law.

Chapter 9: Bob Christie: Christie Law Group, PLLC, Seattle

Bob Christie is the founding principal of Christie Law Group, PLLC. A trial lawyer for over 37 years, Bob has tried nearly 100 cases throughout Washington state and the U.S. District Courts in Washington and Alaska, and argued appeals in all divisions of the Washington Court of Appeals, the Washington State Supreme Court, the Ninth Circuit Court of Appeals, the Federal Circuit Court of Appeals, and the

U.S. Supreme Court (on briefs). Bob is widely recognized as one of the foremost lawyers defending police officers and their agencies in civil rights cases in Washington. He also represents professionals, individuals, and companies in litigation ranging from malpractice, products liability, transportation liability, road design, premises liability, commercial litigation, employment, construction, and many other categories of civil disputes. He works extensively in cases involving death and serious injury, and is often called to serve as trial counsel in defense of significant claims. Working occasionally on behalf of catastrophically injured individuals and damaged business owners, Bob has also achieved several multi-million dollar verdicts and settlements.

Admitted to membership in the Federation of Defense & Corporate Counsel, Bob chaired the Substantive Law Section on Civil Rights and Public Entity Liability. He is now a senior director, and chairs the technology program called FDCC Evolve. Bob also served as co-chair of the Washington Pattern Instruction subcommittee charged with drafting civil rights instructions for use in Washington's superior courts.

Bob writes and lectures frequently on risk management issues, civil rights, governmental entity liability, and trial technology and presentation strategies. The Washington Defense Trial Lawyers (WDTL) just named Bob the Outstanding Defense Lawyer for 2017. He is a 1980 law graduate from the University of Puget Sound, cum laude, and began his career as a clerk for Judge Vernon Pearson in the Washington Court of Appeals. Bob is also licensed in Idaho and Oregon, and resides in Seattle.

Chapter 10: James M. Miller; Akerman LLP, Miami

James M. Miller, a partner at Akerman's Miami office, has been trying civil cases before juries since 1976. He has tried or arbitrated a wide variety of civil cases ranging from antitrust to zoning with intellectual property, trade secrets, products liability, general commercial, and catastrophic torts in between. Jim graduated from the University of Chicago Law School and received his BA, magna cum laude, from the University of Miami. He is currently listed in *Best Lawyers of America*, *Who's Who International: Litigation*, *Benchmark Litigation*, *Super Lawyers Magazine*, and Florida Trend's *Legal Elite*. Jim is a former managing partner of Akerman's Miami Office and former national chair of the firm's litigation department. He is a former chair of the Network of Trial Law Firms.

Chapter 11: Alexandra W. Wahl, Parsons McEntire McCleary PLLC, Dallas

Alexandra W. Wahl is an attorney with the law firm of Parsons McEntire McCleary PLLC, a law firm with offices in Dallas and Houston, Texas. She clerked for the Honorable Jane Boyle, U.S. District Court for the Northern District of Texas. She has substantial trial experience in civil litigation, particularly in probate and commercial disputes. She is also a member of the Texas Bar College.

Chapter 12: John Jerry Glas and Raymond C. Lewis; Deutsch Kerrigan, LLP, New Orleans

John Jerry Glas is the chair of Civil Litigation at the law firm of Deutsch, Kerrigan, LLP in New Orleans, Louisiana. He has tried more than 70 jury trials to verdict and has been enrolled pro hac vice in 11 states. Mr. Glas taught trial practice as an adjunct professor at Loyola University New Orleans College of Law and authored the chapter entitled "Feeding Lions During Closing Argument" in Volume 1 of the ABA's *From The Trenches* series.

Raymond Lewis is a partner at the law firm of Deutsch Kerrigan, LLP in New Orleans, Louisiana. Mr. Lewis is a civil litigator with experience in trial and appellate practice. Before joining the firm, Mr. Lewis served as law clerk for Louisiana state-court judges and attended law school at Louisiana State University, where he was a member of the *Louisiana Law Review*. Mr. Lewis recently co-authored with Mr. Glas the chapter entitled "Dancing with Antaeus: Twelve Unusual Questions to Ask Your Expert" in Volume 2 of the ABA's *From the Trenches* series.

Chapter 13: David R. Pruet III; Lightfoot, Franklin & White, LLC, Birmingham

David R. Pruet III is a partner at Lightfoot, Franklin & White LLC where he has accumulated nearly 20 years of front-line trial and courtroom experience across the Southeast. He prosecutes and defends complex commercial lawsuits in a wide range of industries, including health care, oil and gas, manufacturing, real estate, and banking, and has special expertise in shareholder rights, corporate and trustee fiduciary duties, trade secrets, and non-competition agreements. David is regularly recognized in the Alabama and Mid-South editions of *Super Lawyers*. David is a graduate of Davidson College and the University of Alabama School of Law, where he was a Hugo Black Scholar.

Chapter 15: Lee Hollis; Lightfoot, Franklin and White LLC, Birmingham

Lee Hollis is a partner and member of the Executive Committee of Lightfoot, Franklin and White, LLC in Birmingham, Alabama. Lee has been a trial lawyer for 26 years and represents Fortune 500 companies in high stakes, complex litigation. His practice is varied, consisting of product liability, catastrophic injury, class actions, mass torts, and commercial litigation. Lee was lead counsel at trial in a commercial case which resulted in a $70 million verdict for his client, the largest verdict in Alabama in 2012. Lee practices throughout the Southeast and the nation. Highlights of his practice include a defense verdict in a bus crash case in Mississippi that involved 15 deaths and 15 injuries and defeating class certification and winning summary judgment in an infectious disease case in Louisiana. He is regularly in *Super Lawyers*, *Best Lawyers*, and *Benchmark Litigation*. Lee is a graduate of Washington & Lee University and Vanderbilt Law School.

CHAPTER 1

Internal Investigations

Practical Considerations for Avoiding Pitfalls

W. Scott O'Connell[1]

OVERVIEW

Internal investigations are a necessary tool for entities to get to the root cause of institutional problems that may cause liability and reputational harm. These internal reviews, when handled correctly, can be valuable tools to identify and account for misconduct, to restore brand confidence, to help victims heal, to educate regulators on corrective action and to set the institution on a new path. When handled poorly, the investigation can cause more problems than it resolves.

Every investigation has its own context, parallel processes, and impacted constituencies. Those circumstances must inform and control the internal review process. There are, however, overarching considerations that can help shape the contours of an investigation and set it on a path for success. Detailed in the following sections are practical considerations designed to identify common "traps for the unwary" that can impair or derail the investigation. Careful and thoughtful preparation, together with consistent practices by all team members, can avoid failure. Attention to these issues can be the difference-maker for a successful process.

---

1. The author gratefully acknowledges the research assistance of Annica Bianco, Esq.

THRESHOLD ISSUES

Before undertaking the investigation, it is essential that the following questions be clearly established. Navigating through the many challenges, competing considerations, and interested constituencies that often surround investigations is greatly simplified when the following ground rules guide decision making.

Who Is Your Client?

This is a simple question that can get murky during the investigation. Public companies, private business entities, colleges and universities, churches, and other nonprofit organizations, such as health systems or charitable organizations, are run by individuals. Officers, directors, trustees, and special committees all perform important roles with associated duties in the governance and/or operation of the entity. Any of these constituencies in their respective roles may feel compelled to initiate an internal investigation in furtherance of some important institutional purpose. Any of these constituencies may make contact with outside counsel to get the process started. When such contact is made, the first questions must be: Who is the client? From whom do I take direction? To whom do I direct the report of investigation?

Too often in the private practice of law, it is expedient to conflate the interests, desires, and goals as expressed by a senior executive who is directing a project as being coextensive with the interests of the institution. This is not a surprising circumstance, because all entities operate through the actions of their leaders. Internal investigations bring into sharp focus the potential problems with such conflation. Because the investigation is focused on activities of personnel that may have diverged from the interests of the entity, it is essential that the client be identified and interests segregated, maintained, and pursued. Indeed, actions of individuals instrumental in commissioning the investigation may be part of the inquiry. The potential conflicts resulting from this dynamic are manifest and must be managed to ensure the integrity of the review.

For these reasons, the first action is to identify the client and the person or persons who are permitted to speak for the client with regard to the investigation. Often, because the internal inquiry may directly or implicitly criticize the actions of current management, good practice compels that the oversight of the investigation be vested with an outside director/trustee or a special committee of the board of directors/trustees. This practice helps ensure that the inquiry is not tainted by apparent or actual influence by those who are being investigated. Once defined, these details should be documented in an engagement letter specific to the inquiry.

What Is Your Mandate?

The mandate and scope of an investigation must be defined. Misalignment between the client's expectation and the work contemplated by the investigative team can lead to material problems. Some investigations can be discrete undertakings, yet, as a result of mismanaged expectations, balloon beyond reasonable scale and cost. Other investigations, such as those involving allegations of sexual abuse, may require special considerations for privacy and victim protection. Considerable damage can be caused when an investigation fails to properly balance important considerations such as protecting victims and attempting to get to the truth. The client must set the tone and the rules for what prevails when the search for the truth threatens other constituencies or threatens to cause harm to important cultural values. To paraphrase Hippocrates, on the way to doing something good, do no harm.

With the goal of doing no harm, it is helpful when the client articulates at the beginning of the engagement—as best as it can subject to learning more information as the investigation unfolds—what it wants investigated and what special considerations should prevail. This should include important information such as subject matter, time period, functional area, types of conduct, relevant individuals, documents, data, and other evidence. Also, the client may wish to detail things that should be excluded from investigation. With this information, the investigative team should build a work plan and budget to address the mandate and scope identified. This exercise should quickly reveal any disconnects between the client and the investigative team concerning the invasiveness, disruption, cost, and other collateral consequences resulting from the investigation. Further, the client should provide instructions on any special circumstance—such as the handling of victims—and how the investigation should yield to these important special circumstances. If the scope needs to be adjusted as the investigation proceeds, communicate that to the client and modify the work plan accordingly. In short—get aligned and stay aligned.

Who Are the Intended Recipients of the Report?

Is the report of investigation an internal confidential document not intended for disclosure and subject to privilege protections? Is the report intended for use with regulators, courts, customers, or the public? Is there a possibility of a criminal proceeding, and the attendant prospect of a waiver of the attorney-client and work-product privileges as a condition of a negotiated resolution?[2] All of these are relevant considerations for the logistics of the investigation.

As a practical matter, all investigations start as a privileged undertaking. Care must be taken to mark the report and all drafts with appropriate legends (e.g., "Confidential," "Attorney Client Privilege," "Attorney Work Product Prepared in Anticipation of Litigation"). If some form of disclosure is contemplated, or reasonably anticipated, it is essential that the investigative team not include in the report

---

2. *See infra* at "Voluntary Waiver of Privilege to Earn Cooperation Credit." *See also* "Individual Accountability for Corporate Wrongdoing," Sally Quillian Yates, Deputy Attorney General (Sept. 9, 2015) for further discussion of this issue.

any confidential or privileged information that must be protected, as there would likely be a reasonable argument for waiver in that circumstance.

Often the client simply does not know as the investigation unfolds how the report will be used. In such circumstances, it is a best practice to treat it and all drafts as confidential as well as to maintain all of the formalities of the applicable privileges. It is the client's privilege to waive. In certain circumstances, the client may determine that it needs to disclose the report or use it with regulators, courts, or others. In such situations, it is critical for counsel to determine the scope of the waiver under applicable law. Because the client's decision needs to be informed by the scope of the waiver, this determination ideally should be made early, before the report is drafted, to guide discussions about disclosure. For example, a "subject matter" waiver may expose the client to the disclosure of other privileged information beyond the report of investigation. Similarly, if less than a "subject matter" waiver is permissible in the relevant jurisdiction, a clear writing from the client concerning the scope of the waiver should accompany the disclosure. Finally, if the risk of subject matter waiver is significant, the client may consider appropriate redactions to preserve claims of privilege. Of note, and as discussed more fully later in the chapter, clients and counsel dealing with the government should not assume that a selective waiver will be upheld.

Is the Investigation Team Independent?

Not all internal investigations are the same. Some are prepared for use by third parties, such as regulators or courts, that will scrutinize whether the investigation was performed with sufficient safeguards of independence to bolster credibility and reliability. Where the review and acceptance by a third party is essential, the efficacy of the investigation is only as good as its independence. Even a brilliantly executed investigation may be worthless in the eyes of these third parties if serious questions arise about the team's independence. A critical threshold issue—and one that often needs to be re-examined during the life of the project—is whether the investigation team is sufficiently independent of the client and the issues being investigated.

The contemplated benefit of the investigation for use with third parties is to get an unvarnished report of what actually occurred, the actual or potential consequences, and the suggested remedial or mitigating actions. Investigators acting out of a real or perceived conflict may diminish or erode the impact of the report. Recipients of the report who believe that its conclusions and recommendations were improperly influenced by those who might be impacted by the report may dismiss it out of hand. This is particularly problematic if the intended recipients of the report are regulators, courts, or other constituencies who may question the integrity of the report.

An ongoing business relationship with the client, work performed or advice given concerning the subject being investigated, or a previous reporting relationship to someone at the client who is being investigated, are common examples of circumstances that can undermine a claim of independence. In such a situation, the perception of a conflict may be as damaging as an actual conflict. When such circumstances exist, or arise during the project, the investigation team must examine whether it can perform the independent investigation.

Who Has the Ability to Edit the Report?

Determining who will have the right to review and propose edits before the report of investigation is finalized is another important matter to consider. This is very closely related to the questions defining who the client is and how the independence of the investigation can be assured. While there can be material benefits to having various constituencies (such as directors, trustees, and officers) reviewing the report for accuracy, completeness, and consistency with corporate values and norms, such further review may compromise the independence of the report and, therefore, its efficacy with the target audience. Depending on the scope of the investigation and the circumstances under which it arose, it may be necessary and prudent to restrict review and editing of the final report to a small group of decision makers for the client. For example, if an entity is performing a new investigation because a prior one was viewed as being manipulated by the board of directors or management, to avoid the same pitfalls, the new investigators should run a process that insulates the report from such repeated criticism.

Best practices require that those whose conduct is implicated—including the direct actors as well as officers, directors, trustees, consultants, or lawyers who may have been on watch at the time of the offending conduct—should not be part of the review and finalization process except to confirm facts. Similarly, best practices suggest that those who have a direct or material stake in the report because they were victims or whistleblowers should be managed carefully through the review and finalization process. The investigation team may believe it necessary or advisable to have victims or whistleblowers review portions of the final report to ensure accuracy or that privacy has been protected, but input from those parties into the conclusions or recommendations can be problematic and impugn the independence of the report. Tread carefully into these turbulent areas, and identify clear boundaries as to what is permissible and what is not.

Will the Investigation Require Special Procedures?

Investigations often require interviewing victims of improper conduct or whistleblowers who purport to be witnesses to unlawful or improper conduct. Both categories present unique issues for the client's consideration.

With regard to victims of improper conduct—such as sexual assault—the client may want the investigation team to take special precautions during the interview process and in the final report and work papers. For example, private schools that have reported the results of investigations about past sexual assaults by faculty members and administrators have been accused, after the fact, of being insensitive to the privacy concerns of victims and to the additional harm to the victims caused by the report of investigation. To avoid such criticisms, the use of pseudonyms to anonymize victims is a well-developed convention to protect privacy, yet also report the information learned during the investigation. Unfortunately, it is not always possible to fully protect a victim by simply using a pseudonym. Other facts revealed may allow certain readers to deduce the identity of the victim(s). In such circumstances, the rehabilitation and goodwill expected from the investigative report can be diminished or overshadowed by the revictimization of those originally harmed. Forethought, planning, and clear direction from the client should help avoid such a circumstance.

Will the Investigation Involve "Whistleblowers"?

Similarly, whistleblowers—individuals who disclose suspicions of unlawful, unethical, or prohibited corporate conduct—present special circumstances in an internal investigation. Special handling is essential in light of the protections that a whistleblower may have. A patchwork of federal[3] and state[4] laws provide protections to

---

3. Federal statutes with whistleblower provisions include Affordable Care Act (ACA) § 1558, 29 U.S.C. § 218C; Asbestos Hazard Emergency Response Act (AHERA), 15 U.S.C. § 2651; Clean Air Act (CAA), 42 U.S.C. § 7622; Comprehensive Environmental Response, Compensation and Liability Act (CERCLA), 42 U.S.C. § 9610; Consumer Financial Protection Act of 2010 (CFPA), § 1057 of the Dodd-Frank Wall Street Reform and Consumer Protection Act of 2010, 12 U.S.C.A. § 5567; Consumer Product Safety Improvement Act (CPSIA), 15 U.S.C. § 2087; Energy Reorganization Act (ERA), 42 U.S.C. § 5851; FDA Food Safety Modernization Act (FSMA), § 402, 21 U.S.C. 399d; Federal Railroad Safety Act (FRSA), 49 U.S.C. § 20109; Federal Water Pollution Control Act (FWPCA), 33 U.S.C. § 1367; International Safe Container Act (ISCA), 46 U.S.C. § 80507; Moving Ahead for Progress in the 21st Century Act (MAP-21), 49 U.S.C. § 30171; National Transit Systems Security Act (NTSSA), 6 U.S.C. § 1142; Occupational Safety and Health Act (OSH Act), § 11(c), 29 U.S.C. § 660; Pipeline Safety Improvement Act (PSIA), 49 U.S.C. § 60129; Safe Drinking Water Act (SDWA), 42 U.S.C. § 300j-9(i); Sarbanes-Oxley Act (SOX), 18 U.S.C.A. § 1514A; Seaman's Protection Act (SPA), as amended by § 611 of the Coast Guard Authorization Act of 2010, Pub. L. No. 111-281, 46 U.S.C. § 2114; Solid Waste Disposal Act (SWDA), 42 U.S.C. § 6971; Surface Transportation Assistance Act (STAA), 49 U.S.C. § 31105; Toxic Substances Control Act (TSCA), 15 U.S.C. § 2622; Wendell H. Ford Aviation Investment and Reform Act for the 21st Century (AIR21), 49 U.S.C. § 42121.

4. *See generally Whistleblower Statutes, in* 50 STATE STATUTORY SURVEYS: EMPLOYMENT: EMPLOYEE PROTECTION (Richard A. Leiter ed., 7th ed. 2015), which contains the following compendium of state statutes: *Alabama:* ALA. CODE § 25-5-11.1 (1975), ALA. CODE § 25-8-57 (1975), ALA. CODE § 36-26A-1 (1975); *Alaska:* ALASKA STAT. ANN. § 39.90.100 (West, Westlaw through 2017 Legis. Sess.), ALASKA STAT. ANN. § 18.60.088 (West, Westlaw through 2017 Legis. Sess.), ALASKA STAT. ANN. § 18.60.089 (West, Westlaw through 2017 Legis. Sess.), ALASKA STAT. ANN. § 18.60.095 (West, Westlaw through 2017 Legis. Sess.); *Arizona:* ARIZ. REV. STAT. ANN. § 38-531 (2011), ARIZ. REV. STAT. ANN. § 23-425 (West, Westlaw through 2017 Legis. Sess.), ARIZ. REV. STAT. ANN. § 23-418 (West, Westlaw through 2017 Legis. Sess.); *Arkansas:* ARK. CODE ANN. § 16-123-107 (West, Westlaw through 2017 Legis. Sess.), ARK. CODE ANN. § 16-123-108 (West, Westlaw through 2017 Legis. Sess.); *California:* CAL. LAB. CODE § 1102.5 (West 2016); *Colorado:* COLO. REV. STAT. ANN. § 24-50.5-101 (West 2016), COLO. REV. STAT. ANN. § 24-114-101 (West, Westlaw through 2017 Legis. Sess.); *Connecticut,* CONN. GEN. STAT. ANN. § 4-61dd (West 2015), CONN. GEN. STAT. ANN. § 31-51m (West 2014); *Delaware:* DEL. CODE ANN. tit. 29, § 5115 (West, Westlaw through 2017 Legis. Sess.), DEL. CODE ANN. tit. 19, § 1701 (West, Westlaw through 2017 Legis. Sess.); *District of Columbia:* D.C. CODE § 1-615.51 (West, Westlaw through 2017 Legis. Sess.); *Florida:* FLA. STAT. ANN § 112.3187 (West 2002);

bona fide whistleblowers. While there are clear differences between and among these statutes, one common principle is there can be no retaliation against whistleblowers for disclosing offending conduct. Investigators must be knowledgeable

---

Georgia: GA. CODE ANN. § 45-1-4 (West 2012); *Hawaii:* HAW. REV. STAT. § 378-61 (West, Westlaw through 2017 Act 34); *Idaho:* IDAHO CODE ANN. § 6-2101 (West, Westlaw through 64th Reg. Sess.); *Illinois:* 740 ILL. COMP. STAT. 174/10 (2004), 20 ILL. COMP. STAT. 415/19c.1 (West, Westlaw through 2017 Reg. Sess.); *Indiana:* IND. CODE ANN. § 4-15-10-4 (West 2012), IND. CODE ANN. § 36-1-8-8 (West, Westlaw through 2017 Reg. Sess.), IND. CODE ANN. § 22-5-3-3 (West 2016); *Iowa:* IOWA CODE ANN. § 70A.28 (West 2013), IOWA CODE ANN. § 70A.29 (West, Westlaw through 2017 Reg. Sess.); *Kansas:* KAN. STAT. ANN. § 75-2973 (West, Westlaw through 2017 Reg. Sess.); *Kentucky:* KY. REV. STAT. ANN. § 61.101 (West, Westlaw through 2017 Reg. Sess.), KY. REV. STAT. ANN. § 338.121 (West 2010), KY. REV. STAT. ANN. § 338.991 (West 2010); *Louisiana:* LA. REV. STAT. ANN. § 30:2027 (West, Westlaw through 2017 First Extra. Sess.), LA. REV. STAT. ANN. § 42:1169 (2014); *Maine:* ME. REV. STAT. ANN. tit. 26 § 831 (West, Westlaw through 2017 Reg. Sess.); *Maryland:* MD. CODE. ANN., STATE PERS. & PENS. § 5-301 (West, Westlaw through 2017 Reg. Sess.), MD. CODE ANN., STATE FIN. & PROC. § 11-301 (West, Westlaw through 2017 Reg. Sess.); *Massachusetts:* MASS. GEN. LAWS ANN. ch. 149, § 185 (West, Westlaw through 2017 Ann. Sess.); *Michigan:* MICH. COMP. LAWS. ANN. § 15.361 (West, Westlaw through 2017 Reg. Sess.); *Minnesota:* MINN. STAT. ANN. § 181.931 (West 2013); *Mississippi:* MISS. CODE ANN. § 25-9-171 (West, Westlaw through 2017 Reg. Sess.); *Missouri:* MO. ANN. STAT. § 105.055 (West 2010), MO. ANN. STAT. § 287.780 (West 2010); *Montana:* MONT. CODE ANN. § 39-2-901 (West, Westlaw through Sept. 2016 amendments); *Nebraska:* NEB. REV. STAT. ANN. § 81-2701 (West, Westlaw through 2017 Reg. Sess.), NEB. REV. STAT. ANN. § 48-1114 (West, Westlaw through 2017 Reg. Sess.); *Nevada:* NEV. REV. STAT. ANN. § 281.611 (West, Westlaw through 2017 Reg. Sess.), NEV. REV. STAT. ANN. § 618.445 (West, 2013); *New Hampshire:* N.H. REV. STAT. ANN. § 98-E:1 (2008), N.H. REV. STAT. ANN. § 275-E:1 (2012); *New Jersey:* N.J. STAT. ANN. § 34:19-1 (West, Westlaw through 2017 Legis. Sess.); *New Mexico:* N.M. STAT. ANN. § 50-9-25 (West, Westlaw through 2017 Legis. Sess.); *New York:* N.Y. LAB. LAW § 740 (McKinney 2006), N.Y. CIV. SERV. § 75-b (McKinney 2015); *North Carolina:* N.C. GEN. STAT. ANN. § 126-84 (West, Westlaw through 2017 Reg. Sess.), N.C. GEN. STAT. ANN. § 95-240 (West, Westlaw through 2017 Reg. Sess.); *North Dakota,* N.D. CENT. CODE ANN. § 34-11.1-04 (West, Westlaw through 2017 Reg. Sess.), N.D. CENT. CODE ANN. § 34-11.1-07 (West, Westlaw through 2017 Reg. Sess.), N.D. CENT. CODE ANN. § 34-11.1-08 (West, Westlaw through 2017 Reg. Sess.); *Ohio:* OHIO REV. CODE ANN. § 4113.52 (West, Westlaw through 2017 Reg. Sess.), OHIO REV. CODE ANN. § 124.341 (West 2013); *Oklahoma:* OKLA. STAT. ANN. tit. 74, § 840-2.5 (West, Westlaw through 2017 Reg. Sess.), OKLA. STAT. ANN. tit. 40 § 417 (West, Westlaw through 2017 Reg. Sess.); *Oregon:* OR. REV. STAT. ANN. § 659A.200 (West, Westlaw through 2017 Reg. Sess.), OR. REV. STAT. ANN. § 654.062 (West, Westlaw through 2017 Reg. Sess.), OR. REV. STAT. ANN. § 659A.199 (West, Westlaw through 2017 Reg. Sess.); *Pennsylvania:* 43 PA. CONS. STAT. § 1421 (West, Westlaw through 2017 Reg. Sess.); *Rhode Island:* R.I. GEN. LAWS ANN. § 28-50-1 (West, Westlaw through 2017 Reg. Sess.); *South Carolina:* S.C. CODE ANN. § 8-27-10 (2015), S.C. CODE ANN. § 41-15-510 (West, Westlaw through 2017 Act No. 36), S.C. CODE ANN. § 41-15-520 (2012); *South Dakota:* S.D. CODIFIED LAWS § 20-13-26 (West, Westlaw through 2017 Reg. Sess.), S.D. CODIFIED LAWS § 60-11-17.1 (West, Westlaw through 2017 Reg. Sess.), S.D. CODIFIED LAWS § 60-12-21 (West, Westlaw through 2017 Reg. Sess.); *Tennessee:* TENN. CODE ANN. § 50-1-304 (West 2014), TENN. CODE ANN. § 50-3-106 (West 2008), TENN. CODE ANN. § 50-3-409 (West 2008), TENN. CODE ANN. § 8-50-116 (West, Westlaw through 2017 Reg. Sess.); *Texas:* TEX. GOV'T CODE ANN. § 554.001 (West, Westlaw through 2017 Reg. Sess.), TEX. LAB. CODE ANN. § 21.055 (West, Westlaw through 2017 Reg. Sess.); *Utah:* UTAH CODE ANN. § 67-21-1 (West, Westlaw through 2017 Gen. Sess.); *Vermont:* VT. STAT. ANN. tit. 21, § 231 (West, Westlaw through 2017–2018 Vt. Gen. Assembly), VT. STAT. ANN. tit. 3, § 973 (West, Westlaw through 2017–2018 Vt. Gen. Assembly); *Virginia:* VA. CODE ANN. § 40.1-51.2:1 (West, Westlaw through 2017 Reg. Sess.), VA. CODE ANN. § 40.1-51.2:2 (West, Westlaw through 2017 Reg. Sess.); *Washington:* WASH. REV. CODE ANN. § 42.40.010 (West, Westlaw through 2017 Reg. Sess.), WASH. REV. CODE ANN. § 49.60.210 (West 2011); *West Virginia:* W. VA. CODE ANN. § 6C-1-1 (West, Westlaw through 2017 Reg. Sess.), W. VA. CODE ANN. § 21-3A-13 (West, Westlaw through 2017 Reg. Sess.); *Wisconsin:* WIS. STAT. ANN. § 230.80 (West 2015); *Wyoming:* WYO. STAT. ANN. § 27-11-109(e) (West, Westlaw through 2017 Gen. Sess.), WYO. STAT. ANN. § 9-11-103 (West, Westlaw through 2017 Gen. Sess.).

about these protections and conduct the investigation in ways that do not erode or impair these protections.

It is common during an investigation to learn that there are independent bases to take a job action against the whistleblower, unrelated to his or her disclosures. In some circumstances, the whistleblower's disclosures are nothing more than a cynical attempt to thwart an impending job action. In other circumstances, the whistleblower participated or contributed to the offending activity being investigated. Because of these complicating dynamics, the whistleblower often will have retained counsel who wants to participate in any interview with her/his whistleblower-client.[5] The protections afforded whistleblowers make it more challenging, but not impossible, to get to the truth of the allegations and for the investigators to make appropriate remedial action recommendations, including termination of the whistleblower, if the protections have not been appropriately implicated.[6] All of these issues require careful management and particular attention to the governing law.

---

5. On the duty to cooperate, see Merkel v. Scovill, Inc., 787 F.2d 174, 179 (6th Cir. 1986) (reversing a finding by the district court that the plaintiff's nonparticipation in the investigation was "protected activity," holding that "discrimination against an employee for lack of participation or nonparticipation in an investigation would not be a violation of the ADEA"); Thomas v. Norbar, Inc., 822 F.2d 1089 (holding that since there was no evidence that plaintiff's supervisors had pressured him to lie or give information regarding matters about which he had no knowledge, his refusal to participate in the investigation was not protected activity); City of Hollywood v. Witt, 939 So. 2d 315, 317 (Fla. Dist. Ct. App. 2006) (holding that the verdict on the whistleblower claim could not stand because "the existence of reasons for termination, apart from any alleged whistleblowing, constitutes a defense that is expressly recognized by the whistle-blower act"). On no right to counsel, see In re Carroll, 339 N.J. Super. 429, 440, 772 A.2d 45, 52 (App. Div. 2001) (holding that "the Sixth Amendment right to counsel does not extend to internal investigations"); Williams v. Pima Cnty., 791 P.2d 1053 (Ct. App. 1989) (holding that the right to counsel under the Sixth Amendment applied only to criminal proceedings, and did not confer right to counsel upon an officer being interrogated by sheriff's department during internal affairs investigation).

6. On whistleblower protections, see Somers v. Digital Realty Trust Inc., 850 F.3d 1045, 1048 (9th Cir. 2017) (citing 15 U.S.C.A. § 78u-6) ("No employer may discharge, demote, suspend, threaten, harass, directly or indirectly, or in any other manner discriminate against, a whistleblower in the terms and conditions of employment because of any lawful act done by the whistleblower—(i) in providing information to the Commission in accordance with this section; (ii) in initiating, testifying in, or assisting in any investigation or judicial or administrative action of the Commission based upon or related to such information; or (iii) in making disclosures that are required or protected under the Sarbanes-Oxley Act of 2002 (15 U.S.C. 7201 et seq.), this chapter, including section 78j-1(m) of this title, section 1513(e) of Title 18, and any other law, rule, or regulation subject to the jurisdiction of the Commission."); Grisham v. United States, 103 F.3d 24, 26 (5th Cir. 1997). See 5 U.S.C. § 2302(b)(8) ("The Whistleblower Protection Act was enacted in 1989 to increase protections for whistleblowers by prohibiting adverse employment actions taken because a federal employee discloses information that the employee reasonably believes evidences a violation of any law or actions that pose a substantial and specific danger to public health or safety"). On requirements for a whistleblower protection claim, see Willis v. Dep't of Agric., 141 F.3d 1139, 1144 (Fed. Cir. 1998) (regardless of whether the adverse personnel action is taken in retaliation for a protected disclosure, or is a result of the disclosure, the whistleblower need only demonstrate that the protected disclosure was one of the factors that affected the personnel action); Hickson v. Vescom Corp., 2014 ME 27, ¶ 17, 87 A.3d 704 ("To prevail on a [WPA] claim, an employee must show that (1) he engaged in activity protected by the WPA; (2) he experienced an adverse employment action; and (3) a causal connection existed between the protected activity and the adverse employment action."); see also Galouch v. Dep't of Prof'l & Fin. Regulation, 2015 ME 44, ¶ 12, 114 A.3d 988, 992; see also Miller v. City of Millville, 2014 WL 10122644, at 6 (N.J. Super. L.) ("In order to establish a prima facie case of retaliation under CEPA, the plaintiff must demonstrate the following elements: 1. he reasonably believed illegal conduct was occurring; 2. he disclosed or threatened to disclose the activity

While the whistleblower has certain rights, the investigation team has a mandate that must be fulfilled. When confronted with these dynamics, it is important to understand the governing law and whether the whistleblower protections have been validly implicated, to disaggregate and isolate the issues investigated into those that may receive protection and those that do not, and to make specific recommendations to the client regarding these different buckets of protected and unprotected conduct.

ESTABLISHING THE PRIVILEGE: *UPJOHN* WARNINGS

The ability of an entity to conduct and preserve as privileged an internal investigation rests on certain requirements recognized by the U.S. Supreme Court in *Upjohn Co. v. United States.*[7] The Court recognized an organization's attorney-client privilege when: (1) the communication was made by an entity's employee, (2) to counsel for the entity acting as such, (3) at the direction of corporate superiors, (4) in order to secure legal advice from counsel, (5) concerning matters within the scope of the employee's duties and (6) the employee was aware that the purpose of the questioning was so that the entity could obtain legal advice.[8]

From these principles have sprung standard warnings for witness interviews, called *Upjohn* warnings or sometimes "corporate *Miranda* warnings," designed to ensure that the elements of the attorney-client privilege are established for the benefit of the corporation, not the individual witness. The essential information that the entity's counsel must convey includes instructing the witness that (1) the attorney represents the entity alone and not the individual (unless a joint representation is expressly contemplated, in which case such representation should be carefully delineated); (2) the attorney is investigating facts for the purpose of providing legal advice to the entity; (3) the communication is protected by the attorney-client privilege, and that the privilege belongs to the entity alone, and not to the witness (unless a joint representation is expressly contemplated, which, again, should be carefully considered and delineated); (4) the entity may choose to waive the privilege and disclose the substance of the communication to third parties, including the government; and (5) the communication is confidential and must be kept that way by the witness and not disclosed to third parties except

---

to a supervisor or public body; 3. retaliatory employment action was taken against him; and 4. a causal connection exists between the whistleblowing and the adverse employment action."); Hubbard v. United Press Int'l, Inc., 330 N.W.2d 428, 444 (Minn. 1983).

7. Upjohn Co. v. United States, 449 U.S. 383 (1981). In an earlier case, *Hickman v. Taylor*, 329 U.S. 495 (1947), the Supreme Court recognized and defined the contours of the attorney work-product doctrine, which protects against disclosure of work product prepared by or for counsel in anticipation of litigation.

8. 449 U.S. 383 at 390–91. *Upjohn* articulates the protections available under federal law. While many states have adopted the principles of *Upjohn*, others have not. The investigation team must consult the potentially applicable state law on this privilege issue and conduct the interviews accordingly.

counsel.[9] Care should be taken to make sure that the investigation and the associated privilege belongs to the entity.[10]

Regarding confidentiality, which is distinct from privilege, counsel should be aware of limitations applicable to witness interactions. Counsel can ask a witness to keep an interview discussion confidential, and can explain the purpose and importance of doing so (including preservation of the privilege), but cannot instruct the witness that he or she is forbidden from discussing the matter, especially concerning any communications or potential communications with the government. Nor will written confidentiality agreements be enforceable if they unreasonably restrict the employee's ability to report information to the government. Such restrictions beyond the protection of privilege could be viewed as an effort to obstruct justice.

While an internal investigation can be undertaken for many different purposes, the availability of the privilege turns on the purpose. Many courts apply a "primary purpose test" to determine if the primary purpose of the investigation was to provide legal advice or to prepare for litigation. If so, the attorney-client privilege and work product doctrine protect attorney notes, memoranda, and other materials generated during the investigation.[11] If the primary purpose of the investigation was not to seek legal advice or prepare for potential litigation, however, the privilege and the work product doctrine may not apply.

Practitioners differ on whether *Upjohn* warnings should be provided verbally or in writing and, if in writing, whether the witness should sign an acknowledgment. Some fear that overly formal warnings will chill candor from the witness. Others contend that verbal warnings present proof problems if later challenged. This is a judgment call that must be made in each situation. At a minimum, counsel who elect to forgo the written acknowledgment should document in the memoranda and notes summarizing the interview that the witness received the warnings and confirmed his or her understanding. Privilege challenges from individuals who

---

9. Courts are split on the issue of whether the *Upjohn* privilege extends to former employees. A number of courts have held that *Upjohn* applies to communications with former employees so long as the communication relates to the former employee's conduct and knowledge gained during employment. *See, e.g.*, Export-Import Bank of the U.S. v. Asia Pulp & Paper Co., 232 F.R.D. 103, 112 (S.D.N.Y. 2005); Peralta v. Cendant Corp., 190 F.R.D. 38, 41–42 (D. Conn. 1999); *see also In re* Allen, 106 F.3d 582, 605–06 (4th Cir. 1997) (holding *Upjohn* applies with equal force to former employees). However, not all courts have agreed. *See, e.g.*, Clark Equip. Co. v. Lift Parts Mfg. Co., No. 82 C 4585, 1985 U.S. Dist. LEXIS 15457, 1985 WL 2917, at *5 (N.D. Ill. Oct. 1, 1985) (holding former employees are not the "client," and that "post-employment communications with former employees are not within the scope of the attorney-client privilege"), Newman v. Highland Sch. Dist. No. 203, 381 P.3d 1188 (Wash. 2016).

10. Individual claims of ownership of a corporate privilege are often analyzed under the so-called *Bevill* factors, which include (1) the employee sought legal advice from the company's counsel; (2) in an individual rather than a representative capacity; (3) the attorney, aware of the potential conflict of interest, gave the advice sought; (4) the conversation was confidential; and (5) the substance of the conversation did not involve corporate matters. *In re* Bevill, Bresler & Schulman Asset Mgmt. Corp., 805 F.2d 120, 125 (3d Cir. 1986). Tailoring *Upjohn* warnings to ensure that the witness cannot establish the *Bevill* factors may be appropriate in certain situations.

11. *See In re* Kellogg Brown & Root Inc., 756 F.3d 754 (D.C. Cir. 2014) and *In re* GM LLC Ignition Switch Litig., 80 F. Supp. 3d 521 (S.D.N.Y. 2015).

have close working associations with outside counsel are a common occurrence. In such situations, the individual often associates the outside counsel as representing her/his interests because in past circumstances there has been complete alignment between the individual and the entity. This can lead to confusion on the part of the individual that, if viewed by a court as reasonable, can put the privilege at risk. Where such a situation exists, thought should be given as to whether there is utility and net benefit for written warnings and a signed acknowledgment.

Where joint representation is contemplated, a conflict may arise between the entity and the individual regarding the waiver of the attorney-client privilege. This issue should be addressed in an engagement letter providing the entity with the sole authority to waive the privilege. If the individual is not comfortable with such a delegation, the ability to undertake a joint representation should be revisited.

ETHICAL REQUIREMENTS FOR DEALING WITH WITNESSES

Two important ethical rules govern the investigator's conduct with regard to witnesses. Model Rule of Professional Conduct 1.13(f) details what a lawyer needs to do when dealing with an entity's directors, officers, employees, members, shareholders, and other constituencies that have interests adverse to the client.[12] Specifically, in this situation, further care is required for counsel to state that he or she represents the entity alone. This elevates one of the important aspects of *Upjohn* warnings to the level of an ethical violation if omitted.

Model Rule 4.3 details what an attorney must do when dealing on behalf of a client with any person, including a witness who is not represented.[13] These are particularly tricky situations because the witness often has legitimate questions about the purpose of the investigation and whether it creates jeopardy for the witness, which can risk confusion about the attorney's role vis-à-vis the individual. The investigating team needs to be careful not to provide legal advice to the witness.

---

12. Rule 1.13(f), Organization as Client, states:
    In dealing with an organization's directors, officers, employees, members, shareholders or other constituents, a lawyer shall explain the identity of the client when the lawyer knows or reasonably should know that the organization's interests are adverse to those of the constituents with whom the lawyer is dealing.
13. Rule 4.3, Dealing with Unrepresented Person, states:
    In dealing on behalf of a client with a person who is not represented by counsel, a lawyer shall not state or imply that the lawyer is disinterested. When the lawyer knows or reasonably should know that the unrepresented person misunderstands the lawyer's role in the matter, the lawyer shall make reasonable efforts to correct the misunderstanding. The lawyer shall not give legal advice to an unrepresented person, other than the advice to secure counsel, if the lawyer knows or reasonably should know that the interests of such a person are or have a reasonable possibility of being in conflict with the interests of the client.

For example, if the witness asks if he or she needs representation, the investigator should not answer this question with anything other than "I cannot advise you on that question as I represent the entity and not you." It also may be appropriate to remind witnesses of their ability to consult with their own legal counsel. It is also important to communicate with the client, upfront and later as needed, regarding whether there are any witnesses for whom the client wants to provide individual counsel. Clients can pay for the costs of an employee's counsel if they so choose (or if a relevant policy, such as a director and officer liability policy, requires indemnification). Paying for counsel does not give the client any ability to direct the representation or the employee's decisions, however.[14]

PROTECTING NOTES OF WITNESS INTERVIEWS

The mental impressions, strategy, and analysis of any attorney formulated during an interview of a witness are generally protected from disclosure. Facts learned from a witness, without more, are generally not protectable. As a consequence, when making notes of witness interviews, it is important that the investigator mark the work product as "Attorney Work Product." Additionally, noting that a summary or set of notes is prepared in anticipation of litigation to provide legal advice to the client is prudent. It is helpful to make sure that notes are not a running transcript of the witness's answers to questions, but are rather imbued with counsel's mental impressions. Work product with these features often receives protection from disclosure where mere transcripts of a witness's answers do not.

RECORDING INTERVIEWS AND CREATING TRANSCRIPTS

Recordings are seldom protected, because, unlike notes, the questions and answers simply do not convey the mental impressions, strategy, and analysis of counsel that would warrant opinion work product protection.[15] It is highly probable, therefore,

---

14. *See* MODEL RULES OF PROF'L CONDUCT R. 1.8(f).
15. *In re* Kellogg Brown & Root, Inc., 796 F.3d 137, 148–50 (D.C. Cir. 2015) (holding that fact work product is subject to disclosure on a showing of "substantial need" and "undue hardship" but opinion work product is subject to heightened protection); FED. R. CIV. P. 23(b)(3)(B) (if a court orders disclosure of work product, "it must protect against disclosure of the mental impressions, conclusions, opinions, or legal theories" of counsel, which constitutes opinion work product).

that disclosure of recordings or transcripts may be compelled.[16] Whether such disclosure creates issues for the client is a fact-specific inquiry. Thought should be given to this issue upfront, and the implications of disclosure discussed, before recordings or transcripts of witness interviews are generated.

Other considerations may weigh against recording interviews. There is no uniform rule regarding whether counsel must inform the witness of the recording before it begins and obtain the witness's consent to record. Rather, the legality of one-party recording is an issue that must be examined on a state-by-state basis. In jurisdictions where consent must be obtained, counsel may determine that seeking consent would chill witness candor to the detriment of the interview(s), and may elect to proceed without recording.

COMPELLING WITNESS PARTICIPATION

Employees of public or private entities are usually required to cooperate with internal investigations as a responsibility of employment. Review of the entity's policies and procedures regarding what employees are required to do, as terms of their employment, is a useful first step. Those unwilling to be interviewed may be subject to some form of progressive discipline or job action.[17] The specter of such actions is usually sufficient to secure participation.

Former employees present a different issue. Unless there are contractual requirements that survive the employee's separation from the entity, participation in an internal investigation by a departed employee is entirely voluntary. Participation can often be secured when the witness is informed that some manner of formal process may issue from the government or a potential party to litigation. Often the witness wants to know what those processes will entail and what he or she may be asked to do. When providing this information, it remains important that the entity's counsel not provide legal advice, as prohibited by the Model Rule of Professional Responsibility 4.3, and that counsel clearly define its role as counsel to the entity. Counsel also must assess whether *Upjohn* warnings apply. Additionally, it is prudent to recognize that former employees do not have the same job-related motivations as current employees, and may not heed counsel's request not to discuss the content of the interview.

---

16. *See, e.g.*, United States v. Nobles, 422 U.S. 225 (1975) (affirming the trial court's finding that an investigator's report containing statements by a witness were not protected by, inter alia, the work product doctrine).
17. There often are differences in what actions private entities can take over employees versus public entities. These differences may drive the strategy and tactics employed to secure participation.

WITNESS ACCESS TO COUNSEL

Internal investigations involving private entities ordinarily do not implicate a witness's right to have counsel participate in the interview. Nevertheless, there may be special circumstances—including interviews of victims or whistleblowers—where the client may permit such participation. These are fact-specific determinations made to enhance the efficacy of the investigation. It may be that a witness simply will not cooperate at the level necessary without his or her counsel in the room. The net benefit of getting better cooperation and candor may outweigh the anticipated downsides of participation by the witness's counsel.

When permitting counsel to participate, it is often helpful to set ground rules. Among other things, counsel is there to observe and not participate in the questions and answers. It is not a deposition; there is no right to object and the counsel cannot behave in a way that disrupts the investigation. Further, the counsel needs to agree to maintain the process as confidential.

WORK PAPERS AND DRAFTS OF THE REPORT

All work papers and drafts of the report should be labeled as "Confidential Attorney-Client Communications and Attorney Work Product," and also as drafts. The materials should be treated and maintained as confidential, and should be shared only on a "need-to-know basis." Disclosure should be limited to members of the investigative team or certain select decision makers of the client. Counsel also should be mindful that disclosure of drafts to third parties may waive privilege protections. By maintaining strict formalities, the chances of sustaining the privileges and protections through challenges are increased. Conversely, lack of diligence on these issues puts the protections at risk of waiver, which, as discussed earlier, can vary in scope.

CIRCULATION AND CONTROL OF THE FINAL REPORT OF INVESTIGATION

If the client wants to maintain privilege of the final report of investigation, strict precautions must be used to limit circulation. Counsel should consider issuing individually numbered reports to specifically identified decision makers. Express written warnings should accompany the circulation of the report and should detail the consequences of circulating the report beyond the defined audience. Presenting the report through a secure read-only platform that limits the reader's ability to copy or forward the report may be useful to control circulation to only the intended audience.

DISCLOSURE OF REPORT OF INVESTIGATION AND PRIVILEGE IMPLICATIONS

If the client wants to disclose the report to a third party, careful consideration of the scope of the waiver is important. To the extent permitted by law, the investigative team should help to narrow the breadth of the waiver as much as possible. Detailing what is intended to be waived versus what is not may prove helpful if a third party later moves to compel more information on the basis of partial waiver.

A client considering disclosing some, but not all, of its investigation report should consider that not all jurisdictions recognize selective waivers. Moreover, disclosure of some or all of the report in one proceeding can have an unintended adverse effect in a future or parallel proceeding in which it may be sought, such as a shareholder derivative suit. Care and consideration must be given to the potential effects of even limited waiver of privileged material.

WAIVER OF PRIVILEGES

In addition to disclosure of the actual work product, the use of information obtained through an internal investigation in defense of regulatory or civil claims can result in waiver of associated privileges. Once the material is put at issue and used for offensive purposes, courts are reluctant to maintain privilege protections. The simple reality is that privilege cannot be used both as a sword for offensive purposes and a shield to protect against disclosure. Selective disclosure seldom stands when challenged. Accordingly, if the client needs to use the information obtained during the investigation to defend against regulatory or civil claims, it should do so knowing that the privilege associated with the gathering of this information will likely be waived. This could have a direct effect on future actions, such as shareholder derivative suits and parallel proceedings.

VOLUNTARY WAIVER OF PRIVILEGE TO EARN COOPERATION CREDIT

In recent years, the U.S. Department of Justice (DOJ) has put increased focus on individual accountability for corporate wrongdoing. In September 2015, the

DOJ issued the so-called Yates memo, which detailed new policies and practices for dealing with the prosecutions of corporations. The memorandum emphasizes that "fighting corporate fraud and other misconduct is a top priority" of the DOJ and details "six key steps to strengthen [DOJ's] pursuit of corporate wrongdoing."[18] These steps include (1) to qualify for any cooperation credit, corporations must provide to the department all relevant facts relating to the individuals responsible for the misconduct; (2) criminal and civil corporate investigations should focus on individuals from the inception of the investigation; (3) criminal and civil attorneys handling corporate investigations should be in routine communication with one another; (4) absent extraordinary circumstances or approved departmental policy, the department will not release culpable individuals from civil or criminal liability when resolving a matter with a corporation; (5) department attorneys should not resolve matters with a corporation without a clear plan to resolve related individual cases, and should memorialize any declinations as to individuals in such cases; and (6) civil attorneys should consistently focus on individuals, as well as the company, and evaluate whether to bring suit against an individual, based on considerations beyond that individual's ability to pay.

In the wake of the Yates memo, cooperation credit for timely, diligent, thorough, proactive, and speedy internal investigations now turns on the complete disclosure of facts learned about individuals responsible for the misconduct. Unlike past policy, the Yates memo calls for disclosure of "all relevant facts" relating to individual misconduct. No longer can a corporation lean on the diffuse nature of corporate responsibility. Further, settling the corporate wrongdoing will not occur unless there is a "clear plan" to resolve cases against individuals. Taken together, this has put tremendous pressure on entities to waive privileges associated with the internal investigation in order to do the fulsome disclosure about individual malfeasance necessary to earn cooperation credit as part of the case resolution.

As a practical matter, such a disclosure pits the interests of the corporation to reach a resolution against the individuals responsible for the misconduct. In essence, the corporation is incented to root out corporate wrongdoing at the individual level and help deliver the facts supporting the individual misconduct to the DOJ. Such a dynamic often creates material conflicts between the corporation and the individuals responsible for the misconduct.

The Yates memo's all-or-nothing approach to cooperation credit, and its mandate that the DOJ resolve corporate matters only after articulating a plan to pursue individuals, arguably dissuades corporations from cooperating in investigations. Practically, prolonged investigative effort means that corporations face longer periods of bad press, and that press is less likely to be remediated by acknowledgment of the corporation's cooperation. This complicates internal investigations, with

---

18. The Yates memo can be found at https://www.justice.gov/archives/dag/file/769036/download.

entities and individuals fearing liability potentially assuming recalcitrant or defensive postures earlier on.

JOINT DEFENSE/COMMON INTEREST AGREEMENTS

Practitioners have long used so-called joint defense or common interest agreements to share information gathered between and among counsel for the client and individuals involved in the investigation. This is a useful tool for protecting privilege when interests are aligned. When it becomes evident that interests are not aligned, the client must have a method for exiting the agreement and using its information in an unfettered way.[19]

The Yates memo adds some complexity to this well-used practice. The mandated factual disclosures associated with earning cooperation credit may create tension or limitations on the nature and extent of an agreement that can be entered with counsel for individuals. Certainly, agreements with counsel for individuals responsible for the misconduct presents real issues and may impair the ability to secure cooperation credit. Care must be taken to ensure that benefits associated with such an agreement are not outweighed by the impacts on cooperation benefits.

CONCLUSION

Internal investigations require careful planning, foresight, and execution to avoid many and varied traps. Attention to the threshold issues, care in preserving the applicable privileges, and thoughtful analysis as to when the client may need to waive these privileges to secure appropriate benefits in various proceedings are key drivers for success.

---

19. The nature and extent to which these joint defense/common interest agreements provide protection is an issue of state law.

CHAPTER 2

Timing of Mediation

Pre-Litigation, Early Mediation, or Late Mediation

Andrew R. Kasnetz

INTRODUCTION

As a prefatory comment, not all cases should be mediated. Some need to be tried. Some issues need to be tested. Occasionally, policy or precedent consideration precludes settlement because floodgates may open. Sometimes lawyers and reasonable litigants can also resolve matters on their own. This chapter is not about those cases. It is about all others. So, when the question is—when to mediate? The answer is—it is all about judgment.

As this discussion proceeds, various factors, at least the ones the author thinks are most important, will be discussed. You will likely agree with some, maybe even most, but not others. But, ultimately, the assessment and resulting decision whether and when to mediate (assuming you have a willing client, opposing party, and counsel) will depend on your judgment. Hopefully, some young(er) lawyers will have more of that than the author did at your age. My hope is you will at least consider, if not rely on, some of the discussion points.

So, when to mediate? The simple answer is—whenever the parties agree (or when a judge, generally federal, tells you). While mediation can take place at any stage of a dispute, the choices are generally:

- Pre-suit
- Early on—just after the lawsuit has been filed

- Early(ish)—after a voluntary exchange of information and documents
- After some or all fact discovery
- After some or all expert discovery
- Just before trial
- During trial (rarely)
- After trial but before entry of judgment
- During appeal

There are some general things to keep in the back of your mind. First, as a business/commercial litigator with a fair amount of trial, appellate, and mediation experience, my frame of reference comes from that background. Second, the timing of mediation does, at least arguably, depend on the type of dispute or lawsuit being litigated. For example, commercial fraud cases are inherently factually intensive. You probably do need to examine those e-mails (and perhaps fight for those internal memoranda—are they really privileged?) in order to assess your case. Caveat: (as lawyers say) you do not really need all of those documents to establish a case for punitive damages before mediating. Does anybody really settle a case based on punitives anyway? Another example is when there is clearly a need for expert opinion information, at least reports. This is most likely essential in medical malpractice, products liability, and intellectual property litigation, among others. Sometimes such information is available early and can be freely exchanged, but sometimes not. A final example is matters involving complex, or at least fairly complex, financial issues. This is particularly so in cases where forensic accounting is required or valuation is at the core of the dispute, often concerning property, real or personal, the value of or damage to businesses, and, in particular, lost profits and business interruption.

With all that said, sophisticated lawyers and parties can find traditional and creative ways to share information to make early mediation possible, and perhaps successful, even where such issues are involved.

MEDIATING PRE-SUIT

The first takeaway from this chapter is that pre-suit mediation is rarely done. However, in the right case, pre-suit mediation can be successful in resolving disputes or perhaps, at least, narrowing issues and expediting litigation.

First and foremost, this takes good and confident lawyers (and otherwise busy ones) on both sides to be effective. This is true largely because it will require a fairly free exchange of information and documents and some openness from the key players for the parties to participate and discuss matters freely. The lawyers must facilitate this and provide reassurance that no harm will be done.

So, what is the big upside? Obviously, cost savings. But, everyone knows that. A big factor is often publicity. Certainly, this is true with publicly held companies. This can have even more impact on local or regional companies and individuals who are active and known in their communities. People with public faces are, of course, impacted negatively if litigation ends poorly and in public, but such people can also be hurt by the mere public knowledge of the existence of litigation. In fact, once the litigation becomes public, it often makes it more difficult to resolve. Such people may feel the need to be vindicated. While a good public relations firm can help with this, entrepreneurial-types and others who thrive on brand name recognition may find the need to dig in their heels once publicity starts, or, at minimum, they may resolve the dispute later but pay dearly, or believe they paid dearly, for confidentiality.

The big question for pre-suit mediation is—have emotions cooled sufficiently for sober decisions to be made? Often, a good clue for this is whether there have been significant pre-suit settlement negotiations between the parties with or without lawyer involvement. If yes, a good mediator might just be able to help close the deal.

EARLY MEDIATION

If cases are to be mediated, the majority should be done early or, at least, early(ish). The factors in favor are obvious—cost savings and minimizing distraction. The money aspect is clear to all. The distraction to a litigant is not fully realized until they are in the midst of battle. A mixed factor is the emotional readiness. Emotions are initially high when the lawsuit is filed (for plaintiffs) and served (for defendants). Then, over time, on sober reflection and with the aid of counsel, emotions dissipate. Some early billing and the humdrum of discovery can do that. However, emotions tend to escalate again when depositions are taken, and will rise even higher as trial approaches. Thus, emotionally, early mediation can be the best time.

So, why aren't more cases mediated early? While there are several reasons, the biggest one is that the lawyers get in the way, and this does not refer to running up the fee. Early mediations are contrary to our training and the nerdiness required to be a good lawyer. We are thorough, we need to know (or think we do), to render the best possible advice. This is who we are and how we are trained, and it is mostly a good thing. However, and here is the key (takeaway number two), we also are trained to take a large amount of information, a series of complex cases, and reduce it all to its essence. This is where truly excellent, nuanced lawyering happens. So (takeaway number three), always have that long, initial meeting with the client, perhaps over multiple days. Learn all you can. Ask for key documents and review them. Do research. Then, make your initial assessment. In most cases, you will either be right or close to right. Almost always right enough to mediate meaningfully.

The key variable at this stage should be the client's readiness, informationally and emotionally, not the lawyer's. The client has to be comfortable that its decisions and positions are based on sufficient information. This often turns on whether there is access to enough information and key witnesses. This early process will be more likely successful when the suit is based more on sufficient information than on slightly more than suspicion.

Early(ish) Mediation

For a variety of reasons, the post-suit (very) early mediation may not work, especially if it requires consent of the parties. The next chance is early(ish) mediation. There, good lawyers can arrange for a fairly open, mutual, free exchange of documents. There can even be a joint meeting of some of the principals to discuss the dispute. All can be done with the evidentiary protection regarding settlement discussions. In addition, some limited, mutual, formal discovery can be conducted on an expedited basis. There can be agreement to a simple set of interrogatories, document requests, and even the start of Rule 30(b)(6) depositions, agreeing that both sides can keep the depositions open if the case does not settle. In near ancient parlance, the depositions would be "adjourned" rather than concluded.

Obviously, the same keys of cost savings and limiting distraction exist. To aid the process, getting some early bills out and providing a detailed budget is helpful.

Mediating after Completion of Fact Discovery/Investigation

This is a good time in any litigation to slow down, take a few deep breaths, and provide an updated assessment for the client followed by a long meeting or conference call. Also, check the budget, see where you are, and provide an update if appropriate.

This is an interesting time to assess whether you really are better prepared now to mediate than you were after your initial case assessment. You are now armed with all of the facts, documents reviewed and analyzed, witnesses interviewed, and at least some deposed. Go deep and ask yourself whether you are truly in a significantly better position to mediate than you were at the time of the initial assessment. My guess is that, in most cases, you will conclude that you are no better off, or at least only marginally so. The next question is whether it was worth the money and distraction to get to that point. The answer will vary, but is more than often "no."

All that said, the more important question is—does your client feel more comfortable mediating now? Has the perception that being armed with the facts is helpful and necessary become a reality? If so, then maybe it was worth the time, cost, and distraction. An important question to ask here is whether your particular case turns largely, or at least significantly, on the relative credibility of witnesses. If this is truly the case, and sometimes it is, then witness interviews conducted, depositions taken, and the assessments made of the witnesses, was time well spent and will, perhaps, lead you to a more successful mediation.

MEDIATING AFTER EXPERT DISCOVERY

Whether expert discovery (and how much) is needed prior to the mediation will depend largely on the type of case and key issues involved. As discussed earlier, there are a variety of cases which arguably require some expert opinion/discovery before a meaningful mediation can be conducted.

An initial question to ask is—is liability truly in dispute? And similarly, is expert opinion essential to the proof? If the answers are "yes," then some expert discovery is needed. That can take various forms. In some cases, the mere (complete) answers to an appropriate expert interrogatory might be sufficient. That depends, in part, on how big the case is and how much expense can be justified. In some cases, a voluntary exchange of expert reports might be sufficient. Again, good lawyers should not fear such an exchange. Of course, federal courts require reports to be exchanged while some state courts do not. But, perhaps do it anyway, even if not required. It is only the rare case that you have to do the knock-down, drag out expert depositions to have sufficient information to mediate. Again, ask yourself whether it is really worth the additional cost.

Of course, if full-blown expert discovery is complete, there is little left to know. Thus, the barriers to mediation and settlement, at this stage, have been almost completely removed.

MEDIATING JUST PRIOR TO TRIAL

This is the low hanging fruit on the mediation timeline. This is, by leaps and bounds, the easiest time to mediate.

Both sides have acquired full knowledge of the facts and opinions. Steep costs have been incurred (and hopefully paid). The court has made preliminary rulings on motions to strike defenses, dismissal of certain causes of action, partial summary judgments, and, hopefully, motions in limine.

Most importantly, reasonable fears have fully set in. The reality of the loss of control is as complete as it can be without seeing that jury of your "peers" in the box. Opposing counsel has been assessed. Will they? Can they? Do they really want to . . . go to trial? Are knees wobbling a bit too much?

At this point, if it is a given that the case should be mediated, should be settled, then all barriers, reasonable and unreasonable, to achieving that end have been removed.

EPILOGUE

In writing this chapter, the focus was on the mediation timeline. However, in thinking about this general topic, it is clear there are various barriers to mediation, beyond those discussed. These miscellaneous barriers can impact timing, but often go beyond temporal matters.

IN-HOUSE COUNSEL

In representing good-sized businesses, those large enough to have in-house counsel, sometimes a unique barrier to settlement arises. In-house counsel (the ones hiring you and approving your invoices) were often involved in the drafting of documents or in the decision making that underlies the dispute being litigated. Thus, it is human nature they are invested in the litigation, and are defensive about their decision making. This can affect timing. They may (subconsciously) want to wait to mediate. As the litigation progresses, perhaps there will be a factual revelation they could not have known about or, even better, the court may make a "bad" decision on the law, which requires rethinking settlement posture. Then, when the risk is fully assessed, and reports made to management (or even the board), there may be a real or imagined reason for a change of position.

OPPOSING COUNSEL

In rare circumstances, I have sensed that opposing counsel, under the guise of needing discovery, court rulings, and so on, is really "working the file" in a matter beyond what is necessary. Again, this is likely rare. However, opposing trial counsel, like in-house counsel, might be in the difficult position of defending their own, or perhaps more likely, their corporate partners' work product and advice. This can be tricky and may require a nuanced approach to maneuver around. It is difficult, but possible, to take a tough litigation stance without being (too) critical of the lawyer down the hall.

PHOBIAS ABOUT GIVING AWAY TOO MUCH

A phobia is by definition an unreasonable fear, and such fears generally fall into two categories. First, if we mediate too early, we will give away our strategy and provide too much information voluntarily. These are rarely, if ever, real problems. In modern litigation, disclosure is complete, and contentions are detailed. There are few surprises with all that pre-litigation disclosure requires. If you do not give it up now, you will later. So, you better have a good reason for needing to wait.

Second, there is sometimes a fear of locking in a settlement position or baseline. Again, this is rarely a real problem. If you are candid and (fairly) transparent, you can simply say you are willing to take a certain settlement position now to avoid costs, distraction, and so forth, but that position will change if we fully litigate. Be credible, and be candid. If the other side chooses not to believe you, it is their problem. Again, like so many things, such issues are remedied by having good lawyers on both sides of the case.

FALSE BELIEF IN SUMMARY JUDGMENT

In other rare cases, it may be best to have a unique legal issue resolved before mediation. However, almost always, it is better for both sides to assess, feel, and weigh the risks of adverse rulings. This is an appropriate factor in settlement negotiation which should be in a mediator's wheelhouse.

CONCLUSION

In timing mediation, use your best judgment. And (fourth, and final takeaway), you are generally waiting too long to mediate.

CHAPTER 3

Picking the Right Place

Venue Selection and Jurisdictional Considerations

Tom Waskom

Before bringing an action, a plaintiff must decide two questions: where *can* I file, and where do I *want* to file? A defendant, having been sued, faces a similar set of questions: can I move this case to a different forum and, if so, where would I like to litigate? In many ways, the plaintiff's and defendant's considerations regarding forum are mirror images of one another. This chapter addresses where you can litigate your case, where you want to litigate your case, and what you can do to get your case there.

THE RULES PRESCRIBING WHERE YOU CAN LITIGATE

The most basic questions in picking a forum are these: do I want to be in state or federal court, and which state or district will be most favorable to my claims or defenses? But, it will be the rare case in which a party has every state and every district from which to choose. The options will be limited by the threshold issues familiar to every litigator: personal jurisdiction, subject matter jurisdiction, standing, and venue.

Personal Jurisdiction

In recent years, the scope of personal jurisdiction has been tightening, limiting a plaintiff's choices in selecting a forum. That is true with respect to both specific jurisdiction and general jurisdiction.

A state can exercise specific jurisdiction over an out-of-state entity only with respect to a claim that arises from or relates to the defendant's contacts with the forum.[1] *Bristol-Myers* stands for the proposition that to invoke specific jurisdiction, a court must find that the plaintiff's claims arise from the defendant's contacts with the forum state: "[f]or specific jurisdiction, a defendant's general connections with the forum are not enough."[2] The 678 *Bristol-Myers* plaintiffs included 86 California residents and 592 residents of other states. None of the nonresident plaintiffs claimed that they had been injured in California; rather, they claimed that specific personal jurisdiction existed by virtue of BMS's extensive contacts with California, including its nationwide marketing scheme for Plavix.[3]

The California Supreme Court had held that it could exercise specific jurisdiction over the nonresident plaintiffs' claims, even though they did not claim that they had been injured there, because their claims were substantially similar (if not identical) to those of the California residents who had also brought suit against BMS.[4] The Supreme Court reversed, finding that "[t]he . . . plaintiffs [were] not California residents and do not claim to have suffered harm in that State. In addition . . . all the conduct giving rise to the nonresidents' claims occurred elsewhere."[5] Because the case involved nonresident plaintiffs asserting claims against nonresident defendants based on conduct that allegedly occurred entirely elsewhere, the Court held that "[it] follow[ed] that the California courts cannot claim specific jurisdiction."[6]

The Supreme Court has similarly restricted general jurisdiction in recent terms. To be subject to general jurisdiction, a defendant's contacts with the forum must be "so 'continuous and systematic' as to render [it] essentially at home" there.[7] In most instances, a company is "essentially at home" in the state where it is incorporated and the state where it operates its principal place of business.[8] Although it is possible that a "corporation's operations in a forum other than its formal place of incorporation or principal place of business may be so substantial and of such a

---

1. Bristol-Myers Squibb Co. v. Superior Court, 582 U.S. __, 2017 U.S. LEXIS 3873, at *3–4 (2017); Daimler AG v. Bauman, 134 S. Ct. 746, 754 (2014); Helicopteros Nacionales de Colombia, S. A. v. Hall, 466 U.S. 408, 414 n.8 (1984).
2. *Bristol-Myers*, 582 U.S. __, 2017 U.S. LEXIS 3873, at *14.
3. *Id.* at *7–10.
4. *Id.* at *8–9.
5. *Id.* at *16.
6. *Id.*
7. Goodyear Dunlop Tires Operations, S.A. v. Brown, 131 S. Ct. 2846, 2851 (2011).
8. *Goodyear*, 131 S. Ct. at 2854.

nature as to render the corporation at home in that State," the Supreme Court has noted that such a case would be "exceptional."[9]

Subject Matter Jurisdiction

Subject matter jurisdiction is an issue largely specific to federal courts. Most state courts have plenary jurisdiction, setting aside issues like jurisdictional minimums.[10] Federal courts, on the other hand, only have that subject matter jurisdiction that Congress grants.

The primary bases for subject matter jurisdiction are 28 U.S.C. § 1331 (federal question) and § 1332 (diversity). Section 1331 provides federal district courts "original jurisdiction of all civil actions arising under the Constitution, laws, or treaties of the United States." Under the well-pleaded complaint rule, the federal question must arise from the plaintiff's complaint—not an anticipated defense.[11]

Section 1332 creates two forms of diversity jurisdiction—one long-standing, one a creature of the Class Action Fairness Act of 2005 (CAFA). The former creates jurisdiction over actions in which there is complete diversity of citizenship among the parties (i.e., no plaintiff and defendant are citizens of the same state) and the amount in controversy exceeds $75,000.[12] The latter creates jurisdiction over class actions or certain "mass actions" in which there is minimal diversity (i.e., at least one plaintiff and one defendant are citizens of different states) and the amount in controversy exceeds $5 million.[13]

Title 28 also provides a hodgepodge of other forms of subject matter jurisdiction—for instance, admiralty (§ 1333); patents, copyrights, and trademarks (§ 1338); and civil rights (§ 1343).

Standing

Closely related to subject matter jurisdiction is the concept of standing. Only those plaintiffs with Article III standing may bring an action in federal court. To establish standing, a plaintiff must show it has suffered a concrete and particularized injury that is either actual or imminent, that the injury is fairly traceable to the defendant, and that a favorable decision will likely redress that injury.[14]

---

9. *Daimler*, 134 S. Ct. at 761 n.19; *Carroll*, 2015 U.S. Dist. LEXIS 127207, at *8–9 ("Absent exceptional circumstances, the defendant is only subject to the general jurisdiction of the forum State if it is the defendant's domicile.").

10. In a few states, the selection between different state courts is a strategic consideration. For instance, litigants in Delaware may have the option of choosing between superior court and chancery court. Although beyond the scope of this chapter, that decision can be fraught for the out-of-state litigant. For instance, a party that chooses to file in superior court will waive rights to certain injunctive relief.

11. *See* Louisville & Nashville R.R. Co. v. Mottley, 211 U.S. 149 (1908).

12. 28 U.S.C. § 1332(a).

13. *Id.* § 1332(d).

14. Lujan v. Defenders of Wildlife, 504 U.S. 555, 560–61 (1992).

Recent Supreme Court precedent on standing has narrowed plaintiffs' forum selections (or, at least offered defendants new arguments to challenge that selection). As with personal jurisdiction, the Supreme Court recently narrowed the scope of standing.[15] In *Spokeo, Inc. v. Robins*,[16] the Supreme Court rejected the proposition that a statutory violation, without more, is sufficient to confer Article III standing so long as the plaintiff alleges that *his* statutory rights were violated, thus making his or her interest in the suit individualized and not collective.[17] Even where the alleged harm is particularized to the individual plaintiff, the harm still must be concrete.

The Court explained that Article III is not "automatically satisfie[d] . . . whenever a statute grants a person a statutory right and purports to authorize that person to sue to vindicate that right."[18] While Congress plays an important role in identifying "intangible" harms that should be actionable, the harm identified must be a concrete injury in fact. Thus, a plaintiff "could not, for example, allege a bare procedural violation, divorced from any concrete harm, and satisfy the injury-in-fact requirement of Article III."[19] "[D]eprivation of a procedural right without some concrete interest that is affected by the deprivation . . . is insufficient to create Article III standing."[20]

In contrast, many states have virtually no standing requirement. For instance, the California Supreme Court has noted that while "Article III of the federal Constitution imposes a 'case-or-controversy' limitation on federal jurisdiction . . . [t]here is no similar requirement in our state Constitution."[21] To sue in California, a plaintiff need only be a real party in interest—there is no "injury-in-fact" requirement.[22]

Similarly, in Massachusetts, a plaintiff need not have suffered a concrete injury to recover statutory damages under some consumer protection statutes. For instance, to recover under Massachusetts General Law Chapter 93A, which proscribes deceptive trade practices, a plaintiff need not actually incur a loss—"if he or she is ready, willing, and able to purchase the product or service at a price consistent

---

15. The extent to which *Spokeo* is a wholesale departure from existing doctrine has been oversold by some commentators. Article III limitations on CAFA jurisdiction is not necessarily a new phenomenon. Standing has long been a defense in data breach class actions. *See, e.g.*, Reilly v. Ceridian Corp., 664 F.3d 38 (3d Cir. 2011) (affirming dismissal of data breach claim for lack of Article III standing). And it is a long-standing proposition that "Congress cannot erase Article III's standing requirements by statutorily granting the right to sue to a plaintiff who would not otherwise have standing." Raines v. Byrd, 521 U.S. 811, 820 n.3 (1997) (citing Gladstone, Realtors v. Village of Bellwood, 441 U.S. 91, 100 (1979)). This "requirement of injury in fact is a hard floor of Article III jurisdiction that cannot be removed by statute." Summers v. Earth Island Inst., 555 U.S. 488, 497 (2009).
16. Spokeo, Inc. v. Robins, 578 U.S. __, 136 S. Ct. 1540 (2016).
17. 136 S. Ct. at 1544–45.
18. *Id.* at 1549.
19. *Id.*
20. *Summers*, 555 U.S. at 496.
21. Grosset v. Wenaas, 42 Cal. 4th 110, 1117 n.13, 175 P.3d 1184 (Cal. 2008).
22. *Id.* at 434–35 & n.5 (distinguishing claims arising under California Unfair Competition Law, for which standing requirement was created by referendum).

with the relevant statute," that is typically injury enough.[23] Chapter 93a entitles plaintiffs to recover statutory damages even in the absence of proof of actual damages (in addition to equitable relief, attorney's fees, and other remedies).[24]

Spokeo raises the specter of a new form of strategic pleading to avoid federal jurisdiction in consumer class actions in a way that the data breach cases do not. Plaintiffs now have a clear roadmap for avoiding CAFA removal: find a named plaintiff who has not suffered concrete harm, but who can state a claim under state law. The resulting putative class action is non-removable even where all CAFA requirements are satisfied—and arguably, even if absent class members have concrete injuries and would themselves have Article III standing.

Moreover, *Spokeo* might not merely roll back CAFA jurisdiction over class actions seeking recovery under state consumer protection statutes. There is a real possibility that it could limit federal question jurisdiction in unintended ways. *Spokeo* itself, after all, addressed FCRA violations. Robins likely could have filed suit in California state court seeking recovery for the same statutory violation. Post-*Spokeo*, a defendant could not remove such a case, *even on federal question grounds*. The same is true for other federal statutes for which Congress has created concurrent federal and state jurisdiction, like the Truth in Lending Act or the Telephone Consumer Protection Act. After *Spokeo*, if a plaintiff can allege only a technical violation of these statutes without concrete injury, state courts will essentially have exclusive jurisdiction over a class of federal actions.

So, for instance, a plaintiff could file a putative class action in California state court seeking recovery under the Song-Beverly Credit Card Act,[25] alleging that a store wrongfully asked for his or her zip code during a credit card transaction. Without more, is there a concrete injury? Maybe not. After all, it's a fact pattern closely parallel to Judge Alito's example in *Spokeo* of what would not suffice as a concrete injury for Article III purposes: zip code missteps. But it is also a fact pattern in which federal jurisdiction has been a benefit to defendants.[26] And, it is a fact pattern that might no longer be susceptible to federal jurisdiction.

Venue

The most flexible of the restraints on forum selection is venue. While the federal system and each state has its own set of venue rules, they tend to vary only on the margins. Usually, a plaintiff filing in state court can bring an action in any forum

---

23. Herman v. Admit One Ticket Agency LLC, 454 Mass. 611, 618, 912 N.E.2d 450, 456 (Mass. 2009). Some recent case law suggests that Massachusetts is moving closer to requiring a concrete injury for recovery. *See, e.g.,* Hershenow v. Enterprise Rent-A-Car Co. of Boston, 445 Mass. 790, 797, 840 N.E.2d 526 (Mass. 2006).
24. *See* Aspinall v. Philip Morris Cos., Inc., 442 Mass. 381, 400, 813 N.E.2d 476 (Mass. 2004).
25. Cal. Civ. Code § 1747, *et seq.*
26. *See* Yeoman v. Ikea U.S.A. West, Inc., 2014 U.S. Dist. LEXIS 168968 (S.D. Cal. Dec. 4, 2014) (decertifying class seeking recovery under Song-Beverly for improper request for zip code).

in which the defendant lives, the defendant does business, or the dispute arose. Likewise, under federal law a plaintiff may file a civil action in:

(1)   a judicial district in which any defendant resides, if all defendants are residents of the State in which the State in which the district is located;

(2)   a judicial district in which a substantial part of the events or omissions giving rise to the claim occurred, or a substantial part of property that is the subject of the action is situated; or

(3)   if there is no district in which an action may otherwise be brought as provided in this section, any judicial district in which any defendant is subject to the court's personal jurisdiction with respect to such action.[27]

Some types of federal actions have specific venue rules. As is the case with personal jurisdiction, the Supreme Court recently revisited federal venue statutes and constricted plaintiffs' options for forum selection. The patent venue statute allows suit where the defendant "resides" or "has committed acts of infringement and has a regular and established place of business."[28] In *TC Heartland LLC v. Kraft Foods Group Brands LLC*,[29] the Supreme Court sharply limited venue for patent infringement cases, slashing the ability of patent plaintiffs to pick their forum—in particular, the Eastern District of Texas, where plaintiffs have increasingly chosen to file suit and where nearly half of all patent litigation takes place.

THE FACTORS AFFECTING WHERE YOU WANT TO LITIGATE YOUR CASE

Once a party has decided where it can file, it must choose among its remaining options. Different forums vary in innumerable ways, but there are three sets of factors that have primacy in the forum selection calculus: differences in substantive law; differences in procedural rules; and differences in the forums' judges, juries, and judicial systems.[30]

---

27. 28 U.S.C. § 1391(b).

28. *Id.* § 1400(b).

29. TC Heartland LLC v. Kraft Foods Grp. Brands LLC, 137 S. Ct. 1514 (2017).

30. Notably, these factors all tend to militate in favor of filing in the United States rather than foreign jurisdictions. "[F]iling in the United States is usually in the client's best interest . . . because the United States litigation system offers advantages to the plaintiff which are virtually unparalleled around the world." Michael J. Maloney & Allison Taylor Blizzard, *Ethical Issues in the Context of International Litigation: "Where Angels Fear to Tread,"* 36 S. Tex. L. Rev. 933, 950 & n.61 (1995).

Variations in Substantive Law among Available Forums

For a litigant choosing a forum, the most important criterion is which forum has the most favorable substantive law. "[I]n many situations a state court may be free to apply one of several choices of law," prompting plaintiffs to "select that forum whose choice of law rules are most advantageous."[31]

Choice of forum can effectively decide what rules govern a host of substantive issues. These issues include:

- Type and amount of recoverable damages;
- Scope of common-law duties (e.g., liability for take home exposure in toxic tort suits);
- Contract interpretation (e.g., enforceability of liquidated damages provisions);
- Availability of affirmative defenses (e.g., contributory negligence);
- Capacity to sue;
- Statute of limitations;
- Damages caps;
- Existence of insurance coverage and interpretation of applicable policies; and
- Pre-filing notice requirements.

A court presumptively will apply the substantive law of the forum in which it sits. Application of that law may be challenged, though, either by the defendant or sua sponte by the court. In that event, the court will apply its choice-of-law rules. Broadly speaking, jurisdictions employ two different frameworks for analyzing conflicts of law: lex loci delicti/lex loci contractu (memorialized in the Restatement (First) of Conflicts of Laws) and multi-factor "interests" analysis (memorialized in the Restatement (Second) of Conflicts of Laws). A plaintiff is more likely to convince a court to apply the law of the forum state under the latter framework—the mechanical test prescribed by the former framework makes it difficult for plaintiffs to evade application of the substantive law governing the place where the claim arose.

There also are constitutional limitations on the extent to which a plaintiff's choice of forum can dictate the substantive law governing the case. "[F]or a State's substantive law to be selected in a constitutionally permissible manner, that state must have a significant contact or significant aggregation of contacts, creating state interests, such that choice of its law is neither arbitrary nor unfair."[32] Where such contacts are missing, the state has no interest that can justify the application of the state's substantive law.

---

31. Piper Aircraft v. Reyno, 454 U.S. 235, 250–51 (1981). This principle extends to federal courts sitting in diversity jurisdiction. Klaxon Co. v. Stentor Elec. Mfg. Co., 313 U.S. 487, 496 (1941).
32. Allstate Ins. Co. v. Hague, 449 U.S. 302, 312–13 (1981).

The U.S. Supreme Court applied this rule in *Phillips Petroleum Co. v. Shutts.*[33] In *Shutts*, the plaintiffs brought a putative class action in Kansas for delayed interest payments on royalty contracts against the defendant, a Delaware corporation with its principal place of business in Oklahoma.[34] The class included residents of all 50 states, as well as the District of Columbia and foreign countries.[35] Many of those class members "had no apparent connection to the State of Kansas except for [the] lawsuit."[36] And most of the royalty contracts forming the basis of the class members' claims had no connection to Kansas.[37] Rather than applying the law of the states where those leases were located to determine whether the defendant had improperly withheld interest payments, the Kansas court elected to apply Kansas law to every single individual claim in the case—and it did so despite material conflicts between Kansas law and those other states' laws.[38]

The Supreme Court rejected the application of forum state law to all of the individual claims as unconstitutional:

> Given Kansas' lack of 'interest' in claims unrelated to that State, and the substantive conflict with jurisdictions [where the leases were located], we conclude that application of Kansas law to every claim in this case is sufficiently arbitrary and unfair as to exceed constitutional limits.[39]

Underlying the contacts requirement is the precept that parties should be able to predict which state's law governs their conduct—so for purposes of conduct-regulating rules, due process requires that the conduct have some connection to the forum whose law will be applied. As *Shutts* explained, "[w]hen considering fairness in this context, an important element is the expectation of the parties."[40] The Court found that "[t]here was no indication that when the leases involving land and royalty owners outside Kansas were executed, the parties had any idea that Kansas law would control."[41] Justice Stevens explained this principle in his *Allstate* concurrence:

> The application of an otherwise acceptable rule of law may result in unfairness to the litigants if, in engaging in the activity which is the subject of the litigation, they could not reasonably have anticipated that their actions would later be judged by this rule of

---

33. Phillips Petroleum Co. v. Shutts, 472 U.S. 797, 821–22 (1985).
34. *Id.* at 799.
35. *Id.*
36. *Id.* at 815.
37. *Id.*
38. *Id.* at 816–17.
39. *Id.* at 822.
40. *Id.* (citing *Allstate*, 449 U.S. at 333).
41. *Id.*

law. A choice-of-law decision that frustrates the justifiable expectations of the parties can be fundamentally unfair. The desire to
prevent unfair surprise to a litigant has been the central concern
in this Court's review of choice-of-law decisions under the Due
Process Clause.[42]

Variations in Procedural Rules among Available Forums

In many cases, procedure dictates outcome. As a result, in selecting a forum, a party
and its counsel must carefully consider which of the available forums follows procedural rules most favorable to the party.

The procedural rule with the most immediate importance to a party filing a
new action is the applicable pleading standard. The preliminary question for a litigant will be whether a potential forum requires fact pleading or notice pleading.
Then, if the forum requires notice pleading, the litigant must consider whether
the forum has adopted the heightened "plausibility" standard announced by the
Supreme Court in *Bell Atlantic v. Twombly* and *Iqbal v. Ashcroft*.

For claims other than fraud, malice, or mistake, most forums require only notice
pleading—that is, a pleading with facts sufficient to put the defendant on notice
of the nature of the claims against him. A minority—for instance, Pennsylvania—
require fact pleading. It may be that a litigant feels confident that even before
discovery, he can state facts sufficient to satisfy either pleading standard. If not,
though, a notice-pleading state is obviously preferable.

In the past decade, divisions have developed among notice pleading jurisdictions, with federal courts leading the way. The Supreme Court has, in the eyes of
most observers, heightened that standard. Now, a complaint "must contain sufficient factual matter, accepted as true, to state a claim to relief that is plausible on
its face."[43] The plausibility standard requires a plaintiff to demonstrate more than
"a sheer possibility that a defendant has acted unlawfully."[44] "Threadbare recitals
of the elements of a cause of action, supported by mere conclusory statements, do
not suffice."[45]

The difference in procedure among forums that is perhaps most often outcome-
determinative is the standard for admissibility of expert testimony. In litigation
that hinges on expert evidence, the question of expert admissibility can often be
the central dispositive issue in a case. For the past 25 years, federal courts have
employed the admissibility test set forth in *Daubert v. Merrell Dow Pharmaceuticals*.
Federal courts tend to play the role of gatekeeper much more zealously than state
courts—even those that have adopted the *Daubert* standard. And those states that

---

42. 449 U.S. at 327 (Stevens, J., concurring).
43. Iqbal v. Ashcroft, 556 U.S. 662, 678 (2009).
44. *Id.*
45. *Id.*

continue to employ the *Frye* standard, or some hybrid approach, are often very liberal (some say excessively so) in their admission of expert testimony. Plaintiffs' desire to keep cases in state court (and defendants' efforts to remove those cases) often arises from the different standards employed in this admissibility analysis.

The rules governing summary judgment likewise often prove dispositive. In some jurisdictions, like Texas, a movant can simply file a "no evidence" motion for summary judgment and shift the burden to the non-moving party to demonstrate the existence of a genuine issue of material fact. In other jurisdictions, like California, a movant must painstakingly demonstrate that the discovery conducted in the case has revealed no such genuine issue. And in Virginia, the rules sharply curtail the use of certain types of evidence that can be used in support of summary judgment. Most notably, movants cannot use deposition testimony in support of their motions—a rule that in practice often makes summary judgment unavailable, even though courts in other jurisdictions (or federal courts in Virginia) would find summary judgment appropriate.[46]

Variations in Judges, Juries, and Judicial Efficiencies among Available Forums

Choice of forum in many cases does not turn on questions of the most favorable substantive or procedural law. Often it comes down to questions about potential judges, jury pools, and court systems.

Some jurisdictions have developed reputations as particularly friendly to plaintiffs or defendants—often with good reason. Those reputations are built in some cases on law that is more favorable to one side or the other. But, just as often, there is a popular view that judges or juries are inclined to side with a certain type of litigant.

The most well-known examples are the so-called judicial hellholes, so designated by the American Tort Reform Foundation (ATRF). The ATRF publishes an annual ranking of those jurisdictions that it deems most "plaintiff" friendly. While the purpose of the list is to shame judges and legislators in these states as promoting a purportedly business-unfriendly climate, this ranking could as fairly be used by plaintiffs as a list of suggestions for where they should file.

Some jurisdictions are reputed to have judges that favor plaintiffs. From a national perspective, for instance, plaintiffs with patent claims flock to the Eastern District of Texas, and asbestos plaintiffs disproportionately file in New York state courts in Manhattan (i.e., NYCAL) and Madison County, Illinois.[47] Within states,

---

46. That benefit to plaintiffs in Virginia, though, does not come without trade-offs. For instance, Virginia state courts have no class action mechanism.

47. In Texas, a past magnet for asbestos claims, the combination of legislative tort reform and judicial decisions heightening the causation standard in toxic tort litigation are a case study in how quickly a jurisdiction once perceived as plaintiff-friendly can be transformed.

tort plaintiffs tend to prefer to file claims in urban areas, viewing the jury pools more willing to award higher damages than those in suburban and rural areas.

Some plaintiffs (and some defendants) place a premium on the speed with which their dispute will be resolved. Even across federal courts alone, that varies dramatically. In the Eastern District of Virginia, the average time from filing of a civil action to trial is 10.1 months—the fastest in the nation.[48] The next closest is the Northern District of Alabama, at 14.8 months to trial. The median time to trial in the Western District of New York, on the other hand, is 60.9 months. The Southern District of Florida holds the distinction for being the fastest to disposition, with a median time of 4.1 months—followed by the Central District of California (4.8 months), the Eastern District of Virginia again (5.2 months), and the Northern District of Georgia (5.7 months).

HOW DEFENDANTS CAN MOVE CASES TO THEIR OWN PREFERRED FORUM

Many litigators react to any choice by their opponent by reflexively wanting the opposite. There is some utility to that rule of thumb. But, when faced with a new case, a defendant (and its counsel) should take a measured view of plaintiff's choice of forum. After that analysis, should the defendant and its counsel determine that a change is in the defendant's best interests, counsel can determine whether the defendant has a way to move the case to a more favorable forum. The most useful options for that endeavor are removal to federal court and motions to dismiss, stay, or transfer venue.

Removal

Removal is the most powerful weapon in a defendant's arsenal for affecting choice of forum.

> Except as otherwise expressly provided by Act of Congress, any civil action brought in a State court of which the district courts of the United States have original jurisdiction, may be removed by the defendant or the defendants, to the district court of the United States for the district and division embracing the place where such action is pending.[49]

---

48. *See* http://www.uscourts.gov/statistics/table/na/federal-court-management-statistics/2017/06/30-1.
49. 28 U.S.C. § 1441(a).

However, "[r]emoval statutes do not create jurisdiction. They are instead a mechanism to enable federal courts to hear the cases that are already within their original jurisdiction."[50] Thus, a defendant seeking to remove a case needs two things: a mechanism for removal and a basis for federal jurisdiction.[51]

Once the source of federal jurisdiction is identified, a defendant must navigate the removal statutes, which hide traps for the unwary. Those traps also provide plaintiffs with opportunities to head off removal and keep their cases in state court.

Removable cases generally must be removed within 30 days of service of a complaint.[52] The time for removal does not necessarily begin at service. If an action is not removable when first filed, it can become removable by subsequent events, triggering a new 30-day period for removal:

> If the case stated by the initial pleading is not removable, a notice of removal may be filed within 30 days after receipt by the defendant, through service or otherwise, of a copy of an amended pleading, motion, order or other paper from which it may first be ascertained that the case is one which is or has become removable.[53]

Exactly what constitutes an "other paper" permitting removal is a much-litigated topic.[54]

For actions removed under § 1441(a), the defendant must secure consent or joinder from all other defendants that have been "properly joined and served."[55] Moreover, cases in which subject matter jurisdiction is based on § 1332(a) (i.e., complete diversity of parties) cannot be removed if any defendant "properly joined and served" is a citizen of the state in which the action was filed.[56] In practice, that means that a plaintiff who names a friendly home-state defendant can avoid removal—unless the other defendants can show that the home-state defendant was fraudulently joined.

Complete-diversity actions also must be removed within one year of commencement of the action—with some limited exceptions.[57] Some courts have read an equitable exception into the bar on removals more than a year after commencement. For instance, in *Saunders v. Wire Rope Corp.*,[58] a plaintiff waited nearly a

---

50. Lontz v. Tharp, 413 F.3d 435, 444 (4th Cir. 2005).
51. Not every case in which federal jurisdiction exists is removable. For instance, actions filed in state court against railroads under the Federal Employers Liability Act cannot be removed to federal court even though they are based on a federal question. 28 U.S.C. § 114(a).
52. *Id.* § 1446(b)(2)(B).
53. *Id.* § 1446(b)(3).
54. *See, e.g.,* Lovern v. GMC, 121 F.3d 160, 163 (4th Cir. 1997) (discovery response disclosing the citizenship of the plaintiff is an "other paper" triggering a new 30-day period for removal); *In re* Diet Drugs Prods. Liab. Litig., 2002 U.S. Dist. LEXIS 25285, at *23 (E.D. Pa. Dec. 17, 2002); (plaintiff's first amended designation of expert witnesses omitting expert to testify about non-diverse defendant is an "other paper").
55. 28 U.S.C. § 1446(b)(2)(A).
56. *Id.* § 1441(b)(2).
57. *Id.* § 1446(c).
58. Saunders v. Wire Rope Corp., 777 F. Supp. 1291 (E.D. Va. 1991).

year after commencement to serve the defendant. The defendant then removed more than a year after commencement of the action, and the plaintiff moved to remand.[59] The court denied remand on equitable grounds:

> [W]hile this Court is mindful that removal statutes are to be strictly construed with regard to the jurisdiction of state courts, the Court will not permit crafty trial tactics to deprive a nonresident defendant of a valid statutory right to removal. . . . Proper removal does no violence to state-federal relations.[60]

The court further noted that "[l]itigation is not intended to be a game of chess. Congress did not intend plaintiffs, through gimmicks and artful maneuvering used in connection with the one-year bar to removal, to straightjacket or deprive nonresident defendants or their legitimate entitlements to removal."[61]

Congress, too, has acted to limit the tactics that have in the past enabled plaintiffs to avoid federal courts through strategic pleading. Historically, some plaintiffs tried to thwart removal by alleging less than the jurisdictional minimum under § 1332(a), increasing the demand only after the one-year statutory time for removal had passed. In 2011, Congress amended § 1446. Under the amended statute, "[i]f the notice of removal is filed more than 1 year after commencement of the action and the district court finds that the plaintiff deliberately failed to disclose the actual amount in controversy to prevent removal, that finding shall be deemed bad faith," thus permitting removal.[62]

Where "a plaintiff's right to relief necessarily depends on resolution of a substantial question of federal law," a federal question exists under § 1331, and an action is properly removed to federal court—even if plaintiffs purportedly assert claims exclusively under state law.[63]

Defendants may be able to remove some actions in which federal jurisdiction is not immediately apparent. In limited circumstances, "a federal court [is] able to hear claims recognized under state law that nonetheless turn on substantial questions of federal law, and thus justify resort to the experience, solicitude, and hope of uniformity that a federal forum offers on federal issues."[64] Factors that courts have considered relevant under *Grable* include "(1) resolving [the] federal issue is necessary to resolution of the state-law claim; (2) the federal issue is actually disputed; (3) the federal issue is substantial; and (4) federal jurisdiction will not disturb the balance

---

59. *Id.* at 1282.
60. *Id.* at 1284 (quoting Heniford v. Am. Motors Sales Corp., 471 F. Supp. 328, 338 (D.S.C. 1979)).
61. *Id. But see, e.g.*, Ophnet, Inc. v. Lamensdorf, 2005 U.S. Dist. LEXIS 36260 (D. Mass. Dec. 27, 2005) (declining to set aside the one-year limitation on fraudulent joinder grounds).
62. 28 U.S.C. § 1446(c)(2)(B).
63. Franchise Tax Bd v. Constr. Laborers Vacation Trust Co., 463 U.S. 1, 27–28 (1983); *see also* Merrell Dow Pharmaceuticals Inc., v. Thompson, 478 U.S. 804, 808 (1986) ("We have . . . noted that a case may arise under federal law 'where the vindication of a right under state law necessarily turned on some construction of federal law.'") (quoting *Franchise Tax Bd.*, 463 U.S. at 9).
64. Grable & Sons Metal Prods., Inc. v. Darue Eng'g & Mfg., 545 U.S. 308, 312 (2005).

of federal and state judicial responsibilities."[65] While *Grable* involved a "nearly pure issue of law," exercise of federal jurisdiction will be inappropriate where the case presents a "fact-bound and situation-specific" issue.[66] A federal question will more likely exist where "the meaning of the relevant federal law is unclear."[67] A federal question likely does not exist where "any conceivable legal duty the . . . defendants owed the plaintiffs exists independently of federal law."[68] "[T]he absence of a federal private right of action . . . should be treated as evidence relevant to congressional judgment concerning the proper balance between state and federal jurisdiction."[69]

Other, more exotic grounds for removal also may exist. For instance, the Act of State Doctrine and the federal common law of foreign relations provide a basis for the exercise of federal jurisdiction over state law claims. In *Banco Nacional de Cuba v. Sabbatino*,[70] the Supreme Court ruled that the Act of State Doctrine prevented a federal court from considering the validity of the Cuban government's expropriation of sugar raised in the context of a lawsuit by an instrumentality of the Cuban government to recover proceeds from the sale of sugar and, accordingly, held that the action must be dismissed.[71] Recognizing that the federal interest in relations with a foreign power "should not be left to divergent and perhaps parochial state interpretations," Justice Harlan in *Sabbatino* wrote that "an issue concerned with a basic choice regarding the competence and function of the Judiciary and National Executive in ordering relationships with other members of the international community must be treated exclusively as an aspect of federal law."[72] As the *Sabbatino* Court explained:

> It is plain that the problems involved are uniquely federal in nature. If federal authority, in this instance this Court, orders the field of judicial competence in this area for the federal courts, and the state courts are left free to formulate their own rules, the purposes behind the doctrine could be as effectively undermined as if there had been no federal pronouncement on the subject.[73]

---

65. Singh v. Duane Morris LLP, 538 F.3d 334, 338 (5th Cir. 2008).
66. Empire HealthChoice Assur., Inc. v. McVeigh, 547 U.S. 677, 701 (2006).
67. Adventure Outdoors, Inc. v. Bloomberg, 552 F.3d 1290, 1300 (11th Cir. 2008).
68. *Id.* at 1297.
69. *Id.* at 1302–03 (citing *Grable*, 545 U.S. at 318).
70. Banco Nacional de Cuba v. Sabbatino, 376 U.S. 398 (1964).
71. *Id.* at 436–37.
72. *Id.* at 426.
73. *Id.* at 424. *See also, e.g.*, De Perez v. AT&T Co., 139 F.3d 1368, 1378 (11th Cir. 1998) (recognizing a district court may predicate federal question jurisdiction upon foreign common law of foreign relations where "plaintiffs' complaints are so intertwined with the sovereign interests [of a foreign nation] as to place this case within the purview of the federal courts" but declining to find federal jurisdiction on the facts before it); Torres v. S. Peru Copper Corp., 113 F.3d 540, 543 (5th Cir. 1997) (affirming district court's denial of motion to remand where "plaintiffs' complaint raise[d] substantial questions of federal common law by implicating important foreign policy concerns" in lawsuit alleging damages arising from air emissions from defendant's mining operations); Republic of the Philippines v. Marcos, 806 F.2d 344, 353–54 (2d Cir. 1986) (holding there was federal question jurisdiction over case implicating act of state doctrine "brought . . . under a theory

Venue

Defendants also may move for dismissal or transfer of a case on venue grounds. In federal court, a defendant can seek transfer to a more convenient or appropriate venue under 28 U.S.C. § 1404(a). Critically, a venue transfer under § 1404(a) might provide a defendant with a more favorable jury pool, or a more defense-friendly court—but it will not improve the defendant's position with respect to the governing law. Where a defendant wins transfer under § 1404(a), "the transferee district must be obligated to apply the state law that would have been applied if there had been no change in venue."[74]

The more powerful weapon for defendants is the motion to dismiss on forum non conveniens grounds. The doctrine of forum non conveniens empowers a court to decline to exercise jurisdiction when "trial in the chosen forum would establish oppressiveness and vexation to a defendant . . . out of all proportion to plaintiff's convenience, or when the chosen forum is inappropriate because of considerations affecting the court's own administrative and legal problems."[75]

As the Supreme Court has stated, "[t]here is a local interest in having localized controversies decided at home."[76] Further, if a defendant can "show[] that trial in the chosen forum would be unnecessarily burdensome, dismissal is appropriate."[77] Courts will consider both public and private factors in determining whether a case should be dismissed in favor of adjudication in a different forum.

The private factors relevant under forum non conveniens include (1) the relative ease of access to sources of proof; (2) the availability of compulsory process for obtaining attendance of unwilling witnesses, and the cost of obtaining attendance of willing witnesses; (3) the ability to implead parties that should properly be present for resolution of the dispute; (4) the possibility of view of the premises, if view would be appropriate to the action; and (5) all other practical problems that make trial of a case easy, expeditious, and inexpensive.[78] The Supreme Court has explained that

> To examine "the relative ease of access to sources of proof," and the availability of witnesses, the district court must scrutinize the substance of the dispute between the parties to evaluate what proof

---

... akin to a state cause of action for conversion" against the former head of state of the Philippines because the "claim raises, as a necessary element, the question whether to honor the request of a foreign government that the American courts enforce the foreign government's directives"); Herero People's Reparations Corp. v. Deutsche Bank AG, No. 01-cv-01868, 2002 U.S. Dist. LEXIS 27982, at *9 (D.D.C. May 30, 2002) (holding act of state doctrine potentially applicable where plaintiffs' complaint alleged wrongful acts by government of Imperial Germany, as this "implicat[ed] this area of federal common law [and t]herefore, these claims fall under federal court jurisdiction.").

74. Van Dusen v. Barrack, 376 U.S. 612, 639 (1964).
75. American Dredging Co. v. Miller, 510 U.S. 443, 447–48 (1994) (quoting *Piper*, 454 U.S. at 241).
76. *Gulf Oil*, 330 U.S. at 509.
77. *Piper*, 454 U.S. at 252 n.19.
78. *See Piper*, 454 U.S. at 241 n.6 (quoting *Gulf Oil*, 330 U.S. at 508).

is required, and determine whether the pieces of evidence cited by the parties are critical, or even relevant, to the plaintiff's cause of action and to any potential defenses to the action.[79]

In the analogous context of motions to transfer venue under 28 U.S.C. § 1404(a), courts have held that "[t]he convenience of witnesses is said to be the most important factor."[80]

The public interest factors include (1) administrative difficulties flowing from court congestion; (2) the local interest in having localized controversies decided at home; (3) the interest in having the trial of a diversity case in a forum that is at home with the law that must govern the action; (4) the avoidance of unnecessary problems in conflict of laws, or in the application of foreign law; and (5) the unfairness of burdening citizens in an unrelated forum with jury duty.[81]

Most, if not all, states have adopted some type of forum non conveniens doctrine, and many have adopted the *Piper* factors. As is true of other issues, though, federal courts tend to apply the *Piper* factors with greater rigor than do state courts, and are generally seen as more willing to dismiss cases on forum non conveniens grounds. As a result, if a defendant in state court intends to file a forum non conveniens motion, it will often be to his benefit to remove the case first.

This can be true even if the existence of federal jurisdiction is an extremely close question. Where a federal district court is confronted with both a complicated jurisdictional question and a comparatively straightforward forum non conveniens motion, the court can grant the forum non conveniens motion and dismiss the case without first determining that it has jurisdiction.[82] That is because forum non conveniens is a quasi-jurisdictional issue.

In *Sinochem*, the court decided a forum non conveniens motion before ruling on personal jurisdiction. But, at least one court has followed *Sinochem* in the context of subject matter jurisdiction. In *Auxer v. Alcoa Inc.*,[83] the defendant removed five mass tort actions filed in Pennsylvania state court by a total of 243 Australians and one Pennsylvanian. While the question of subject matter jurisdiction was close, the forum non conveniens question was less so. The district court deferred on a motion to remand, and instead granted a motion to dismiss the five actions on forum non conveniens grounds, a ruling that the Third Circuit affirmed.

---

79. Van Cauwenberghe v. Baird, 486 U.S. 517, 528 (1988) (quoting *Gulf Oil*, 330 U.S. at 508).

80. Saminsky v. Occidental Petroleum Corp., 373 F. Supp. 257, 259 (S.D.N.Y. 1974); *accord* Los Angeles Mem'l Coliseum Comm'n v. Nat'l Football League, 89 F.R.D. 497, 501 (C.D. Cal. 1981); *see also* 15 WRIGHT, MILLER & COOPER, FEDERAL PRACTICE AND PROCEDURE 2D § 3851, at 415 (1986) (convenience of the witnesses is "[p]robably the most important factor").

81. *See Piper*, 454 U.S. at 241 n.6 (quoting *Gulf Oil*, 330 U.S. at 509).

82. *See* Sinochem v. Int'l Co. v. Malay Int'l Shipping Co., 549 U.S. 422 (2007).

83. Auxer v. Alcoa Inc., 406 Fed. Appx. 600 (3d Cir. 2011).

CHAPTER 4

Seeking and Preparing Litigation Holds

Howard Merten, Paul M. Kessimian,
and Christopher M. Wildenhain

INTRODUCTION

The search for truth is at the heart of the justice system.[1] Preserving information to sustain that search is a fundamental part of the civil discovery regime. To that end, the law obligates litigants to take reasonable efforts to preserve relevant and discoverable information whenever litigation is reasonably anticipated, threatened, or pending against them.[2]

This chapter explores the concept of litigation holds, the consequences of failing to use them, the process of preparing and implementing litigation holds and

---

1. Nixon v. Adm'r of Gen. Servs., 433 U.S. 425, 477 (1977) ("the functioning of our adversary legal system, depends upon the availability of relevant evidence in carrying out its commitments both to fair play and to the discovery of truth").
2. *See* Sedona Conference, *The Sedona Conference Commentary on Legal Holds: The Trigger & The Process*, 11 SEDONA CONF. J. 265, 267 (2010) [hereinafter Sedona]; *see also* Yelton v. PHI, Inc., 279 F.R.D. 377, 384 (E.D. La. 2011) ("fundamental to the duty of production of information is the threshold duty to preserve documents and other information that may be relevant in a case").

associated practical and legal considerations. Although written with corporate/ organizational clients in mind, much of this chapter's content is applicable to litigation hold issues that individuals often confront (albeit usually on a smaller scale in the individual's case). Likewise, this chapter deals with litigation holds in the context of federal practice and procedure, but the principles are relevant in state court proceedings as well, given the existence of preservation duties there. The first section defines the litigation hold and the reasons clients should issue them. The second section addresses when the duty to preserve attaches and the best practices for communicating the litigation hold request. The third section describes how to acquire the information needed to communicate and implement the litigation hold. It focuses on determining who to notify of the obligation to preserve, setting limits on the scope of preservation, and gaining knowledge of the scope of existing information to effectuate the litigation hold in a defensible manner. The fourth section provides an overview of the key elements of a written litigation hold, and the fifth section examines the responsibilities of clients and counsel to monitor compliance with the litigation hold following transmission of the initial hold notice.

LITIGATION HOLDS, PRESERVATION OBLIGATIONS, AND THE CONSEQUENCES OF SPOLIATION[3]

The Purpose of the Litigation Hold

A litigation hold is a mechanism for initiating, directing, and maintaining a client's efforts to satisfy its duty to preserve relevant information and tangible evidence when the client reasonably anticipates litigation.[4] Often written—but not necessarily so—the hold alerts recipients to this duty and advises as to the actions they must take, or refrain from taking.

Depending on the client and the available documents and information infrastructure, the steps for compliance can become very complicated quickly. This is because the preservation duty requires litigants to "identify, locate, and maintain" information that is "relevant to the claims or defenses of *any* party" or "relevant to the subject matter involved in the action."[5] The duty extends to documents or

---

3. This chapter focuses on the responsibility of a litigant to preserve its own documents and the process and best practices for satisfying that obligation. That is, its focus is on inward-looking litigation holds. Outward-looking litigation holds designed to alert adversaries of their duty to preserve with an eye towards protecting the information the sender wishes to discover and laying the groundwork for a motion for spoliation sanctions in the event the adversary does not comply are beyond the scope of this chapter.

4. Sedona, *supra* note 2, at 267.

5. Apple Inc. v. Samsung Elecs. Co., Ltd., 881 F. Supp. 2d 1132, 1137 (N.D. Cal. 2012) (emphasis added); *see* Sedona, *supra* note 2, at 267 (noting obligation to take "reasonable and good faith actions to preserve relevant and discoverable information and tangible evidence").

tangible things made by persons likely to have discoverable information, as well as "documents prepared for those individuals, to the extent those documents can be readily identified."[6] Moreover, if a document retention policy calls for the destruction or disposal of any such relevant matter, the litigant must "immediately suspend" such policy once the duty to preserve arises.[7]

Although this does not mean that the litigant must "keep every shred of paper, every e-mail or electronic document, and every backup tape," the preservation duty remains quite broad.[8] Responsibility for complying, moreover, falls not just on litigants.[9] Rather, counsel must oversee the preservation efforts, monitoring their clients' "efforts to retain and produce relevant documents."[10] Failure to do so can result in sanctions against counsel directly.[11]

Why Do a Litigation Hold? Because Bad Things Can Happen Otherwise

Taking preservation obligations seriously cannot be overemphasized. Spoliation can ruin a client's case and even expose it to civil liability in some jurisdictions. "Spoliation is the destruction or significant alteration of evidence, or the failure to preserve property for another's use as evidence in pending or reasonably foreseeable litigation."[12] In persuading clients of the seriousness of the duty to preserve and why substantial (and expensive) preservation efforts may be needed, counsel should not hesitate to describe the various penalties the client may incur for failing to preserve relevant evidence. The consequences run the gamut from discovery sanctions and causes of action for spoliation to loss of evidence helpful to the spoliator. All, however, represent painful self-inflicted wounds. And there should be no mistake—opposing counsel will press these issues aggressively. There is a growing body of caselaw addressing sanctions for failure to preserve data.[13]

Discovery Sanctions for Spoliation

Among the most common and obvious consequences of spoliation are discovery sanctions. These can range from "awards of attorneys' fees, to more serious

---

6. *Apple Inc.*, 881 F. Supp. 2d at 1137.

7. *Id.*

8. Marshall v. Dentfirst, P.C., 313 F.R.D. 691, 697 (N.D. Ga. 2016).

9. *Yelton*, 279 F.R.D. at 384.

10. Major Tours, Inc. v. Colorel, No. 05-3091 (JBS/JS), 2009 WL 2413631, at *2 (D.N.J. Aug. 4, 2009).

11. *See, e.g.,* Richard Green (Fine Paintings) v. McClendon, 262 F.R.D. 284,292 (S.D.N.Y. 2009) (considering whether monetary sanction for failure to preserve should fall on spoliator or its counsel and deferring resolution to allow spoliator and counsel to either allocate sanction among themselves or submit issue to court for decision).

12. West v. Goodyear Tire & Rubber Co., 167 F.3d 779, 779 (2d Cir. 1999); *accord Marshall*, 313 F.R.D. at 694; CTB, Inc. v. Hog Slat, Inc., No. 7:14-CV-157-D, 2016 WL 1244998, at *8 (E.D.N.C. Mar. 23, 2016).

13. *Infra* notes 14–38 and accompanying text.

sanctions, such as dismissal of claims or [an instruction to] the jury that it may draw an adverse inference."[14] Federal courts draw authority to issue discovery sanctions from their inherent powers to manage their own affairs and from Rule 37[15] of the Federal Rules of Civil Procedure.[16]

Inherent Power Spoliation Sanctions

"Federal courts possess inherent powers necessary to manage their own affairs so as to achieve the orderly and expeditious disposition of cases."[17] Such powers include "the ability to levy appropriate sanctions against a party who prejudices its opponent through the spoliation of evidence that the spoliating party had reason to know was relevant to litigation."[18] Historically, courts relied primarily on inherent power to address spoliation of all manner of documents and electronically stored information (ESI) because Rule 37 only authorized sanctions for violations of court orders.[19] Their discretion was broad.[20] This changed with the 2015 amendments to Rule 37, which put ESI beyond the reach of the federal courts' "inherent power" sanctions and set new rules for ESI spoliation sanctions.[21] Except in limited cases, therefore, inherent power spoliation sanctions now only address failures to preserve paper documents and other tangible evidence.[22]

But where inherent powers still govern, courts retain wide discretion to craft an appropriate sanction to remedy prejudice to the non-spoliating party. The full panoply of sanctions includes harsh penalties, such as dismissal of claims, exclusion of evidence, and adverse inference instructions.[23] The standard for "inherent power" sanctions, moreover, varies across the federal circuits, with some jurisdictions making available the harshest penalties even in cases of careless, non-intentional destruction of evidence.[24] Before the 2015 amendments to the Federal Rules of Civil Procedure, ESI also was subject to this malleable "inherent power" standard.

---

14. *Apple Inc.*, 881 F. Supp. 2d at 1135.
15. All further references to "Rule __" are to the Federal Rules of Civil Procedure unless otherwise noted.
16. Sedona, *supra* note 2, at 268.
17. Browder v. City of Albuquerque, 187 F. Supp. 3d 1288, 1295 (D.N.M. 2016) (internal citation and quotation marks omitted).
18. *Apple Inc.*, 881 F. Supp. 2d at 1135.
19. Sedona, *supra* note 2, at 268.
20. *See, e.g.*, Adkins v. Wolever, 554 F.3d 650, 651 (6th Cir. 2009) (recognizing that "federal court's inherent powers include broad discretion to craft proper sanctions for spoliated evidence").
21. *See infra* notes 25–32 and accompanying text.
22. Amended Rule 37 applies in all cases filed on or after December 1, 2015, and in all cases filed beforehand, unless the court determines that its application would not be practical or just in that particular case. FED. R. CIV. P. 37(e) advisory committee's note to 2015 amendment. *Compare* Learning Care Grp., Inc. v. Armetta, 315 F.R.D. 433, 440 (D. Conn. 2016) ("Here, the Court finds that applying the new rules to this motion would be neither just nor practicable, because the parties first raised this issue in September 2015, prior to the application of the new rules."), *with Marshall*, 313 F.R.D. at 695 ("The Court concludes that applying the amended version of Rule 37(e) would be just and practicable, including because the amended to [sic] Rule 37(e) does not create a new duty to preserve evidence.").
23. *Apple Inc.*, 881 F. Supp. 2d at 1135; *see infra* note 24 and accompanying text.
24. FED. R. CIV. P. 37(e) advisory committee's note to 2015 amendment ("Federal circuits have established significantly different standards for imposing sanctions or curative measures on parties who fail to preserve

Amended Rule 37(e)

As discovery of ESI grew exponentially in amount and relevance to federal litigation throughout the early twenty-first century, the ease with which it could be lost or rendered inaccessible increased the risk that major, case-changing sanctions would issue for the unintentional loss of ESI. The 2015 amendments to the Federal Rules were designed to foreclose this possibility by completely rewriting Rule 37(e) and putting ESI spoliation beyond the courts' "inherent authority."[25] As amended, Rule 37(e) provides:

> If electronically stored information that should have been preserved in the anticipation or conduct of litigation is lost because a party failed to take reasonable steps to preserve it, and it cannot be restored or replaced through additional discovery, the court:
>
> (1) upon finding prejudice to another party from loss of the information, may order measures no greater than necessary to cure the prejudice; or
>
> (2) only upon finding that the party acted with the intent to deprive another party of the information's use in the litigation may: (A) presume that the lost information was unfavorable to the party; (B) instruct the jury that it may or must presume the information was unfavorable to the party; or (C) dismiss the action or enter a default judgment.

The amended rule "specifies [the] measures a court may employ if [electronic] information that should have been preserved is lost, and specifies the findings necessary to justify these measures."[26] It forbids the issuance of sanctions except "upon finding prejudice to another party from loss of the information."[27] Moreover, the amended rule restricts courts' authority to use the "very severe measures" described

---

electronically stored information."); *compare Browder*, 187 F. Supp. 3d at 1295–96 (ordering production of privileged documents, allowing plaintiff to present evidence that defendant lost a phone, and awarding costs and attorney's fees to plaintiff for grossly negligent spoliation); Czuchaj v. Conair Corp., 13cv1901 BEN (RBB), 2016 WL 4161818, at *6–7 (S.D. Cal. Apr. 1, 2016) (ordering an adverse inference instruction to remedy spoliation of hair-dryers returned to defendant by consumers where defendant exhibited a "conscious disregard" for duty to preserve), *with CTB, Inc.*, 2016 WL 1244998, at *9 ("Where a spoliator's conduct is merely negligent, the adverse inference instruction is not an appropriate sanction." (internal quotation marks and citations omitted)); *Yelton*, 279 F.R.D. at 385 ("If the court's inherent power . . . provides the source of the sanctioning authority . . . the court's ability to sanction is limited by the party's degree of culpability, which must be greater than mere negligence.").

25. *Marshall*, 313 F.R.D. at 694–95 ("This amendment "forecloses reliance on inherent authority or state law to determine when certain measures should be used.").

26. FED. R. CIV. P. 37(e) advisory committee's note to 2015 amendment.

27. *Id.*

at subdivision (e)(2) to only where "the party that lost information acted with the intent to deprive another party of the information's use in the litigation."[28]

Although amended Rule 37(e) cabins and controls courts' use of sanctions for spoliation of ESI, it does nothing to remove the threat of painful consequences from spoliation.[29] The harshest sanctions may be reserved for destruction of information with an intent to deprive another party from using it, but that does not mean that all case-changing sanctions are so restricted.[30] Courts are still empowered to remedy negligent ESI spoliation that prejudices another party and "it may be that serious measures are necessary to cure that prejudice."[31] Such sanctions include "forbidding the party that failed to preserve information from putting on certain evidence, permitting the parties to present evidence and argument to the jury regarding the loss of information, or giving the jury instructions to assist in its evaluation of such evidence or argument," provided there is no instruction that the jury "may draw an adverse inference from the loss."[32] Regardless of any interpretation of the amendment, sanctions remain as a serious reminder of the importance of preservation.

Spoliation Causes of Action

Beyond discovery sanctions, a minority of state high courts have held that spoliators may be civilly liable for a failure to preserve documents where the spoliation deprives the plaintiff of a cause of action.[33] These jurisdictions include Alabama, Alaska, Connecticut, the District of Columbia, Idaho, Illinois, Louisiana, Montana, New Mexico, Ohio, and West Virginia.[34] In these jurisdictions at least, civil

---

28. *Id.*; *see also* Bagley v. Yale Univ., 318 F.R.D. 234, 237 (D. Conn. 2016) (observing that the 2015 amendments reject cases "that authorize the giving of adverse-inference instructions on a finding of negligence or gross negligence" (internal citations omitted)).

29. *See Marshall*, 313 F.R.D. at 695.

30. FED. R. CIV. P. 37(e) advisory committee's note to 2015 amendment.

31. *Id.*

32. *Id.*

33. Margaret M. Koesel & Tracey L. Turnbull, *Spoliation of Evidence* 81 (2d ed. 2006).

34. Some courts limit the applicability of tort actions for spoliation to the parties to the underlying lawsuit (i.e., "first parties") or to non-parties (i.e., "third parties"). *See* Smith v. Atkinson, 771 So. 2d 429, 432 (Ala. 2000) (recognizing claim against third parties for spoliation may be pursued under "doctrine of negligence"); Hazen v. Mun. of Anchorage, 718 P.2d 456, 463 (Alaska 1986) (recognizing "common-law cause of action in tort for intentional interference with prospective civil action by spoliation of evidence"); Rizzuto v. Davidson Ladder, Inc., 905 A.2d 1165, 1173 (Conn. 2006) (adopting the tort of first-party intentional spoliation); Holmes v. Amerex Rent-A-Car, 710 A.2d 846, 847 (D.C. 1998) (adopting a cause of action for negligent or reckless spoliation); Yoakum v. Hartford Fire Ins. Co., 923 P.2d 416, 424 (Idaho 1999) (recognizing that spoliation of evidence can be pursued through a "claim for intentional interference with a prospective civil action"); Boyd v. Travelers Ins. Co., 652 N.E.2d 267 (Ill. 1995) (holding that "action for negligent spoliation can be stated under existing negligence law"); Oliver v. Stimson, 993 P.2d 11, 18 (Mont. 1999) ("it is necessary to recognize the tort of spoliation of evidence, which may be negligent or intentional, as an independent cause of action"); Coleman v. Eddy Potash, 905 P.2d 185, 189 (N.M. 1995) (recognizing "intentional spoliation of evidence as a distinct category of tort liability"), overruled on other grounds by Delgado v. Phelps Dodge Chino, Inc., 34 P.3d 1148 (N.M. 2001); Smith v. Howard Johnson Co., 615 N.E.2d 1037, 1038 (Ohio 1993) (recognizing tort for willful interference with or destruction of evidence between first and third parties); Hannah v. Heeter, 584 S.E.2d 560, 567–68, 571 (W. Va. 2003) (recognizing intentional spoliation as tort against first and third parties and negligent spoliation as tort against third parties only); *see generally* Koesel

damages—as well as the costs of defending a spoliation lawsuit—are another danger of ignoring the duty to preserve.

Loss of Evidence Helpful to the Client's Claims or Defenses

Although avoiding sanctions and exposure to civil liability are important reasons to implement a litigation hold, counsel and clients should not lose sight of the other key purpose of litigation holds: shielding helpful documents in the client's possession from inadvertent destruction. In instances where data is lost due to inaction or inadvertence, helpful, even critical, evidence also may be lost.[35] In such circumstances, negligent clients turn what may be a helpful document into a "bad document" because the jury may be instructed to assume the document was harmful to the spoliator.[36] The spoliator, therefore, may be as much of a victim as its adversary—perhaps more so, given that the spoliator's harm is its own doing.[37] As such, litigation holds are not only important to insulating clients from the court and their adversaries but also to protecting the substance of the clients' claims and defenses. Counsel should not forget this when impressing the importance of preservation upon their clients.

Well-Executed, Broad Preservation Ultimately Saves Clients Money

In many critical ways, especially in modern litigation often dominated by electronic discovery issues, data preservation and collection set the stage for all that follows. Responding to discovery and the coding and review of documents all rest on a client's initial effort in identifying and preserving relevant information. Some clients may balk at the often expensive and time-consuming process sometimes required to properly comply with a client's preservation obligations. But that expense will likely pale in comparison to having to redo a document review of tens or even hundreds of thousands of documents because data sources were missed at the outset. Document preservation should not be looked at solely as a burden to be endured. It

---

& Turnbull, *supra* note 33, at 81–90, 102–06 (collecting cases).

    Intermediate appellate courts in California and Louisiana have held that spoliation causes of action exist under their respective state laws. *See* Velasco v. Commercial Bldg. Maint. Co., 215 Cal. Rptr. 504, 506 (Cal. Ct. App. 1985); Robertson v. Frank's Super Value Foods, Inc., 7 So. 3d 669, 673–74 (La. Ct. App. 2009).

35. *Yelton,* 279 F.R.D. at 392 ("Because we do not know what has been destroyed, it is impossible to accurately assess what harm has been done to the [innocent party] and what prejudice it has suffered." (brackets in original and internal citation omitted)).

36. The 2015 amendments to Rule 37(e) have mitigated this risk in the case of ESI, but it remains a reality for non-ESI. *See supra* notes 25–32 and accompanying text.

37. *See* Coach, Inc. v. Dequindre Plaza, L.L.C., No. 11-cv-14032, 2013 WL 2152038, at *14 (E.D. Mich. 2013) ("Thus, this is a case where the destroyed goods were likely just as helpful to the party being accused of spoliation as the party claiming prejudice."); Rimkus Consulting Grp., Inc. v. Cammarata, 688 F. Supp. 2d 598, 607–08 (S.D. Tex. 2010) (commenting that loss of relevant evidence may be harmful as well as helpful to spoliator).

is the foundation for large parts of what will follow in the ensuing litigation. Cheap cement in a foundation will doom a construction project. Inadequate preservation—as daunting and expensive as doing it well is—may end up costing the client significantly more.[38]

PREPARING TO WRITE A LITIGATION HOLD

Timing Is Everything: When a Litigation Hold Is Necessary

The duty to preserve arises when litigation is reasonably anticipated, threatened, or pending. Although receipt of a complaint or a subpoena (in the case of third parties) can be obvious triggers, they are hardly prerequisites to initiate the duty to preserve.[39] Rather, the duty may arise well before the service of a complaint, regardless of "whether the organization is bringing the action, is the target of the action, or a third party possessing relevant evidence."[40] For example, the initiation of a regulatory investigation, the filing of an administrative charge, receipt of a notice of claim, or an accident resulting in serious injury all could trigger the duty,[41] sometimes years before the litigation commences.[42]

There is no bright-line rule for deciding when a client should reasonably anticipate litigation, thus triggering its duty to preserve. Rather, identifying the trigger requires a "good faith and reasonable evaluation of the facts and circumstances as they are known at the time."[43] The analysis can shift depending on whether the litigant is a plaintiff or defendant. For prospective plaintiffs, the test is often when

---

38. That said, as discussed *infra*, reasonableness and proportionality—not perfection—are the touchstones here, but those are in the eye of the beholder and most often measured in hindsight. It is best to err on the side of caution, however, to avoid preservation disputes to the extent possible.

39. *See* Sedona, *supra* note 2, at 271; *see also* Orbit One Commc'ns, Inc. v. Numerex Corp., 271 F.R.D. 429, 436 (S.D.N.Y. 2010) (stating that the "obligation to preserve evidence arises when the party has notice that the evidence is relevant to litigation—most commonly when suit has already been filed . . . but also on occasion in other circumstances, as for example when a party should have known that the evidence may be relevant to future litigation" (internal citations omitted)).

40. Sedona, *supra* note 2, at 271; *see CTB, Inc.*, 2016 WL 1244998, at *8 ("A duty to preserve arises not only after litigation has been commenced, but 'also extends to that period before the litigation when a party reasonably should know that the evidence may be relevant to anticipated litigation.'" (internal citations and quotations omitted)).

41. *See* Sedona, *supra* note 2, at 271–74.

42. *Major Tours, Inc.*, 2009 WL 2413631, at *4 (holding that duty to preserve was triggered by defendants' receipt of September 11, 2003, letter alleging racial profiling, "even though the complaint was not filed until June 15, 2005").

43. Sedona, *supra* note 2, at 272; *see* United States ex rel. Baker v. Cmty. Health Sys., Inc., No. CIV. 05-279 WJ/ACT, 2012 WL 12294413, at *4 (D.N.M. Aug. 31, 2012) ("When litigation is 'reasonably foreseeable' is a flexible fact-specific standard that allows a district court to exercise the discretion necessary to confront the myriad factual situations inherent in the spoliation inquiry.").

the party determined that "legal action is appropriate."[44] This could include seeking advice of counsel, sending a cease and desist letter or taking specific steps to commence litigation.[45] For defendants, on the other hand, "credible information that [they are] the target of legal action may be sufficient to trigger the duty to preserve."[46] Credibility (or a lack thereof) may depend on "the nature of the threat itself" or from "past experience regarding the type of threat, the person who made the threat, the legal bases" for the threat or any of a number of factors.[47] For example, "the trigger point for a small dispute . . . might occur at a later point than for a dispute that is significant in terms of business risk or financial consequences."[48]

In the case of corporate defendants, identifying the trigger point can be particularly difficult. Where one employee or agent of the corporation comes upon facts that—when known by the right person—could lead the corporation to reasonably anticipate litigation, has that triggered the duty to preserve?[49] "Often, the answer will depend on the nature of the knowledge, the potential litigation, and the agent."[50] Courts, for example, have held that widespread knowledge among employees, but especially management, that a plaintiff may sue the corporation can trigger the duty to preserve.[51] Generally, "[a]n agent's knowledge is imputed to the corporation where the agent is acting within the scope of his authority and where the knowledge relates to matters within the scope of that authority."[52] Consequently, the knowledge of managerial figures increases the prospect that the duty to preserve has attached.[53]

But that, unfortunately, does not necessarily end the calculus. As the corporation (or new corporate personnel) acquires further information, it may need to re-evaluate a prior conclusion that litigation was or was not anticipated, thus triggering the duty to preserve or a cessation of preservation efforts.[54]

---

44. Sedona, *supra* note 2, at 271.
45. *Id.*
46. *Id.*
47. *Id.* at 272.
48. *Id.*
49. *Id.*
50. *Id.*
51. *See, e.g.*, Zubulake v. UBS Warburg LLC ("Zubulake IV"), 220 F.R.D. 212, 217 (S.D.N.Y. 2003) (holding duty to preserve was triggered when "almost everyone associated with [plaintiff] recognized the possibility that she might sue," including plaintiff's supervisors). At the same time, however, "merely because one or two employees contemplate the possibility that a fellow employee might sue does not generally impose a firm-wide duty to preserve." *Id.*; *see generally* Tim Winslow & Jason Malone, *Don't Hold Back: When and How Corporate Counsel Should Implement A Litigation Hold*, 51 Jurimetrics J. 245, 246–54 (2001) (discussing triggers for the duty to preserve).
52. Sedona, *supra* note 2, at 271 (quoting *In re Hellenic, Inc.*, 252 F.3d 391, 395 (5th Cir. 2002)).
53. *See, e.g.*, Broccoli v. Echostar Comm'ns Corp., 229 F.R.D. 506, 510–11 (D. Md. 2005) (holding that defendant employer was placed on notice of potential litigation and thus had a duty to preserve documents as soon as the plaintiff employee informed two supervisors of another supervisor's sexually harassing behavior); *Zubulake IV*, 220 F.R.D. at 217 (concluding that knowledge of various employees, including plaintiff's supervisors, triggered duty to preserve).
54. Sedona, *supra* note 2, at 271.

Tell Signs of the Litigation Hold Trigger

Identifying when the client should reasonably anticipate litigation, thereby triggering the duty to preserve, is simple in theory and in hindsight. Theory and hindsight, however, are the province of the courts. In practice, circumstances are rarely as clear and the analysis is far trickier. The difficult reality is that "a variety of events may alert a party to the prospect of litigation."[55] "Often these events provide only limited information about" the prospective litigation such that "the scope of information that should be preserved" or whether the duty to preserve has been triggered at all "may remain uncertain."[56] To that end, the Federal Rules Advisory Committee has cautioned: "It is important not to be blinded to this reality by hindsight arising from familiarity with an action as it is actually filed."[57]

This is not to suggest that deciding when the duty to preserve attaches is always a complex analysis. Sometimes, the answer may be as plain as reading the date on the complaint or subpoena. But for those circumstances where the answer is not as clear—whether because critical personnel have left the client, the client has delayed counsel's involvement, the threat itself is vague, or any other reason—the Sedona Conference has developed a set of factors to assist counsel and clients in considering whether the duty to preserve has attached:

- The nature and specificity of the complaint or threat;
- The party making the claim;
- The business relationship between the accused and accusing parties;
- Whether the threat is direct, implied, or inferred;
- Whether the party making the claim is known to be aggressive or litigious;
- Whether a party who could assert a claim is aware of the claim;
- The strength, scope, or value of a known or reasonably anticipated claim;
- Whether the company has learned of similar claims;
- The experience of the industry; and
- Reputable press and/or industry coverage of the issue either directly pertaining to the client or of complaints brought against someone similarly situated in the industry.[58]

---

55. Fed. R. Civ. P. 37(e) advisory committee's note to 2015 amendment; *see, e.g.*, First Am. Title Ins. Co. v. Northwest Title Ins. Agency, LLC, 2:15-cv-00229, 2016 WL 4548398, at *3 (D. Utah Aug. 31, 2016) (holding that defendant's duty to preserve was triggered upon receipt of preservation notice from plaintiff); *CTB, Inc.*, 2016 WL 1244998, at *11 (providing that plaintiff's preservation duty triggered when it notified trademark office of defendant's alleged infringement); *Baker*, 2012 WL 12294413, at *5 (holding that government's preservation obligations attached when defendants rejected government's settlement offer); Caston v. Hoaglin, No. 2:08-CV-200, 2009 WL 1687927, at *3 (S.D. Ohio June 12, 2009) (involving motion to issue subpoenas for the purposes of requiring preservation of relevant information); Keithley v. Homestore.com, Inc., 629 F. Supp. 2d 972, 977 (N.D. Cal. 2008) (concluding duty to preserve was triggered when plaintiff sent defendant letter indicating that it assumed defendant "wishes to litigate this matter").

56. Fed. R. Civ. P. 37(e) advisory committee's note to 2015 amendment.

57. *Id.*

58. Sedona, *supra* note 2, at 276.

These factors are hardly exhaustive and the weight and relevance counsel should give any particular factor depends "on the nature of the [client] and the nature of the litigation."[59] They can be a useful starting point, however, in identifying when the preservation duty attaches.

Should the Hold Communication Be in Writing?

Once the duty to preserve arises, counsel and the client must promptly communicate and implement a litigation hold to alert relevant document custodians of their preservation obligations and guide preservation efforts. But must the hold be in writing? Or is an oral hold sufficient?

Courts have struggled to answer the question consistently. Some have treated the failure to issue a written hold as evidence of per se gross negligence in complying with preservation obligations and therefore sanctionable.[60] In recent years, however, courts have moved away from this draconian approach to a more nuanced position.[61] Although courts still recognize oral holds as "problematic" and potentially insufficient "to fulfill a party's discovery obligations" in some circumstances, they acknowledge that there may be cases where simply issuing an oral hold could satisfy the duty to preserve.[62] For example, "in a small enterprise," one court has noted, "issuing a written litigation hold may not only be unnecessary, but it could be counterproductive, since such a hold would likely be more general and less tailored to individual records custodians than oral directives could be."[63]

Despite such judicial acknowledgments, however, such conditions will be rare and clients and counsel take a risk in assuming their case fits within those special parameters. Instead, the best (and safest) measure in most circumstances remains to communicate the hold orally *and* in writing. Indeed, counsel and clients should take advantage of both means of communication to ensure proper dispersal and compliance with the litigation hold. The purpose of the hold request, after all, is to ensure that potentially relevant information is preserved, not just to check the box that a hold has been sent.

---

59. *Id.*
60. *See* Pension Comm. of the Univ. of Montreal Pension Plan v. Banc of Am. Secs., LLC, 685 F. Supp. 2d 456, 465 (S.D.N.Y. 2010).
61. *See* Chin v. Port Auth. of N.Y. & N.J., 685 F.3d 135, 162 (2d Cir. 2012) (abrogating *Pension Comm.* and holding that failure to issue a litigation hold is not gross negligence per se and not sanctionable by default); *First Am. Title Ins. Co.*, 2016 WL 4548398, at *2 (providing that oral litigation hold is not per se violative of duty to preserve).
62. *First Am. Title Ins. Co.*, 2016 WL 4548398, at *2; *see also Orbit One Commc'ns*, 271 F.R.D. at 441 ("Indeed, under some circumstances, a formal litigation hold may not be necessary at all"); Sedona, *supra* note 2, at 283 (noting that litigation hold should be in a form, which may include e-mail, written hard copy or, in some cases, oral notice, which is appropriate to the circumstances).
63. *Orbit One Comm'ns, Inc.*, 271 F.R.D. at 441.

ACQUIRING INFORMATION TO COMMUNICATE, EFFECTUATE, AND MONITOR THE HOLD: WHO NEEDS TO PRESERVE DOCUMENTS AND WHAT DO THEY NEED TO PRESERVE?

Implementing a litigation hold is primarily an exercise in gathering and interpreting facts. Counsel must work with the client to identify whom to alert of the duty to preserve, the documents they must preserve, the details of any records retention/destruction policies, and the additional cost, if any, to the client in suspending those policies.

Identifying the Recipients of the Litigation Hold

Recall that the duty to preserve does not extend to every document in the litigant's possession, custody, or control, but to only those persons likely to have discoverable information, also known as "custodians."[64] Most often, custodians will be "the 'key players' in the litigation, i.e., the people identified in a party's initial disclosure and any subsequent supplementation thereto."[65] "Because of the distributed nature of ESI," however, it will be frequently necessary "to communicate a legal hold notice not only to relevant data-generating or -receiving custodians, but also to appropriate data stewards, records management personnel, information technology personnel, and other potentially knowledgeable personnel."[66]

The Custodians

Although the client can easily direct counsel to its information technology (IT) and record management people, establishing the custodians whose data the client must preserve can sometimes be a more complex ordeal. Ultimately, the allegations of the claim/dispute control who are the custodians. Sometimes, a preservation notice, complaint, or subpoena will provide counsel with everything they need to know about these persons. Other times, however, counsel will need to draw that information out from the client contact after reviewing the available facts. Counsel should ask:

- Who are the people involved in the dispute or with knowledge of the facts underlying it?
- What was their level of involvement/knowledge, if known?

---

64. Sedona, *supra* note 2, at 277 ("the typical legal hold process focuses on key custodians and data stewards, who are asked to take steps to preserve relevant information and help prevent losses due to routine business operations.").

65. Zubulake v. UBS Warburg LLC ("Zubulake V"), 229 F.R.D. 422, 433 (S.D.N.Y. 2004).

66. Sedona, *supra* note 2, at 283.

- Do they still work for the client? If not, where are they now?[67]
- Are there any reasons to think the custodian may be prone to delete material when notified of the dispute?
- Do any third-party consultants or agents possess relevant documents/data?
- Does the client still engage these third parties?

With answers to these questions, counsel should be able to move forward with an assessment of what documents must be preserved.

But the process is not always easy. The client contact may not have all the answers, particularly when the claim is hazy or critical pieces of information are missing that would otherwise establish a custodian's tie to the issues. In such circumstances, identifying the custodians can be just as elusive as determining when the duty to preserve has been triggered. Counsel may need to interview known custodians or review their documents to establish a complete list.

Another potential complication rests with the fact that some cases may involve a large number of people who likely possess discoverable information, posing issues as to both the scope and cost of preservation efforts. "CCs" on e-mails, for example, can multiply the number of relevant documents and custodians at a dramatic pace. The litigant should attempt to sort out such issues with opposing counsel via pre-suit negotiation, if appropriate, or as part of the Rule 26(f) conference, with resort to the court in the event negotiations fail.[68] As with other discovery demands, principles of proportionality apply to preservation efforts.[69] Courts (and litigants), therefore, should keep in mind both the scope of the dispute, the amount in controversy, the significance of the issues, and the cost of preservation in assessing how many custodians the hold should cover.[70]

---

67. Where a former employee is a key custodian, the litigant has a duty to preserve and produce upon request former employees' relevant documents in the litigant's possession, custody, or control. *See* Pippins v. KPMG LLP, 279 F.R.D. 245, 254 (S.D.N.Y. 2012) (holding that defendant in class action brought by audit associates must preserve hard-drives of all former audit associates). Courts have split over whether this duty extends to relevant documents in the possession of former employees. *Compare* Exp.-Imp. Bank of the U.S. v. Asia Pulp & Paper Co., Ltd., 233 F.R.D. 338, 341–42 (S.D.N.Y. 2005) (holding that a corporation must "exhaust the practical means at its disposal to obtain the documents from" former employee); *In re* Folding Carton Antitrust Litig., 76 F.R.D. 420, 423 (N.D. Ill. 1977) (suggesting that an employer may have control over documents in the possession of a former employee if that individual is still receiving economic benefits from the employer), *with* Cache La Poudre Feeds, LLC v. Land O'Lakes, Inc., 244 F.R.D. 614, 627 (D. Colo. 2007) (collecting authority as to employer's obligation to contact former employees believed to possess responsive documents and declining plaintiff's invitation that court compel defendant to make such effort); Miniace v. Pac. Mar. Ass'n, No. C 04-03506 SI, 2006 WL 335389, at *2 (N.D. Cal. Feb. 13, 2006) (denying motion to compel production of documents in possession of former directors of defendant).
68. *See infra* notes 91–99 and accompanying text.
69. *See* Sedona, *supra* note 2, at 278 (citing *Rimkus Consulting Grp., Inc.*, 688 F. Supp. 2d at 613).
70. Fed. R. Civ. P. 26 and advisory committee's notes to 2015 amendment; *see Rimkus Consulting Grp., Inc.*, 688 F. Supp. 2d at 613 ("Whether preservation or discovery conduct is acceptable in a case depends on what is reasonable, and that in turn depends on whether what was done—or not done—was proportional to that case and consistent with clearly established applicable standards.").

When attempting to negotiate the scope of a litigation hold with opposing counsel, be mindful of the type of claim and their client's preservation obligations. In commercial disputes, where all parties face similar issues, negotiating may come easier than in a personal injury claim, where the other side has limited preservation obligations. In the latter cases, early recourse to the courts may be necessary.

Third Party Consultants/Service Providers/Agents

As part of the custodian analysis, counsel must also account for the client's third party consultants, service providers, and agents, because the duty to preserve extends not only to documents in the litigant's possession, but also to documents within the litigant's control, as defined by Rule 34.[71] A "party has control over documents when it has the 'right, authority, or practical ability to obtain the documents from a non-party to the action.'"[72] This is typical of the relationship between principals and their consultants/agents.[73] Accordingly, third party consultant/agent materials may be often within a litigant's control, even if not in the litigant's possession, and, the litigant, therefore, has a duty to ensure that the third party consultant/agent preserves that information.[74]

Deciding What Must Be Preserved

The Legal Scope of Preservation: All That Is "Relevant," "Reasonable," and "Proportional"

As discussed in the first section, the duty to preserve is broad. Once litigation is reasonably anticipated, litigants must "identify, locate, and maintain" information that is "*relevant* to the claims or defenses of any party" or "*relevant* to the subject matter involved in the action."[75] The duty attaches to documents or tangible things

---

71. Sedona, *supra* note 2, at 279 ("Some sources of information under the control of third parties may also be deemed to be within the control of the organization because of contractual or other relationships.").

72. GenOn Mid-Atl., LLC v. Stone & Webster, Inc., 282 F.R.D. 346, 354 (S.D.N.Y. 2012) (internal citations omitted).

73. *See id.* (noting that consultant's ongoing relationship with plaintiff put relevant documents in consultant's possession within plaintiff's "practical control"); *see also* Libertarian Party of Ohio v. Husted, No. 2:13–CV–953, 2014 WL 3928293, at *2 (S.D. Ohio Aug. 12, 2014) (identifying "explicit contractual right" as an example of the type of relationship that gives a party control over documents possessed by another); Mazzei v. Money Store, No. 01cv5694 (JGK)(RLE), 2014 WL 3610894 (S.D.N.Y. July 21, 2014) ("A principal is deemed in control of the documents held by its agents.").

74. *See GenOn Mid-Atl., LLC*, 282 F.R.D. at 355 (holding that third-party consultant that maintained continuing relationship with principal was within principal's practical control and therefore principal "had a duty to ensure that those [third-party consultant] materials were adequately preserved."). Some courts, moreover, hold that even where the litigant knows of potential evidence held by a third party, but lacks the ability to affect its preservation, the litigant "still has an obligation to give the opposing party notice of access to the evidence or of the possible destruction of the evidence if the party anticipates litigation involving that evidence." *Id.* at 354 (internal citations omitted).

75. *Apple Inc.*, 881 F. Supp. 2d at 1137 (emphasis added); *see* Sedona, *supra* note 2, at 268 (noting that party must take "reasonable steps to preserve what it knows, or reasonably should know is relevant in the action,

made by persons likely to have discoverable information—"the key players in the case"—as well as "documents prepared for those individuals, to the extent those documents can be readily identified" and are relevant.[76]

Relevance, of course, is in the eye of the beholder, an amorphous concept that, at its worst, is bound only by an opposing party's imagination. Some courts attempt to place limits on the preservation obligation by noting that "relevance means *only* that the materials sought are reasonably calculated to lead to the discovery of admissible evidence."[77] In other words, "relevance" for preservation purposes "means relevance for the purposes of discovery."[78] But this is not a particularly meaningful limit, given that "relevance for purposes of discovery . . . is an extremely broad concept."[79] "There is," moreover, "no 'bad document' exception."[80] In such circumstances, litigants may feel as if they have no choice other than to retain "all relevant documents . . . in existence at the time the duty to preserve attaches."[81]

Relevance is key to establishing the world of information that may require preservation, but it is not the sole guidepost for what clients must preserve. Rather, the "touchstone" for managing the scope of preservation is reasonableness and proportionality.[82] To that end, Rule 26(b)(1) limits the scope of discovery to not just what "is relevant to any party's claim or defense," but also "proportional to the needs of the case." In assessing proper compliance with the preservation duty, therefore, parties in the first instance (and courts in review), should ask what steps are reasonable and proportional.[83] Like the trigger for the preservation duty itself, the "reasonable and proportional" inquiry is fact-specific. As one court stated: "Whether preservation or discovery conduct is acceptable in a case depends on what is reasonable, and that in turn depends on whether what was done—or not done—was proportional to that case and consistent with clearly established applicable standards."[84] Factors for consideration "include the nature of the issues raised in the matter, the

---

is reasonably calculated to lead to the discovery of admissible evidence, is reasonably likely to be requested during discovery and/or is the subject of a pending discovery request" (internal citation and quotation marks omitted)).

76. *Apple Inc.*, 881 F. Supp. 2d at 1137.

77. *Czuchaj*, 2016 WL 4161818, at *2 (citing Oppenheimer Fund, Inc. v. Sanders, 437 U.S. 340, 351 (1978)) (emphasis added).

78. *Orbit One Commc'ns, Inc.*, 271 F.R.D. at 436–37.

79. *Id.* (internal citation and quotation marks omitted). To some degree, defining "relevance" in the same fashion for preservation and discovery purposes is unavoidable. To do otherwise risks putting too much reliance on subjective understandings of what is and is not important in a particular matter. As one court recognized: the "argument of an accused spoliator that it did not violate its duty to preserve evidence because it retained the 'relevant' information and only deleted 'irrelevant' information rings particularly hollow." *Baker*, 2012 WL 12294413, at *11 (quoting Goodman v. Praxair Servs. Inc., 632 F. Supp. 2d 494, 517 n.12 (D. Md. 2009)). Thus the "ultimate decision of what is relevant is not determined by a party's subjective assessment filtered through its own perception of self-interest." *Id.* (internal citation omitted).

80. *Yelton*, 279 F.R.D. at 384.

81. *Orbit One Commc'ns, Inc.*, 271 F.R.D. at 436–37.

82. Sedona, *supra* note 2, at 279.

83. *Id.* at 270 & n.35.

84. *See Rimkus Consulting Grp., Inc.*, 688 F. Supp. 2d at 613.

accessibility of the information, the probative value of the information, and the relative burdens and cost of the preservation effort."[85]

Given the fact-specific nature of the "reasonable and proportional" inquiry, the analysis is hardly predictable. Perhaps unsurprisingly, therefore, courts have handled questions as to what is reasonable preservation unevenly. For example, one court has held that "as a general rule," a "litigation hold does not apply to inaccessible backup tapes" which "may continue to be recycled."[86] But in the same breath, the court held such tapes had to be preserved, when the party in possession knew which "tapes [contained] the documents of 'key players.'"[87] Likewise, some courts have held that, although litigants must preserve all relevant documents, this duty does not extend to "multiple identical copies" of those documents.[88] Other courts, however, have questioned the usefulness of the rule, noting that it may not always be correct, particularly when the recipients or time of receipt is important to the litigation.[89]

Thus, although "reasonableness and proportionality" are "good guiding principles," they remain "highly elastic" concepts, such that "they cannot be assumed to create a safe harbor for a party that is obligated to preserve evidence but is not operating under a court-imposed preservation order."[90] For this reason, a litigant must weigh any decision not to preserve with care and, if possible, consult opposing counsel or seek guidance from the court.

The Practical Scope of Preservation—The 26(f) Conference

The only way of establishing a scope of preservation with defined limits understood by all parties, which the court can memorialize in a preservation order, is through communication with opposing counsel. To that end, the Federal Rules of Civil Procedure specifically seek to foster such conferences early in the life of a case. Rule 26(f) "requires discussion of issues about preserving discoverable information" prior to the Scheduling Conference required by Rule 16(b).[91] These discussions, moreover, need not wait for the filing of the complaint but, where appropriate, can (and should) begin in the pre-suit phase.

In setting an acceptable scope of preservation, counsel should discuss the number and identities of custodians whose documents will be searched, the type of information involved, whether the litigation hold extends to active, historical, and/or future data, the relevant timeframe, and the cost to preserve and potentially

---

85. Sedona, *supra* note 2, at 270.
86. *Zubulake IV*, 220 F.R.D. at 217.
87. *Id.* at 218.
88. *See, e.g., id.*
89. *See Orbit One Commc'ns, Inc.*, 271 F.R.D. at 442 (observing that it "may not always be obvious what constitutes an 'identical' copy" and discussing circumstances where it could be important to retain all copies of a document").
90. *Id.*
91. *See* Sedona, *supra* note 2, at 268.

restore information.[92] Where the parties cannot reach agreement on preservation issues, they should promptly seek judicial guidance on the matter.[93] Quick resort to the court may help resolve confusion as to the proper scope of preservation and reduce the prospect that relevant data might be lost by deferring resolution of the disagreement.[94]

In resolving a preservation dispute, the court should consider whether the request is reasonable and proportional to the needs of the case, including the amount in controversy, the significance of the issues, and the scope of the case.[95] "The court should [also] be sensitive to party resources[.] [A]ggressive preservation efforts can be extremely costly, and parties (including governmental parties) may have limited staff and resources to devote to those efforts."[96] Likewise, the 2015 Advisory Committee notes to amended Rule 37 provide that courts should recognize that a "party may act reasonably by choosing a less costly form of information preservation, if it is substantially as effective as more costly forms."[97] Finally, in bringing an issue to the court, the party arguing that preservation is unreasonable or disproportionate should "provide specifics about these matters in order to enable meaningful discussion of the appropriate preservation regime."[98]

Discussion of preservation issues in conferences under Rule 26(f) work to potentially spare litigants and the courts of the cost and frustration of high stakes fights over motions for spoliation sanctions. Through discussion (pre-suit and post-complaint) and, if necessary, motion practice during the early stages of the litigation, litigants can turn the nearly boundless theoretical scope of preservation into a substantive, understandable, case-specific set of preservation rules and root them in a court order.[99]

The Nuts and Bolts of Preservation: What Kind of Documents Are at Issue and Where Are They Located?

To ensure a productive Rule 26(f) conference and effectively articulate any concerns as to the reasonableness of preservation efforts to the court, counsel must

---

92. *See id.* at 280–81.

93. Fed. R. Civ. P. 37(e) advisory committee's note on 2015 amendment.

94. *Id.*

95. Fed. R. Civ. P. 26(b)(1); *see* Sedona, *supra* note 2, at 278; *see also Rimkus Consulting Grp., Inc.*, 688 F. Supp. 2d at 613.

96. Fed. R. Civ. P. 37(e) advisory committee's note on 2015 amendment. *But see Orbit One Commc'ns, Inc.*, 271 F.R.D. at 442 ("Proportionality is particularly tricky in the context of preservation. It seems unlikely, for example, that a court would excuse the destruction of evidence merely because the monetary value of anticipated litigation was low.").

97. Fed. R. Civ. P. 37(e) advisory committee's note on 2015 amendment.

98. *Id.*; *see, e.g., Apple Inc.*, 881 F. Supp. 2d at 1140 (rejecting defendants' claim that the added cost of "extending the retention policy" justified defendants' failure to do so, where defendant had apparently not considered or provided the court with estimates for the cost of less expensive alternative methods of preservation).

99. Fed. R. Civ. P. 37(e) advisory committee's note on 2015 amendment ("Preservation orders may become more common, in part because Rules 16(b)(3)(B)(iii) and 26(f)(3)(C) are amended to encourage discovery plans and orders that address preservation.").

have a firm grasp of the type and volume of relevant documents in the client's possession, custody, or control, the client's information technology infrastructure, and how the records are kept.[100] This is not just a practical necessity, but part of counsel's duty to ensure proper implementation of the litigation hold. "Once a 'litigation hold' is in place, a party and her counsel must make certain that all sources of potentially relevant information are identified and placed 'on hold.'"[101] In doing so, counsel and the litigant should "consider the sources of information within [the litigant's] 'possession, custody, and control' that are likely to include relevant, unique information."[102] "The most obvious of these sources are those that the [litigant] physically has in its possession or custody," such as filing cabinets and the e-mails on its servers at headquarters, but could also include sources like "thumb drives, company furnished laptops, and PDAs used by employees for business purposes."[103]

As with so much of the litigation hold process, identifying the relevant document sources, types, and retention policies is case specific. To acquire this knowledge, counsel must interview the custodians, and the client's IT/records management personnel, on a variety of matters. Suggested questions for each follow.[104]

Where significant portions of the relevant data is electronic, understanding and keeping track of document sources, types, storage media, and retention policies can rapidly become a highly technical affair. In matters involving ESI, therefore, counsel and the client should consider retaining the services of an e-discovery consultant to assist in the process of interviewing custodians and, particularly, the client's IT and records management personnel. These consultants specialize in the identification and collection of ESI. Thus, they can provide substantial assistance in ensuring that counsel asks the right questions to exhaust the client's knowledge as to relevant document sources and the workings of the client's information technology infrastructure.[105]

Additionally, retention of a qualified, proven e-discovery consultant offers a number of potentially critical important advantages. They can offer expert support in any litigated discovery battle. They are separate from the client and can offer some objectivity. They can help insulate the client and be of tremendous assistance in helping counsel convince the client what steps are necessary, why they are

---

100. Identifying what documents are substantively relevant is a case-specific exercise, dependent on the allegations of the complaint and the subject matter of the dispute, as described briefly at *supra* notes 75–90 and accompanying text. Defining "substantively relevant" documents is more of a matter of document review and assessment based on case-specific facts, rather than a question of document preservation. It is distinct, therefore, from the acquisition of an understanding of the potentially relevant world of information and issues associated with preserving all or a part of that information.

101. *Zubulake V*, 229 F.R.D. at 432.

102. Sedona, *supra* note 2, at 279.

103. *Id.*

104. *See infra* notes 105–118 and accompanying text.

105. *Yelton*, 279 F.R.D. at 387 ("As the *Zubulake* court noted, '[o]ne of the primary reasons that electronic data is lost is ineffective communication with information technology personnel.'" (internal citation omitted and brackets in original)).

necessary, and—importantly—why the client's in-house technology personnel may not be the best choice for the work.

In other circumstances, counsel may be dealing with a sophisticated client that has substantial experience with litigation holds, dedicated staff, and existing protocols. If so, consult early and directly with such resources.

Questions for Custodians

As part of implementing the litigation hold, counsel should speak with the custodians about their duty to preserve relevant documents, as well as the location of those documents, and methods they used to communicate about the matter in dispute.[106] Such questions may include:

- When did the custodian become aware of the dispute and the facts underlying the dispute?
- When did the custodian first start communicating about the dispute or the facts underlying the dispute?
- Excluding this interview, when did the custodian last communicate about the dispute or the facts underlying the dispute?[107]
- By what means did the custodian communicate about the dispute or the facts underlying the dispute (e.g., in-person conversations; phone calls; text messages; letters; inter-office memoranda; corporate e-mail; personal e-mail; social media; instant messaging application for phone, tablet, or computer)?
- Were there any meetings regarding the dispute?
- If so, were there documents at the meetings? Where are those documents now?
- Do you keep paper documents about the dispute or the facts underlying the dispute?
- Do you throw out paper documents or delete e-mail/electronic documents related to the litigant's business?
- Have you deleted/thrown out any documents/e-mails related to the dispute?
- If so, when?[108]

In most cases, counsel will speak with the custodian before collecting documents for review. That said, where the "custodian is the subject of the investigation

---

106. *Baker*, 2012 WL 12294413, at *2 ("It will also involve communicating with the 'key players' in the litigation, in order to understand how they stored information.").

107. Although the complaint, subpoena, or other facts may provide counsel with all they need to know as to the relevant timeframe, when the custodian became involved in the dispute and began communicating about it can be useful information to have in terms of setting a period for any electronic search of that custodian's relevant documents.

108. If the custodian reveals that he or she has disposed of documents after the duty to preserve attached, counsel should immediately instruct the custodian to cease further deletion/destruction of documents relevant to the substance of the litigation and review available avenues to recover the lost information.

or litigation," collection of information prior to notice to the custodian "may be prudent in light of the risk that . . . he or she might take steps to delete or destroy relevant information if aware of the circumstances."[109] Counsel should make this determination in consultation with supervisory client personnel (e.g., general counsel).

A separate issue emerges where it is not feasible for counsel to speak with every custodian, given the size of the company or the scope of the lawsuit. In such circumstances, "counsel must be more creative" and should seek to leverage technology to ensure sufficient litigation hold implementation.[110] For example, it may be possible to run a systemwide keyword search, such that counsel could solicit a broad list of search terms from opposing counsel for preservation purposes only and "then preserve a copy of each 'hit.'"[111] E-discovery consultants can be of great assistance in developing and defending such strategies.

Questions for the Client's IT and Records Management Personnel

Speaking to the custodians about the duty to preserve and the relevant documents in their possession is only half the battle. "Once the duty to preserve evidence is triggered, a party must [also] suspend any existing policies related to deleting or destroying files and preserve all relevant documents related to the litigation."[112] Thus, counsel "must become familiar with the client's document retention policies, which involves speaking with information technology" and records management personnel to ensure adequate application of the litigation hold.[113]

These interviews are where e-discovery consultants can really prove their worth, as they can speak the same language as IT personnel—and translate for counsel—to ensure all requisite and important questions are asked and answered. Frequently, it will be preferable for the e-discovery consultant to lead the interview with client IT and records personnel, with counsel present to answer legal questions on preservation, ask questions, and make sure everyone has a complete understanding of what will be done. Topics for discussion should include:

- What is the IT infrastructure like?
- How is information communicated/processed?
- Does the client issue phones, tablets, laptops, or home computers to employees?
- Where are paper documents stored (e.g., filing cabinets, warehouses, desk drawers)?

---

109. Sedona, *supra* note 2, at 283.
110. *See Zubulake V*, 229 F.R.D. at 432.
111. *Id.* at 432 & n.75. Opposing counsel would then provide a narrower, more targeted set of search terms in connection with requests for production, which would be run only against the body of preserved data identified by the broader set of preservation hits. *Id.* at 432.
112. *Czuchaj*, 2016 WL 4161818, at *1 (internal quotation marks and citations omitted).
113. *Baker*, 2012 WL 12294413, at *2.

- If not saved locally on company issued devices, where can key custodians' electronic documents be found (e.g., servers, shared drives)?
- What are the client's ESI backup procedures?[114]
- Can backup tapes be identified as storing information created by or for key custodians?[115]
- If so, where are the tapes stored? Can they be segregated?[116]
- Does the client use third party service providers to assist in data management and storage?[117]
- Describe any document/data retention policies?
- How often does ESI drop from active status to inactive/archive status?
- Is it possible to suspend the data retention policies as to certain custodians only?
- How difficult would it be to restore ESI to active status once it is archived/rendered inactive?
- What would the cost of restoration be?
- What is the cost of, or problem, with just stopping all destruction of documents/ESI indefinitely?
- What is the cost of preserving everything opposing counsel wants preserved?

As part of the interview, counsel and the consultant also should be prepared to field questions from the client relative to the impact of the litigation hold on the client's business. For example, the client may ask, "when may we resume operation of our regular document retention policies"? The answer, here, is most often "when the litigation that triggered the hold is no longer pending or reasonably anticipated" or when the court orders otherwise. Similarly, if the costs of complying with an adversary's preservation demands are too great, the client might ask, "what steps we can take to obtain relief?" In this case, counsel should discuss with the client appropriate motion practice available through the courts, its cost and potential outcomes.[118]

---

114. *Zubulake V*, 229 F.R.D. at 432 ("This will invariably involve speaking with information technology personnel, who can explain system-wide backup procedures and the actual (as opposed to theoretical) implementation of the firm's recycling policy.").

115. *Id.* at 427 ("I further held that [l]itigants are now on notice, at least in this Court, that backup tapes that can be identified as storing information created by or for key players must be preserved." (internal quotation marks and citation omitted)).

116. *Id.* at 434 ("Counsel must also make sure that all backup media which the party is required to retain is identified and stored in a safe place."); *see also id.* ("By taking possession of, or otherwise safeguarding, all potentially relevant backup tapes, counsel eliminates the possibility that such tapes will be inadvertently recycled.").

117. Examples may include "information held by outsourced service providers, storage facilities operators, and application service providers (ASPs). With respect to those sources, the organization should consider providing appropriate notice concerning the need to preserve material that is likely to be relevant." Sedona, *supra* note 2, at 279 (footnote omitted).

118. *See supra* notes 91–99 and accompanying text.

WRITING THE LITIGATION HOLD

What Does the Litigation Hold Need to Say?

As discussed earlier in the chapter, once the duty to preserve attaches, counsel and the client must implement a litigation hold as soon as possible to alert relevant document custodians of their preservation obligations and to guide preservation efforts. In most circumstances, the best practice is to prepare a written litigation hold. Counsel will rarely have a perfect understanding of the custodians or the full scope of available information at the time of writing the hold, but should not let the perfect be the enemy of the good. Much of the fact-gathering process described earlier in the chapter will have just begun and should continue after the initial written litigation hold goes out. As counsel obtains new information, it should update and recirculate the hold to both past recipients and new custodians as appropriate.[119]

In writing the hold document, counsel "should review relevant pleadings or other documents and then describe the litigation in a way that will be understood by those with responsibility for preserving documents."[120] The litigation hold should generally include the following elements, as well as the contact information of the transmitter of the hold and/or counsel. A mock litigation hold memorandum featuring the following components is included at Appendix A.[121]

1. *Introduction.* The introduction to the litigation hold should advise that (1) an event has occurred that has triggered a duty to preserve relevant documents, (2) the recipients have been identified as a potential custodian of said documents, and (3) severe penalties could befall the client (and the recipients) if the recipients do not follow the instructions outlined in the memo.

2. *Subject Matter of Dispute/Issue.* This portion of the litigation hold summarizes the facts necessary for recipients to understand what documents are relevant to the issue or dispute that triggered the duty to preserve. For example, a litigation hold issued following the service of a subpoena might list the topics listed in any schedules attached to the subpoena.

3. *Documents That May Be Relevant.* This section of the hold reiterates the clients' legal duty to preserve—and not destroy—potentially relevant

---

119. Sedona, *supra* note 2, at 270 (noting that litigation hold notice should be "periodically reviewed and, when necessary, reissued in either its original or an amended form").

120. *Id.* at 283.

121. The mock litigation hold memorandum at Appendix A is also consistent with the Sedona Conference's recommended content of a written litigation hold. The Sedona Conference recommends that initial and subsequent litigation holds: (1) "describe the matter at issue," (2) "provide specific examples of the types of information at issue," (3) "identify potential sources of information," (4) "inform recipients of their legal obligations to preserve information," (5) "include reference to the potential consequences to the recipient and the organization of noncompliance," and (6) identify whom recipients "should contact if they have questions or need additional information." *See* Sedona, *supra* note 2, at 283.

documents and ESI. It then provides a non-exhaustive list of examples of such documents. Substantive relevance, of course, will vary depending on the case. In a contract dispute, for instance, potential examples may include documents and ESI related to the formation of the contract, the circumstances at the closing of the transaction, or any documents in a particular timeframe regarding the other parties to the contract.

4. *Forms of Documents and ESI That Must Be Retained.* This part of the litigation hold communicates the breadth of the legal definitions of "documents" and "ESI" in litigation and instructs the recipients to be over-inclusive in their efforts to collect and preserve documents and ESI. It calls for the retention of all relevant paper documents and ESI in the recipients' possession, includes non-exhaustive examples of each, and specifically requests the preservation of non-identical duplicates of documents.

5. *Avoiding Inadvertent Destruction of Documents.* This section of the hold alerts recipients as to the client's obligation to ensure that relevant documents and ESI are not lost or at risk for deletion due to document retention/deletion programs and processes that automatically delete or destroy documents at set intervals of time. It also informs recipients that they may be called to give testimony about document and data preservation efforts.

6. *Do Not Discuss with Unauthorized Persons.* This portion of the litigation hold cautions recipients about discussing the content of the litigation hold memorandum or the underlying dispute/issue, except in response to requests from the client's management or counsel.

7. *Protect the Privilege.* This segment of the litigation hold informs recipients that the documents in their possession, custody, or control regarding this matter may be protected by either the attorney-client privilege or work product doctrine. It advises as to various points for the recipient to keep in mind about preserving the privilege when creating correspondence and having conversations about the issue/dispute that triggered the litigation hold.

8. *Help Identify Additional Custodians.* As noted earlier, counsel may not always know the custodians at the time counsel must prepare the initial written litigation hold. In recognition of this reality, the hold should inform recipients that it is important that all persons who may be custodians receive a copy of the hold document and that the litigant/counsel keep track of all persons who received the notice, in the event the court (or opposing counsel) makes inquiry into the client's collection and preservation efforts. Thus, this part of the hold document requests that recipients review the distribution list attached to the litigation hold memo and notify the sender immediately if the recipients know of a person who may be a custodian who is not on the list. Critically, it asks that recipients not forward the notice until they have contacted the sender and received permission to do so.

9. *Distribution List.* As discussed at point 8.

Written Litigation Holds and the Privilege

Courts diverge as to whether, and in what circumstances, the attorney-client privilege or work product doctrine shields litigation hold memoranda from discovery.[122] They also have applied varying reasons as to when the privilege may not apply or must give way.[123] Regardless of whether they conclude litigation hold memoranda are privileged, however, courts appear to agree that the facts underlying preservation efforts (e.g., what steps were taken, who was notified) are generally discoverable.[124]

Although hardly a picture of clarity, the available precedent suggests certain measures that litigants and their counsel can use to increase the odds of protecting a privilege claim over the hold memoranda. For example, the client should instruct outside counsel to prepare and transmit the litigation hold to custodians to avoid a characterization of the hold as a directive from management, as distinct from "legal advice" from counsel.[125] To that end, if the communication is to come from anyone within the company it should come from in-house counsel. That said, given the case law discussed *supra* and the responsibility for preservation imposed on the client *and* outside counsel who have appeared in the action, outside counsel often send the hold directly to custodians.

Additionally, counsel should draft the hold to reflect legal advice as to compliance with document preservation concerns, and structure the document to avoid

---

122. *Compare* Bagley, 318 F.R.D. at 239 (deeming the contention that litigation hold memorandum is privileged as "something of a stretch"); *In re* Blue Cross Blue Shield Antitrust Litig., No. 2:13-CV-20000-RDP, 2015 WL 10891632, at *6 (N.D. Ala. Nov. 4, 2015) ("litigation/preservation holds and memoranda . . . issued by a corporate party to its employees for the purpose of giving instruction and direction concerning documents and records to be preserved, even where that instruction arises from legal advice from counsel, are not shielded by the attorney-client privilege."), *with* Neighborhood Assistance Corp. of Am. v. U.S. Dep't of Housing & Urban Dev., 19 F. Supp. 3d 1, 22 (D.D.C., 2013) ("To be sure, litigation hold letters are generally privileged"); Muro v. Target Corp., 250 F.R.D. 350, 360 (N.D. Ill. 2007) ("[T]he litigation hold notices, on their face, appear to be privileged.").

123. *See, e.g., Blue Cross Blue Shield*, 2015 WL 10891632, at *4 (concluding that litigation hold representing managerial instructions to employees was not privileged); United States ex rel. Barko v. Halliburton Co., 74 F. Supp. 3d 183, 191 (D.D.C. 2014) (concluding litigation hold was not privileged where defendant widely dispersed hold document among employees without any direction that the document be kept confidential); *Major Tours, Inc.*, 2009 WL 2413631, at *2 (D.N.J. 2009) ("Although in general hold letters are privileged, the prevailing view, which the Court adopts, is that when spoliation occurs the letters are discoverable.").

124. *See, e.g., Bagley*, 318 F.R.D. at 241 ("Courts have recognized the need for plaintiffs to obtain information relating to litigation hold notices, such as whether a notice was actually issued and what steps were thereafter taken to collect and preserve relevant documents and data."); *Blue Cross Blue Shield*, 2015 WL 10891632, at *5 ("Because it [preservation] is a duty inherent in litigation, it must always be subject to supervision and inquiry by the court. Whether a party has fulfilled the duty of preservation cannot be hidden behind a claim of work-product."); Brown v. West Corp., 287 F.R.D. 494, 499 (D. Neb. 2012) ("While such [litigation hold] letters are themselves privileged, the information surrounding the letters is not.").

125. *See, e.g., Bagley*, 318 F.R.D. at 240 (concluding that litigation hold notices issued by university counsel were more akin to "forceful *instructions*" to employees, rather than legal "*advice* as to what to do" (emphases in original)); *Blue Cross Blue Shield*, 2015 WL 10891632, at *6 (holding that litigation hold was not privileged, where corporate legal department issued hold to employees "for the purpose of giving instruction and direction concerning documents and records to be preserved by those employees").

it from appearing as a list of instructions untethered from legal advice.[126] Finally, counsel and the client should exert control over the distribution of the litigation hold to ensure its transmission to the requisite custodians and clearly instruct recipients as to the importance of keeping the document and its content confidential.[127] Although the facts of the case and the disposition of the court will still loom large in the privilege calculus, litigants can improve their chances of withstanding efforts to discover the actual holds by taking such steps.

OBLIGATIONS AFTER THE HOLD GOES OUT

Monitoring Compliance

"While the traditional role of counsel is to 'inform the client of its duty to preserve potentially relevant documents in the client's custody or control and of the possible consequences of failing to do so'" and the ultimate responsibility for preservation rests with clients, counsel should take steps to ensure that litigation holds are not send-and-forget propositions.[128] Rather, some courts hold that counsel have a "continuing responsibility to ensure that the parties preserve relevant information."[129] "This responsibility obligates counsel to do more than simply notify all employees of a litigation hold and expect that the party will then retain and produce all relevant information."[130] Counsel instead "must oversee compliance with the litigation hold, monitoring the party's efforts to retain and produce the relevant documents."[131] For example, counsel can arrange for the periodic recirculation of the litigation hold "so that new employees are aware of it, and so that it is fresh in the minds of all employees," and check-in with custodians to remind them "that the preservation duty is still in place."[132] Failure to take these or other steps may result in sanctions.[133]

---

126. *See Muro*, 250 F.R.D. at 360 ("The court has examined the litigation hold notices *in camera*. Each seem to be communications of legal advice from corporate counsel to corporate employees regarding document preservation.").

127. *See Barko*, 74 F. Supp. 3d at 191 (D.D.C. 2014) (concluding litigation hold notices were not privileged where defendant distributed the notices to large groups, encouraged recipients to share notices with employees who may not have received the first notice, and failing to direct "employees not to discuss the litigation hold notices outside the company").

128. Sedona, *supra* note 2, at 278 (internal citation omitted).

129. *Browder*, 187 F. Supp. 3d at 1295; *accord Bagley*, 318 F.R.D. at 238; *Major Tours, Inc.*, 2009 WL 2413631, at *2.

130. *Browder*, 187 F. Supp. 3d at 1295.; *see Baker*, 2012 WL 12294413, at *11 (observing that the litigant and counsel cannot just assume hold information will "trickle down" to appropriate personnel, with preservation of documents and ESI to follow).

131. *Czuchaj*, 2016 WL 4161818, at *3 (quoting *Zubulake V*, 229 F.R.D. at 432).

132. *Zubulake V*, 229 F.R.D. at 433–34.

133. *See Apple Inc.*, 881 F. Supp. 2d at 1150 (holding that defendant's failure to monitor preservation efforts "in the face of its biweekly destruction policy once litigation holds issued, warrants sanctions").

Reiterating litigation holds also may have salutary effects. At the outset of a dispute, custodians—much like counsel—may not have a complete understanding of the scope of the dispute or the documents that might relate to it. Revisiting these issues may prompt the identification of further documents. Counsel should consider updating the hold, or preparing a cover letter, providing further information on how the dispute has developed.

Ultimate Responsibility Rests with the Client

The monitoring obligation, at least in part, reflects a perception by some courts that convincing clients of the importance of preservation and gaining comfort that they are complying with the duty to preserve are the most difficult parts of implementing a litigation hold. They view counsel as "more conscious of the contours of the preservation obligation" than the client.[134] Such courts reason that "a party cannot reasonably be trusted to receive the 'litigation hold' instruction once and to fully comply with it without the active supervision of counsel."[135]

At the same time, however, courts recognize that a "lawyer cannot be obliged to monitor her client like a parent watching a child."[136] This is particularly so for outside counsel, who cannot be on-site with the client at all hours. "At some point," therefore, "the client must bear responsibility for a failure to preserve."[137] To that end, litigants "should develop ways to regularly monitor a legal hold to ensure compliance."[138] This could "include requiring ongoing certifications from custodians and data stewards, negative consequences for noncompliance, and audit and sampling procedures."[139]

There is nothing, of course, stopping counsel from suggesting such steps as a part of satisfying their (and their clients') preservation obligations. But, the success of such continuing preservation safeguards depends on commitment and involvement on the part of client personnel. "At the end of the day, the duty to preserve and produce documents [ultimately] rests on the party."[140] "Once that duty is made clear to a party, either by court order or by instructions from counsel, that party is on notice of its obligations and acts at its own peril."[141]

---

134. *See, e.g., Zubulake* V, 229 F.R.D. at 433.
135. *See, e.g., id.*
136. *See, e.g., id.*
137. *Id.*
138. Sedona, *supra* note 2, at 286.
139. *Id.*
140. *Zubulake* V, 229 F.R.D. at 436.
141. *Id.*

CONCLUSION

Implementing a litigation hold is a multiple step process requiring fact-specific inquiries and analyses to gauge when the duty to preserve is triggered, the scope of relevant preservation, and how the hold should be communicated. It is a process that continues from the pre-litigation stages through the conclusion of the case. In undertaking this process, counsel and the client have a heavy burden, particularly where the information is electronic and voluminous. Even the best-laid preservation plans, moreover, can be upset by unexpected turns of events. But, by following the procedures outlined in this chapter, paying close attention to the facts of the case, and impressing upon the client the importance of complying with preservation duties and the significant consequences of not doing so, counsel will improve the odds of implementing a successful litigation hold and avoiding (or defeating) adverse motion practice.

APPENDIX A

MOCK LITIGATION HOLD MEMORANDUM

Privileged & Confidential
Attorney-Client Communication
Attorney Work Product

Litigation Hold Memorandum—Please Do Not Forward

To: Schedule A Attached Hereto
           (Distribution List of Potential Custodians at ABC Bank)
From: Outside Counsel
Date: As Soon As Possible After the Duty to Preserve Attaches
Subject: Document Preservation Obligations Respecting Subpoena

Please read the following memorandum in its entirety. Please acknowledge, by return email, that you have read this memorandum, and that you will comply with its instructions.

1. Introduction

On April 1, 2017, Seller issued a subpoena (the "Subpoena") to ABC Bank, directing it to produce its business records and other information related to a series of transactions between Seller and Buyer between June 2016 and September 2016. The Subpoena derives from litigation between Seller and Buyer in the Columbia Superior Court. Seller alleges that Buyer has breached various contracts with Seller, misrepresented Buyer's assets and intentions, and deceived Seller and ABC Bank into transacting with Buyer. Seller, therefore, maintains that ABC Bank is a potential witness to Buyer's alleged misconduct and requests that ABC Bank make a production of documents pertaining to Seller's litigation.

Receipt of the Subpoena triggers a duty to suspend routine document retention policies and to implement a litigation hold to ensure the preservation of potentially relevant documents and electronically stored information ("ESI"). Accordingly,

Privileged & Confidential   **Please Do Not Forward**

we have determined that ABC Bank will preserve all documents and communications relating to the subject matter described in the Subpoena. We have previously instructed ABC Bank to preserve (and cease) any deletion of any documentation verbally but are following up with this written hold. Because the failure to preserve relevant documents and data can result in severe sanctions against ABC Bank and/ or its employees, your immediate assistance is required to preserve all such information, and it is critical that you follow the instructions below.

If you have any questions about this notice and/or your obligations to preserve information and documents, please contact me at (555) 555-5555. Also, please note that you may receive future, follow-up requests relating to this memorandum.

2. Subject Matter of the Subpoena

The subpoenas seek information regarding

(1) Buyer;

(2) Buyer's relationship with ABC Bank; and

(3) the following properties: (i) 123 Third Street, Columbia City, Columbia; (ii) Four Finance Square, Columbia City, Columbia; 75 Stock Place, Columbia City, Columbia; and 300 West Tornado Plaza, Columbia City, Columbia (collectively, the "Properties").

3. What Documents May Be Potentially Relevant to the Subpoena?

ABC Bank has a legal duty to preserve—and not destroy—documents and ESI that may be potentially responsive to the Subpoena. In order to ensure ABC Bank's compliance with the Subpoena, it is important to cast a wide net when defining what may be relevant to the Subpoena, even if such documents or ESI may not appear relevant to you. Please preserve any documents and ESI that relate to the Subpoena in any way. Such documents could include, but are not limited to:

a) All records related to Seller, Buyer, or the Properties;

b) To the extent that a document does not fall within ABC Bank's devoted files for Seller and Buyer: All records and documents, including correspondence, electronic mail, notes of conversations, or any other records related to SELLER's or BUYER's dealings with each other and/or ABC Bank;

c) All records and documents, including correspondence, electronic mail, notes of conversations, reports of investigation, or any other records related to ABC Bank's due diligence of Buyer and the closing of ABC Bank's loans to finance Buyer's acquisitions of the Properties from Seller;

d) Your communications with Buyer, Seller, and personnel associated with Buyer and Seller, including emails, letters, notes, logs of instant messages, and recorded voicemails;

e) The contents of loan files for the above referenced Properties; and

f) To the extent that a document is not in one of the loan files for the Properties: all applications, financial statements, guaranties, credit reports, mortgages, payment histories (including copies of checks front and back), discharges, promissory notes, and all correspondence in any form including electronic mail or messages, concerning Seller, Buyer, or the Properties.

As set forth in the Subpoena, the time period for which documents must be identified and preserved pursuant to this notice is March 1, 2016 to December 31, 2016. Additional notices may be sent as this matter progresses. If you are unsure about the relevance of a document, please be cautious and preserve it.

4. The Forms of Documents and ESI That You Must Retain

Because the definitions of "document" and "ESI" will be broadly construed by a court, you must retain all documents in your possession, custody or control (including without limitation correspondence, emails, letters, facsimiles, notes, presentations, reports, summaries, phone records, calendars, contracts, agreements, drawings, graphs, photographs, data compilations), as well as all ESI (*e.g.*, emails and attachments, Word documents, Excel spreadsheets, PowerPoint presentations, PDFs, text messages). In addition, you must preserve and retain any non-identical duplicates or documents, including drafts, electronic documents with tracked changes, handwritten or electronic notes or comments, highlighting and any other annotations. You must retain all internal communications and reports, as well as all communications with any of the parties or any third party relating to the parties (such as accountants, consultants or financial advisors). Should you have any voicemail that fits within the above categories, please make sure those electronic files are preserved or obtain a transcription of those voicemails and preserve the paper copy of the transcription.

In short, please be over-inclusive in your efforts to collect and preserve documents and ESI.

Privileged & Confidential   Please Do Not Forward

5. Avoiding Inadvertent Document and ESI Destruction

ABC Bank must ensure that all potentially relevant documents and ESI, such as email and other computer files, are adequately preserved so that they are not at risk for deletion due to programs or processes that automatically delete information at set intervals of time (this would include processes that automatically delete emails that remain in an account for a certain period of time).

Please note that you may be called upon to give testimony about your document and data preservation efforts. No one is permitted to destroy or delete relevant evidence that could be helpful to any party or that may support any claim or defense.

6. Please Do Not Discuss This Matter with Unauthorized Persons

Please be circumspect in your communications and *refrain* from speaking about this matter except in response to requests from ABC Bank's management or counsel. Any inquiries from any source outside of ABC Bank, including any press inquiries, should be immediately directed to ABC Bank's management or counsel.

As discussed in Item No. 7 below, privileges applicable to communications (whether written or oral) or documents regarding this matter may be waived if you disclose those communications or information to another, unless an attorney representing ABC Bank is present during, or has approved in advance, the communication or discussion.

7. Help Us Maintain the Attorney-Client Privilege

Communications and other documents in your possession, custody or control regarding this matter may be protected by either the attorney-client privilege or work-product doctrine. *You play an important role in maintaining, and avoiding the potential waiver of, these privileges.* Any such conversations must occur in the presence of corporate or litigation counsel for ABC Bank and in order for such communications to remain privileged (and not be discoverable) they (1) must be between an ABC Bank employee and corporate or litigation counsel; (2) cannot include any outsiders/third parties; and (3) must remain confidential. Please keep these three points in mind when creating correspondence and having conversations about this matter.

In addition, potentially privileged communications or documents should not be shared with or forwarded to outsiders and/or third parties without first discussing with corporate or litigation counsel.

Privileged & Confidential   Please Do Not Forward

8. Help Us Identify Additional Custodians

It is important that this notice be received by all persons who may be custodians. It is also important that I keep track of all persons who have received this notice, in the event that the Court makes inquiry into our collection and preservation efforts. Therefore, if you know of an employee who may be a custodian who is not on the attached distribution list, or has not been advised of his or her preservation obligations, please notify me immediately using the contact information provided below.

Please do not forward this notice without first notifying me and receiving permission to do so, however.

Thank you in advance,

/s/ Outside Counsel

Outside Counsel,

Counsel, Counsel, & Lawyers LLP

One Attorney Lane

Columbia City, Columbia 55555

Phone: 555-555-5555

Privileged & Confidential   **Please Do Not Forward**

SCHEDULE A:
Distribution List (To Be Supplemented)

1. Employee A
2. Employee B
3. Employee C
4. Employee D
5. Employee E

CHAPTER 5

Discovery in the Modern Age

Conducting and Resisting E-Discovery

J. Michael Showalter

In some ways, computers changed everything. Some people have 20,000 personal photos on their phones and no camera. Virtually any song in your computer can play immediately. Our watches keep track of our heart rates and how many steps we take each day. And Facebook! We can find out what several hundred of our high school classmates did today, yesterday, and (for some) each day for the past ten years.

The amount of information available to us and stored by electronic devices is breathtaking. This may be good news for our social lives, but not necessarily for litigation. When litigation begins—in most cases—all of this information is fair game. And lawyers' heads have been spinning for two decades as they figure out how to deal with this information explosion. The problem of electronically stored data adds significant technical issues to problems lawyers have themselves addressed for generations.

This chapter suggests that, in fact, computers have not changed anything in terms of how cases and, specifically, discovery should be managed. The same skills lawyers have used for decades—combined with a modicum of technological fluency—remain important. The meaningful difference in the process is that it now occurs on spreadsheets and laptops, and not pieces of paper with pens and pencils— and that's a positive development. Although the legal framework for conducting discovery has changed somewhat to account for technology, many paradigms—how to conduct it, and how to think about it—really have not.

While it is possible that some litigators' practices have not been radically altered by e-discovery, even straightforward matters that hinge on whether the traffic light was red or green, can involve electronic data like cameras, e-mails, police reports, vehicle data, or Facebook postings. Technological devices, and not shrewd cross-examination, frequently provide insight into what really happened. Getting these materials requires thinking holistically about your case early enough that the materials still can be preserved, collected, and put to use.

PLANNING, CONSISTENCY, AND TRANSPARENCY

Planning, consistency, and transparency are important in addressing e-discovery issues and are helpful in the same manner as they would be in any other life activity. As an example, you may run marathons. There, preparation matters. If you train, you do well; there are few surprises and no magic days.[1] Likewise, consistency is rewarded. You can run a certain pace for a certain time; if you undershoot, you fail. If you overshoot, you also fail. If you plan and then do what you can always do, you perform well. And, if you are trying to tell someone where you will be when you are running, you need to be able to fairly estimate what you *can* do, not what you hope that somehow you could do assuming you were 20 pounds lighter and the law of gravity was temporarily suspended.

Discovery (including e-discovery) is no different. Preparation and planning matter.

1. In general, use good information management practices.
2. Once litigation is foreseeable, develop a plan to address foreseeable issues in the litigation and be willing to reasonably discuss it with opposing counsel.
3. Know what you are talking about in terms of technology, or find someone who does.
4. Be proactive, and not reactive.
5. Hope your adversary is also doing one, two, three, and four. If they are not, hope for a good judge: you will need the court's help.

Further, you should consider the same things when conducting discovery that you consider when resisting it.

Most cases start with suggestions. The facts of this case line up this way, and not that way. Our people are in the right. Universally, we frame broad discovery plans

---

1. I would argue that magic days do happen in the endurance world (see Riccardo Riccò's incredible wins in Stage 6 and 9 of the 2008 Tour de France), they just also involve people cheating (see Riccardo Riccò's positive drug test less than a week later).

seeking to uncover all facts related to a dispute. We are frequently better at shining light in every corner of an adversary's world than at framing a discovery plan narrowly tailored to the needs of a particular case.

Litigators are not accustomed to narrowing their requests. Whether we admit it or not, we prefer that no rock goes unturned. From the outset of a case, we plan cases as if the issues require resolution of truth at a metaphysical level and not through the lens of reasonableness through which people generally guide their lives.

Waste results when the parties fail to remember that litigation is a process to resolve disputes and not an end unto itself. Too many documents are collected, from both sides. Litigation dollars are spent on wild goose chases, acrimony occurs, and positions harden. Courts become involved—generally, but not always, forcing compromises that could have been realized from the outset. The purpose of this chapter is not to halt this process; it is to try to structure a process that can manage risk no matter what your adversary's position might be.

HAVE GOOD INFORMATION MANAGEMENT PRACTICES

The discovery story should start long before scorched-Earth litigation does. In almost every case, document discovery drives litigation cost. If a client has good information practices, it's far easier to get one's arms around how much litigation should cost and how long one needs to produce necessary documents. Good information management practices reduce the variables that parties need to deal with in litigation.

Often the first dose of reality comes from learning about your client's information practices. While some clients are sophisticated and can manage items in-house with great speed and efficiency, others cannot. Documents are housed in many places: on a network, on phones, in "the Cloud." Every custodian's e-mail inbox has 10,000 messages. Key documents related to the affirmative case are in a country where they may be virtually inaccessible. Attorneys need to factor these challenges into their game plan going forward. Oftentimes, the plan should include disclosing these problems to opposing counsel.

The first step in any litigation relationship should be to understand your client's information management practices and stress the need to have a proactive and sound strategy to manage information, both with respect to the ongoing litigation and beyond. These practices include, at a minimum, having formal records and information practices in place and applying them consistently; maintaining and/or disposing of information pursuant to these policies; and having appropriate technology to consistently manage information across an enterprise.

BUILD A PLAN

Litigators can build a plan by knowing what documents you have, what documents you need, and what you are prepared to do if those documents do not exist. In federal court, the Federal Rules of Civil Procedure outline in great detail various "to dos," but their list is not exhaustive. In any case, a case plan needs to address three issues:

- What a party's "offensive" needs in a case really are;
- What issues will affect the party's preservation, collection, and review of documents; and
- What happens if documents the party believes exist at the outset do not?

The "plans" that a party puts together as part of court-required case management planning certainly incorporate some aspects of these issues. But the required case management plan should not be the end of the planning. Litigation is too expensive for a party to not consider end games from the outset. Related technical questions litigators should evaluate include the following:

- How are you going to collect, review, and produce documents? How is the other party going to do so? Should an order set forth these expectations?
- How much time do you really need to get through document discovery?
- Do you have many privileged documents to deal with? If so, have you considered whether to use a "categorical" log, or do you even need a log from the other side at all?
- Do you need a protective order to deal with confidential information?

These issues are worthy of separate discussions, but one overarching point is worth making. In most cases, your plan should include some form of checklist showing what tasks have to happen, when, and who is responsible. In smaller cases, it is possible to keep track of all details on one piece of paper. In the largest cases, keeping track of what is supposed to happen, what did happen, and when might be a full-time job. But, every litigator must have some sort of process to do this.

Identifying Offensive Needs in a Case

Discovery is nearly always broader than what is contemplated by the Federal Rules of Civil Procedure. A good example are cases involving the federal law Comprehensive Environmental Response, Compensation, and Liability Act (CERCLA). Under CERCLA, proof of liability is simple: Did someone own or operate a site? Did they transport waste somewhere, or arrange for someone else to do so? If the answer to any of these questions is "yes" (and subject to a few limited exceptions), liability is established. After liability is established, CERCLA cases, which are frequently bifurcated, then move into an allocation phase, which seeks to allocate cleanup costs.

CERCLA cases provide good examples of disconnects that occur between the documents a party thinks it needs and what it actually needs. Liability is broad and intended to be easy to establish. Ownership and operation can be established from public records. Who transported wastes somewhere can be established from bills of lading. Nevertheless, virtually every CERCLA case starts with a massive collection of documents from every possible person who touched the property. Litigation holds issue to every possible custodian; every document they have is collected; clients begin a massive internal and external spend. And, this investment will likely not meaningfully affect the outcome of the liability case.

While this is what typically happens, it is not what is supposed to happen under the amended Federal Rules of Civil Procedure. From the beginning of the case, crucially *with the assistance of the* court, the parties are supposed to work together to plan what discovery should occur, what should not occur, and when. Specifically, Federal Rules of Civil Procedure Rule 16 directs federal courts to play an active role in case planning. Sometimes this meaningfully happens; sometimes it does not. There are a few reasons courts may not play an active role in case management. Sometimes, this is because parties are not really sure what they want or need to establish their case. Other times, this failure results from courts (literally) "phoning it in" rather than taking their case planning role seriously. The system planned by the Federal Rules works only if all participants are engaged.

This said, parties themselves *should* be able to collectively work together to evaluate what evidence is "key" to resolving their case. If the case can be structured in a way to limit inquiry into particular topics, the parties can dramatically reduce the amount of electronic information that needs to be collected and evaluated.

This point cannot be emphasized enough. *If your client is concerned about e-discovery costs, focus the case.* If issues are not being litigated, the chances that anyone will have to preserve, collect, review, and produce documents regarding them decrease dramatically. If your adversary will not listen, the court might. If the court will not, well . . . at least you tried.

Issues with Preservation, Collection, and Review

While all case plans should contemplate preserving, collecting, and reviewing documents, the past few years have shifted these issues—most particularly preservation—from "hot button" to "pretty boring." When "e-discovery" issues were first addressed by courts, most disputes centered on preservation. Decisions like *Zubulake v. UBS Warburg, LLC,*[2] found that case-dispositive sanctions were appropriate for

---

2. Zubulake v. UBS Warburg, LLC, 220 F.R.D. 212 (S.D.N.Y. 2003).

failure to preserve relevant documents once litigation was reasonably foreseeable. *Zubulake* brought forth a wave of litigation where parties focused their attention on non-merits-related metanarratives focused on who received legal holds and when. Over time—and often with explicit recognition in essence that "things happen"— courts now largely limit the most serious sanctions to situations where there is true bad faith. In 2015, Federal Rules of Civil Procedure Rule 37 was modified to reflect courts' new approach.

With draconian sanctions for somewhat routine situations off the table, preservation, collection, and review of documents has shifted from a legal problem to a technical one. In almost every case with substantial discovery, non-lawyers perform the forensic collection of documents. Increasingly, technology-assisted review is being used to shift review functions from being lawyer-focused to technical.

Litigators should consider two points when they are planning their document collection and review. First, file structures and hierarchies are not magical. In most situations, file structures function like drawers in a cabinet or rooms in a house. If one can discern how they operate, that knowledge can dramatically expedite review—particularly when it comes to non-e-mail-related attorney work product. This knowledge can also save your clients huge amounts of money—if you are only collecting and reviewing 1 percent of a party's total amount of documents one document at a time, you can save a similar percentage of review costs.

Second, in a world where much information is global—even though cases remain local—it is important to assess early on if relevant documents are located outside the United States. Many countries have different views of privacy. These views can complicate, if not totally frustrate, civil discovery typically conducted in the United States. To the extent "foreign" documents or information are relevant to a particular case, it is important to identify this fact early enough in a case so that issues can be addressed.

What Happens When Documents Cut Off the Endgame

All litigation comes to an end. On television, the end usually involves a trial and a lawyer in a nice suit. This is no longer a standard end-game for most types of civil litigation. Ninety-five percent of civil cases end either as the result of a dispositive motion or through negotiated resolution. Unsurprisingly, discovery—electronic and traditional—plays a role in these resolutions.

In many cases, the case team that collects and produces documents develops an understanding of the facts of the case that diverges from the understanding they had at the outset. Initial strategies are cut off by bad documents. Failed memories are refreshed by old e-mails. Depositions establish that facts that seemed certain to be true are, in reality, supported only by fallible human beings. To the extent one can establish at the *beginning* of the case what factual linchpins exist and evaluate their merits before lawyers and their friends in the e-discovery industry begin spending money, the world (and your practice) will be better off.

Create a Production Plan

Production planning combines management of the logistics of review with the psychology of production. Particularly with the advent of technologies like TAR (technology-assisted review) and more robust claw back orders, it can be possible to produce a large volume of documents early in a case if it is either required by the court or advantageous for the party's strategy.

Litigators must, therefore, set internal benchmarks early in a case for what should be produced and when. These benchmarks facilitate litigation budgeting, making sure the appropriate number of reviewers (if any) are hired, and getting through even the largest of cases without too much "real life" disruption. As one might expect, this is a non-legal, project management issue.

If you have meaningful internal benchmarks, you can be more successful negotiating with adversaries (as long as your relationship remains cordial). Here are some examples:

- A case involves the meaning of an ambiguous contract and damages. The parol evidence as to the meaning of the contract involves a relatively small amount of documents; damages evidence, in turn, is voluminous. Rational parties may agree to "stage" the parol evidence discovery before the parties engage in a settlement conference or mediation and delay the damages discovery until later.
- An environmental case involves dozens of parties with the main question being whether parties sent waste to a landfill decades ago. The plaintiff has performed investigation and remediation work on the landfill for decades and has generated hundreds of thousands of documents likely consisting of millions of pages. Here, it may be rational for all involved to focus collection and review of "old" documents—which are likely paper—in contrast to the more voluminous environmental investigation and remediation documents.

Protective Orders and Privilege Logs

Litigators should discuss protective orders and privilege logs at the beginning of a case, but they rarely do. Instead of negotiating a protective order at the outset, parties tend to wait until "confidential" documents are ready to be produced and only then raise the issue.

Experienced attorneys generally know from the outset of a case what information is sensitive enough to require a protective order. Obvious topics include medical records, intellectual property, and critical business financial information. Further, many protective orders are straightforward and can be built from models.[3]

The existence of electronic documents has fundamentally changed privilege logs. In one way, it has made creating privilege logs easier because an electronic collection of documents lets you fill in many of the fields (to:, from:, date:, etc.) automatically from document metadata. But, the volume of electronic documents makes privilege logging more difficult—where logging a few dozen paper documents could make for a boring afternoon, logging tens of thousands of documents using the traditional manner (i.e., a spreadsheet) can be extremely time- and resource-intensive. If an average reviewer can code 40 documents per hour for privilege, coding tens of thousands of documents can take months.

Litigators can make this task easier by using so-called categorical logs. Although courts are beginning to accept categorical logs as a default, some jurisdictions still require you to get opposing counsel's agreement. Where a party knows it will have a significant quantity of privileged documents at the beginning of a case, it should raise the issue in the early phases of litigation.

FIND A TRANSLATOR

It may be that the preceding section of this chapter made your eyes glaze over. Many lawyers do not know anything about e-discovery, but there's a whole industry of people to help you adjust to changes in technology.

It is possible—and potentially required—for technical experts rather than attorneys to address e-discovery issues. Some court rules now require each party to appoint a technical representative to resolve e-discovery issues. This requirement can be a good thing, because having technical personnel involved with cases at a deep level generally results in cost savings, so long as counsel exerts sufficient oversight over their activities.

Keeping these things in mind, it makes sense to include technical team members from the time a new matter comes in the door. Indeed, sophisticated clients often require non-lawyer technical staff to be involved in litigation. Technical team members can manage collection efforts. They can work with clients to deal with contracting issues. They can figure out what review platform is "best" for a particular case; assess whether cost savings can be achieved through use of technology; and generally facilitate the just, speedy, and inexpensive resolution of disputes

---

3. While many electronic documents are protected from disclosure by protective orders, there must be an independent basis—other than their electronic nature—that renders them confidential.

contemplated by the Federal Rules of Civil Procedure. Litigators should not wait until problems arise. Waiting may lead the legal team to make decisions on its own that may be costly and are hard to undo.

BE PROACTIVE, NOT REACTIVE

Like much in life, the key to winning the e-discovery portion of cases is to anticipate and get ahead of potential problems. Most of this chapter focuses on case planning because, if a good plan is in place, it becomes largely self-executing.

After planning internally, the next phase of "winning" e-discovery is to manage disputes with opposing counsel. One maxim to live by is that *for most aspects of e-discovery*, it is exponentially cheaper to do things once. This often means disclosing issues to opposing counsel and seeking to negotiate an agreement before you conduct the work. Potential examples of where litigators might benefit from proactive disclosure:

- Parties are often required at the beginning of cases to disclose potential documents. It may be that documents are duplicative. Instead of collecting duplicative documents, one side may approach the other side and propose to collect documents from some custodians, but not all.
- Documents are often collected using search terms. Search terms are inexact. If you disclose search terms before you apply them, you can limit potential duplicative searching.
- You will solve problems if you enter into a comprehensive ESI agreement in the very early stages of a case.
- A party knows that there is key financial data contained in a proprietary database. Rather than seeking to image the database, a party could disclose the existence of the database and offer to print relevant reports.
- A party wants to use TAR to review documents. The party might work with the opposing counsel to populate "seed sets" that will help build the algorithms TAR programs use to assess documents.

Your management of one part of your case can affect other parts, and all the parts matter. E-discovery is one part of discovery. Discovery is one part of a case. A case, in turn, is often one aspect of a series of relationships among clients, opposing counsel, and the court. E-discovery cannot exist in isolation. Any short-term benefit in most cases that comes at significant long-term costs simply is not worth it. If you raise issues with the other side before problems develop, you can engage in horse trading (the fun part of practicing law) and collaboration that results in cost-savings and better outcomes.

HOPE FOR A GOOD JUDGE

When horse trading and collaboration do not work, you will need to rely on a knowledgeable, available, and fair judge.

Frequently, it is uncertainty—rather than a dispute itself—that causes a party problems. The transaction costs of resolving disputes can be high: if a 25-page briefing is allowed for discovery motions, parties will use it. This adds expense and it adds time. Resolving problems in a timely manner with or without motions saves money and helps the case move on. Early (and frequent) court involvement generates certainty and precludes posturing. It forces parties to focus on the important parts of cases. Parties are more likely to work out disputes on their own if getting the court on the phone is a realistic threat. If you do not have an involved, educated judge, e-discovery disputes can be particularly problematic for two reasons:

- First, many attorneys are inexperienced in e-discovery disputes. In the absence of experience, parties tend to fall back on formalisms like "every relevant document needs to be collected, no matter where it exists and if it is duplicative" or "parties who make privilege claims need to substantiate them with a formal, 'traditional' log." In a case involving hundreds or even a thousand total documents, both of these positions may be reasonable. In a case involving hundreds of thousands or millions of potential documents, they surely are not.

- Second, many courts remain inexperienced in addressing e-discovery disputes and end up frustrated with lawyers who do not work things out on their own. Consider the experience of trying to explain why your client should not be obligated to produce even paper documents with all of their staples removed for 15 minutes to an indifferent judge. A judge who is unwilling to engage on this issue will likely be unwilling to engage in more technical disputes such as whether parties must cooperate in producing "seed sets" required for technology-assisted review.

There is a possible work-around for cases assigned to disengaged judges: you may try to retain a mediator to help you negotiate the procedural parts of this case. Although mediators cost money, in a case of sufficient size, their services could exponentially exceed all costs.

SPECIAL POINTS FOR "RESISTING" DISCOVERY

It goes without saying that every client—and litigator—will resist discovery. There are two reasons for this: because responding to discovery generally costs a lot and because scoring points is more fun than playing defense. In a large case, it takes a long time to catalog all potential sources of discovery. There are e-mails, cloud drives, laptops, cell phones, personal computers—the list is endless.

In general, as a baseline, parties can seek to discover information from any and all of these things, provided the information has some bearing on the case. But even if it has some bearing on the case, the real question is whether the information is likely to be truly helpful. If the answer to this question is a plain "no," as was discussed in this chapter's section on case planning, the next question is whether this discovery is necessary.

If the question of whether a particular type of document is a proper subject of discovery was not resolved as part of creating a case management plan, resolving it likely will require motion practice. Because discovery motions involve concrete things, the following points should be kept in mind:

- It is important to build a record showing your client acted in good faith. This paper record should include information dating back to the beginning of the case: what the case management plan says; why an adversary's discovery requests are not consistent with it; and what steps have been taken—or would need to be taken—to respond to the relevant discovery.
- Where the objections to discovery are based on proportionality, that is, the burdensomeness of a particular discovery request as it relates to the importance of the documents, courts increasingly require parties to substantiate their costs. Technical staff overseeing an electronic review can generally assist you in calculating what efforts would need to be undertaken to complete a particular task and how much it would cost. This information can then be submitted in a declaration to a court in support of a party's burdensomeness objections.

The other main difference in responding to discovery (rather than producing documents that support a side's case) relates to timing. Here are two examples:

- The time period for resisting discovery is generally compressed. For instance, in the Eastern District of Virginia, the default rules require that objections to requests for production need to be served 14 days after service of the discovery request. For a party that did not begin proactively identifying and addressing issues, two weeks is no time at all.
- Sometimes "final" answers are required before full review is complete. Initial responses to requests for admission and interrogatories could be due before a party has performed most of its electronic collection and review. While parties may supplement their responses, it can be frustrating—for both parties—when one produces incomplete answers early in litigation.

CONCLUSION

Discovery is the offensive line play of litigation in that it involves a huge effort that only gets noticed when something goes wrong. This chapter sought to identify problems that litigators routinely face and identify common-sense solutions. Boiling it all down, litigators should focus on diligence, reasonableness, and transparency when they are dealing with discovery issues.

What goes around comes around regarding e-discovery. Diligence, reasonableness, and transparency are often the best tools to avoid problems. Make a plan for what information you need. Have the means to understand what the other side is, or is not, producing. Hope for a technically competent adversary and a judge willing to engage as appropriate. And, realize at a gut level that if you are asking for more information from the other side than you really need, they will likely respond in kind and be unreasonable in their requests to you. Stepping back from this reality for a second, no court wants to hear lawyers engage in finger-pointing about reasonableness when it can be avoided through planning and negotiation.

CHAPTER 6

Expedited or Pre-Suit Discovery

Laurence Kurth

PRE-SUIT AND EXPEDITED DISCOVERY FOR LITIGATION

Virtually every state jurisdiction, plus federal courts, allows for some avenue of finding out the facts of a potential claim before a lawsuit is filed.[1] Some of those avenues must comply with a strict set of rules and stay within the parameters of the Rules of Civil Procedure, while others require simply a laptop and a good internet connection. Regardless of the approach, knowing the lay of the landscape before committing to a petition may be good lawyering.

Additionally, circumstances may arise pre-suit that necessitate prudent use of allowable formal discovery. The ill health of a critical witness, or party, are examples. The potential spoliation of evidence or a short document retention policy may also require you to act *now*.

This chapter explores both formal and informal approaches to special discovery needs. Together, these real-time alternatives hopefully will provide you useful advice in crafting your case.

---

1. *See* ALA. R. CIV. P. 27 (Alabama allows pre-suit discovery regardless of need to perpetuate evidence. N.Y.C.L.R. § 3102© McKinney 2005); OHIO CIV. R. 34(D)(1); PA. R. CIV. P. 4003.8(a),(b); VT. R. CIV. P. 27. Further, most states, except Kansas, recognize a form of an equitable bill of discovery. Jeffrey J. Kroll, *The Art and Science of Pre-Suit Discovery*, 45 TRIAL 28–29 (Mar. 2009).

RULE 27 OF THE FEDERAL RULES OF CIVIL PROCEDURE

The Law

Prior to 2011, and the pronouncement of the *Twombly* and *Iqbal* federal decisions,[2] trying to get a federal district court to allow you to conduct discovery prior to filing a petition and engaging in Rule 26(f) discovery conference was a crapshoot. What you might think as a reasonable basis to seek pre-suit discovery—"In order to determine if the cause of action is viable"—was frowned upon and rarely resulted in the desired order to proceed.[3] Since 1938, when the pre-lawsuit discovery rule was first codified, it has remained basically the same.[4] It was designed to perpetuate testimony, and in most federal circuits, that alone.[5] The original rule did not contemplate a pre-suit litigant asking the court to maintain the status quo by preserving physical evidence, or retaining documents. Preserving tangible items or documents, photographs, or especially digital content did not occur to the original rule drafters as the necessity it is today.[6]

It took eight years and literally an act of Congress[7] to expand the reach of the rule to encompass evidence presentation under Federal Rule 34, or inspection of evidence under Federal Rule 35. The performance of mental examinations were now also permitted.[8] Nonetheless, while the potential items you could seek for logically expanded, the manner to obtain the relevant data remains the same. The "Mother, may I" control of the Federal District Court remains firmly in place.[9]

The Practical Approach

All pre-suit discovery under the federal rules (and some state systems discussed later) require a petition to the court.[10] That petition must contain catch phrases to bring it into conformance with what the rule allows. Those catch phrases include

---

2. Ashcroft v. Iqbal, 556 U.S. 662 (2009 (allowing civil litigation to be dismissed by district courts much easier); Bell Atlantic Corp. v. Twombly, 550 U.S. 544 (2007) (Plaintiffs must include enough facts in their complaint to make it plausible.).

3. CHARLES A. WRIGHT, ARTHUR R. MILLER & RICHARD L. MARCUS, FEDERAL PRACTICE AND PROCEDURE § 2072 (2d ed. 2002).

4. Sidney Hardy & Heather Nagel, *Expansion of Pre-Suit Discovery in Federal Courts: Preparing for the Brave New World*, FED'N OF DEF. & CORPORATE COUNSEL (2011).

5. *See* Nevada v. O'Leary, 63 F.3d 932, 935 (9th Cir. 1995).

6. Curtis Quay, *Pre-Complaint Discovery in Federal Court* (2000).

7. Congress amended Rule 27 in 1946, expanding pre-suit discovery pursuant to Rules 34 & 35; *see* FED. R. CIV. P. 27(b)(3).

8. Nicholas Kronfeld, *The Preservation and Discovery of Evidence Under Federal Rule of Procedure 27*, 78 GEO. L.J. 593 (1990).

9. *See In re* Yamaha Motor Corp., USA, 251 F.R.D. 97 (N.D.N.Y. 2008).

10. MICHAEL SMITH, O'CONNOR'S FEDERAL RULES CIVIL TRIALS § 4.2 (2017).

demonstrating the requirements of Rule 27 have been satisfied.[11] These requirements are:

1. The proponent needs to take a deposition to preserve testimony.
2. That if that testimony is lost, then there will be irreparable harm.

Types of Pre-Suit Discovery Allowable under the Federal Rules

Federal Rule of Civil Procedure Rule 27 allows only certain types of pre-suit discovery in the federal system. If the plaintiff satisfies certain requirements described further on, and obtains leave of court, he or she may take depositions in line with the court's orders.[12] You should consider this avenue to preserve testimony when the circumstances dictate. Examples include occasions when a key witness is ill, elderly, or may become unavailable by virtue of leaving the jurisdiction or other exigency which will render the evidence unobtainable.[13]

A second reason for seeking pre-suit discovery is where you might have doubting questions about the legal theory and degree of merit for your case. This early discovery assists evaluation of causes of action and may help to establish the merits of the action and assists in avoiding allegations of sanctions under Federal Rule 11(c).[14]

First, assess what you are trying to accomplish by setting such an early deposition even before you file the complaint or petition. As plaintiff, do you really need to go to the expense of this procedure? Are you ready to conduct discovery at a point when you are not yet clear about your final objectives, witnesses, motions or trial strategy? Is it worth the cost when it will in effect alert all defendants to your claims?

If you have decided that circumstances do indeed dictate time is of the essence, then the second step will be to draft a petition and seek the court's permission to perpetuate testimony.[15] That petition must satisfy certain requirements:

1. It must be verified.
2. It must be filed in the federal district court where any reasonably adverse party resides.

---

11. *See In re* Deiulemar Compagnia Di Navigazione S.P.A., 198 F.3d 473 (4th Cir. 1999); *In re* Bay County Middlegrounds Landfill Site, 171 F.3d 1044 (6th Cir. 1999); Penn. Mut. Life Ins. Co. v. U.S., 68 F.3d 1371 (D.C. Cir. 1995).
12. *See* FED. R. CIV. P. 27.
13. Jay Grenig, *Taking and Using Depositions Before Action or Pending Appeal in Federal Court,* MARQ. L. SCHOLARLY COMMONS (2004).
14. Penn. Mut. Life Ins. v. U.S., 68 F.3d 1371, 1373 (D.C. Cir. 1995).
15. *See* FED. R. CIV. P. 27.

3. It must clearly state the name(s) of the person(s) to be deposed in order to perpetuate that testimony.
4. It must be filed in the petitioner's name.

The contents of the petition must further state:

- That the petition will be filed in a federal court,[16] but that it cannot be presently filed, or filed on the plaintiff's behalf;
- The subject matter of the lawsuit and the plaintiff's specific interest in that suit;
- The facts sought to be established;
- The names and descriptions of those parties adverse to the petition, and include their contact information;
- Identify the proposed deponents including name, address, and anticipated testimony.

There also are requirements under the federal rules for notice and service of the parties.[17] The notice must include the notice date and time for a hearing, and must be served 21 days before the hearing. Service should occur under the guidelines of Rule 4 of the Federal Rules of Procedure.

Alternative service is available. If you do not have an accurate address or clear locations for the potential opposing parties, you can petition the court for service by publication or other alternate method of notice and service to which the court agrees.

If alternate service is your only choice, you will be required to obtain a court order. Along with that order, your court will need to appoint counsel to represent the missing party[18] at the pre-suit deposition.

The primary purpose of both the motion and the argument to the court is for you to convince the judge[19] that if you are not allowed to perpetuate the evidence, it would create a "failure or delay of justice."[20] You should also prepare a specific order for the court which recites all required elements.[21] The order should specify:

1. Who shall appear for the deposition;
2. The topics of the deposition; and
3. States the manner of how the deposition should be taken.[22]

---

16. *See Penn. Mut. Life Ins.*, 68 F.3d at 1374.
17. FED .R. CIV. P. 27(2).
18. In the event one of the anticipated defendants is not competent, then Rule 17(c) requires notice to the guardian, committee, conservator, or fiduciary.
19. The standard you will have to prove is not admissibility at trial but, rather, the evidence must be *relevant* and not just cumulative. *In re* Bay City Middlegrounds Landfill Site, 171 F.3d 1044, 1046 (6th Cir. 1999).
20. *See In re* Deivlemar Compagnia Di Navigazione S.P.A., 198 F.3d 473, 486–87 (4th Cir. 1999).
21. FED. R. CIV. P. 27(3).
22. An order may also conform to the rules and orders in FED. R. CIV. P. 34 and FED. R. CIV. P. 35.

It is important that you be fully prepared before you take the pre-suit deposition. While of course it is best for you to always be fully prepared for any deposition, the pre-suit deposition brings added concerns. Because it can be used for any purpose in the subsequent lawsuit pursuant to Federal Rules of Civil Procedure Rule 32(a), some courts may not allow you a second bite at the apple.

MOST STATES ALLOW PRE-SUIT DISCOVERY UNDER STATE RULES OF CIVIL PROCEDURE

All states which allow depositions before suit also require you to obtain leave of court prior to conducting such pre-suit discovery.[23] Usually, the state rules require petitioning the court and, much like the federal rules, that petition must set out the person(s) to be deposed; the evidence sought; that the plaintiff is in anticipation of litigation; and the exigency which necessitates the discovery must take place now. A good example to use as a template is the State of Texas.

The Law

Texas has an extensive state statute. Texas Rule of Civil Procedure Rule 202[24] allows such a process (Former Texas Rule of Civil Procedure Rule 187[25] for depositions). Rule 202 governs all discovery before suit, including rules governing how a deposition designed to perpetuate testimony occurs.

Under Texas Rule 202, you begin the process by preparing a petition to be filed in the proposed state court venue. It is filed in the county where the deponent resides, or where the proper venue of the lawsuit should be when a lawsuit is filed.

While the Texas rules appear more liberal than the federal rules, there are still state-centric requirements not imposed under federal case law. Examples include that the petition must specifically recite that either, "the Petitioner seeks to investigate a potential claim by or against the Petitioner" or that "the Petitioner anticipates an action where the Petitioner is a party."[26] However, not every request for a Rule 202 deposition will be granted because the court must have both subject matter jurisdiction.[27] For example, a plaintiff cannot seek a Rule 202 deposition to investigate a claim that falls below the court's amount of damages for subject matter jurisdiction. So, you should be careful when drafting the petition to include a

---

23. Texas Rules of Civil Procedure 202 was codified in 2008, and the prior Rule 187 was enacted in 1990 and was subsumed by Rule 202 as well as Texas Rule 737 governing bills of discovery.
24. *Id.*
25. *Id.*
26. Texas Rules of Civil Procedure 202.2(d)(1),(2).
27. *In re* DePinho, 505 S.W.3d 621, 624 (Tex. 2016); *In re* Doe, 444 S.W.3d 603, 608 (Tex. 2014).

prayer for damages that places your case within the minimal jurisdictional levels of the court.[28]

Nor can a petitioner use the 202 deposition to investigate a potential federal action.[29] In *In Re Doe*,[30] the court held Rule 202 was not an available option to investigate a potential federal antitrust suit. Likewise, a plaintiff cannot use a Rule 202 deposition to take depositions or conduct pre-suit discovery concerning a claim that is not yet "ripe." The case cannot be contingent or remote.[31] It must be at a sufficient stage so the facts are developed to a point where it can be shown an injury likely occurred.[32]

The Practical Approach

You should be sure your ultimate lawsuit will meet or exceed the jurisdictional limit of the court where you intend to file the petition. Be mindful that all state jurisdictional requirements will be necessary. For example, in the Texas case of *In re City of Dallas*,[33] the plaintiff, wanting the pre-litigation deposition of a municipal worker to establish tortious interference, failed to include the amount in controversy. Because of this failure, the Dallas District Court could not ascertain from the pleadings whether it had subject matter jurisdiction and, as a result, the petition failed.[34]

Personal jurisdiction is a prerequisite.[35] Be sure the ultimate defendant of your anticipated litigation has sufficient minimum contacts with the state. You should plead enough facts so a court may conclude it has sufficient jurisdiction.[36] *In re Doe*[37] is a Texas example of how lack of personal jurisdiction may torpedo your efforts. The petitioner in that litigation sought to file a defamation action against a blogger. The problem was the erstwhile plaintiff did not know the anonymous blogger's actual identity. To secure that identity, the plaintiff sought the deposition of "Google" in a pre-trial petition. The petition failed because the ultimate defendant was anonymous and unknown, and because the petitioner could not assure the district court it would have actual personal jurisdiction.[38]

Much like the federal rules and the Texas rules, your state will typically require proper notice to be given to all those parties and potential parties with an interest in the litigation. Various state rules differ as to the number of days' notice, but you must

28. *See In re* City of Dallas, 501 S.W.3d 71 (Tex. 2016).

29. *See In re Doe*, 444 S.W.3d.

30. *In re Doe*, 444 S.W.3d at 608.

31. *In re DePinho*, 505 S.W.3d.

32. *See* Waco I.S.D. v. Gibson, 22 S.W.3d 849, 851–52 (Tex. 2000).

33. *In re City of Dallas*, 501 S.W.3d 71.

34. 501 S.W.3d 71, 73–74.

35. *In re Doe*, 444 S.W.3d at 604.

36. Tex. R. Civ. P. 202.2.

37. *In re Doe*, 444 S.W.3d at 604.

38. *See In re Doe*, 444 S.W.3d 604–05.

set the deposition and provide sufficient reasonable notice for the parties to attend and participate. Only where you prove in the interest of "justice" or in the interest of "imminent necessity" will a time limit be shortened; for example, where an illness or infirmity may render the deponent incapacitated in the immediate future. To secure the attendance of the witness, you will need to subpoena him/her/it.

Hearing and Order

Your state rules may, like Texas, require a hearing to satisfy required findings. Notice of the hearing, like notice of the deposition, must be served on all parties of interest. Those items that you will need to prove at the hearing are a showing that without this deposition there would be a failure of justice, or justice will be delayed or, at least in Texas, that the discovery to be gained by allowing the petitioner to take the deposition outweighs the burden or expense to the deponent. You should clearly spell out each of these findings in the order to be signed by your court. Likewise, be sure your order includes each of those elements required by your own state court rules.

Alternatively, the lawyer representing the deponent may include requirements or limitations of some sort in the order. For example, the respondent may petition you to pay all costs or that the witness may have to be reimbursed costs, or the deposition be limited as to time, or place. As another example, at least one case required a doctor to monitor the health of a fragile deponent.[39]

Likewise, ensure your order includes the means and manner of obtaining or conducting the deposition or discovery you need. Include either that it will be an oral deposition or by written questions, and especially include if the deponent shall bring documents, or a subpoena duces tecum, if allowable under your state rules.[40]

Use of the Deposition

So long as there is a "privity" of parties, then the deposition may be used like any other deposition that is taken once the lawsuit begins. At least in Texas, you also apply the same rules for taking the deposition. All of the usual objections are appropriate. While case law appears silent on the specific issue, there is no reason the deposition could not be taken by videotape or by other means other than stenographically if your state allows such procedures. Even though not all the parties in the trial were present or available to attend the pre-suit deposition, it still qualifies as a statement against interest of the deponent. The deposition also may be used as impeachment evidence against the deponent.[41]

---

39. *See In re* Fernandez, No. 04-99-00841-CV (Tex. App—San Antonio 1999, orig. proceeding) and Valley Baptist Med. Center v. Gonzalez, 18 S.W.3d 673 (Tex. App.—Corpus Christi 1999).
40. *See In re* Akzo Nobel Chem., Inc., 24 S.W.3d 919 (Tex. App.—Beaumont 2000, orig. proceeding).
41. Nathan L. Hecht & Robert H. Pemberton, *A Guide to the 1999 Texas Discovery Rules Revisions* (Nov. 11, 1998).

Nonetheless, a district court may restrict your use of the deposition. An example in Texas, under Rule 202.5, is a court may restrict or totally prohibit the use of the deposition in the event a party objects, and proves it was not given adequate notice to participate in the deposition.[42]

INFORMAL DISCOVERY

In addition to petitioning the court to take depositions, you can find out facts on your own.

The Internet

The easiest, cheapest and the most obvious of pre-litigation informal discovery tools is the internet. I always "Google" my opposition's client, and my own client, too. There is a veritable wealth of information available about anyone who does not screen and delete information that gets out on the web. While you are at it, you might as well Google your opposition, and your own prospective experts.

Social network sites, and references to the subject of your search, are available by checking all available search engines. Do not just stick with the one that comes up when you open your browser. You should make the effort to look at *all* the most common search engines, such as Google, Yahoo, and Bing. Do not stop with the first page. "Gems" of information are often found five pages into the search.

No search would be complete without a check of Facebook, YouTube, and LinkedIn. Because Facebook allows the poster to include all sorts of details about background, education, and experiences, it is a good place to start. Also, there are "walls" that contain areas where the Facebook user posts what is going on in his or her life. Always check to see what posts were made on the day of the incident which is the basis of the potential suit.

There are usually photographs, and possibly videos. There has been more than one instance where a personal injury claimant alleges serious injury, but then cannot wait to post Facebook pictures of his or her latest rock climbing vacation, 5K exploit, or golf tournament victory. Opposing parties may post videos or photos where they show themselves doing exactly what they claim *not* to be able to do. On one occasion, a man actually posted on the internet an instructional video on "How to properly do leg presses" where he pushed 175 pounds of weight on a machine, after filing a lawsuit alleging serious leg injury from an accident. On another occasion a claimant posted a video where he was dancing when he claimed debilitating back injury. Most accounts are relatively secure and set to "private," thus full access would require your subject to accept a "friend request," which under the Model Rules of Professional Conduct is violative of Rule 4.2. Because it has

---

42. *In re* Does 1 & 2, 337 S.W.3d 862, 863 (Tex. 2011).

proven over the years to be such a valuable source of information, clients should be advised to avoid the temptation of Facebook and stay off the social media sites. Because most attorneys advise their clients to avoid social media, you may not be as lucky in finding your own "gems," but do not give up digging.

Simple Interviews

Get yourself a head start on the acquisition of facts. Interview your client extensively; interview family members of your client; interview anyone who offers first-hand information. Determine what causes of action you need to prove or what causes of action you need to defend, and pair the witness with the proof you need. There is always the case where a witness is deposed, and you discovery the witness has never been interviewed, not even by the party seeking to depose the deponent.

Inspect the Scene of the Accident

Much in the same vein as talking to witnesses, it is strongly recommended that you visit the scene. Even if it is several states away, you can always "visit" by using a "Google Earth" app or similar internet device. Some lawyers prepare for litigation, but never leave the four walls of the office. You can take your own reference photographs with your smartphone. Similarly, if it is a products case, get hold of an exemplar product early on. Not only does that familiarize you with how the product may work, but you will be surprised at how products can be changed, models updated or simply discontinued in the years that may elapse before trial.

Court Records

Most courthouse filings are now available online. Investigate whether the party has already been sued. In that way, you can find out if your case is unique, or is your client tenth in a line on a list of similar lawsuits? What a wealth of information on strategy, causes of action, experts, and probable defenses you will gain by looking at another lawyer's work. Why plow the field anew? Also found in court records are marriage records, which can provide that thread you need to start your social media search.

FOIA Requests

Freedom of Information Act requests to governmental agencies yield results. It takes no time to write a letter. Be sure to follow the requirements of your jurisdiction.

Westlaw/Lexis

This is a good tool to cross-check other research you have obtained, or may shed light on assets, criminal litigation history, or associated businesses, and so on.

CONCLUSION

Whether it is formal, and conducted under federal or state rules, or whether it is surfing the web in the comfort of your living room, be sure you are demonstrating the thoroughness that is the bulwark of effective representation.

CHAPTER 7

Initial Case Assessment

Preliminary Fact and Legal Evaluations

Michael D. Shalhoub and Jill Owens

The sun is shining. It is a warm and glorious day. Maybe the golf course is calling, or the beach, or the chair in your yard to enjoy some quality family time. In any event, briefcase in hand, or backpack slung over your shoulder, you are leaving the office early for some well-deserved down time. You are out the door, and your cell phone rings with a call forwarded from your desk. You do not recognize the out-of-town number, but because you are who you are, you answer. The caller is a potential new client, referred to you by a satisfied former or existing client, who wants to talk about a new lawsuit. It does not matter whether it is a plaintiff case or a defense case, you are being asked to represent a new client. You now have preliminary work and analysis to do. Sometimes it can await your much-needed trek to the beach. Sometimes it needs to be dealt with promptly.

A thorough, systematic, early initial case investigation is crucial. Its absence can create frustration later for the client, the lawyer, insurance adjuster, or in-house counsel, as the case moves into later phases. Facts not discussed at the outset may become lost or confounded by fading memories. Important documentation not required to be preserved, gathered, and provided at the earliest stage of the representation may become lost. Witnesses not identified, investigated, located, and their evidence gathered and stories "pinned down" early may move, retire, forget, or leave a client's employment, and in doing so potentially become hostile to the client's litigation interests. The savvy trial lawyer learns to avoid pre-trial regrets about what should have been done during early investigation and factual and legal evaluation.

The attorney who undertakes a disciplined, systematic case investigation will also appear to the client, whether an in-house attorney or private individual, as organized and efficient. On the other hand, a haphazard start will lead to later frustration and a mental note by the client of the attorney retracing steps. A busy client will not take kindly to being asked a second time for documents already provided at the outset of the litigation, but not reviewed and assimilated or cataloged properly to avoid a repetitious request. Such perceptions can have obvious implications on a client's decision regarding which attorney to retain the next time they are sued, or need to bring a lawsuit or claim.

Attorneys for plaintiffs, as a matter of ethical obligations, and as a practical matter, have much more work to do up-front from the standpoint of initial fact gathering and legal evaluation than defense lawyers. Naturally, plaintiff's counsel must be first to plead and generally bear the burden of proof at trial, so their evaluation of the facts and applicable law necessarily pre-dates the complaint.

As to plaintiff's counsel's ethical obligations, Federal Rule of Civil Procedure Rule 11(a) requires every pleading to be signed by the attorney of record. Rule 11(b)(3) provides that by presenting a court with a signed pleading, the signer is certifying that based on "inquiry reasonable under the circumstances," to the best of their knowledge, information, and belief the facts plead have evidentiary support, or, if so identified, will have such support after a reasonable opportunity for further investigation or discovery. The phrasing of Rule 11(b)(3) signifies that reasonable inquiry into the evidentiary basis for factual allegations contained in an initial pleading is not optional. Thus, plaintiff's attorneys engaged on a new matter are required to pause before filing a complaint with the court, and not do so until they have investigated the factual and legal bona fides of the intended claims.

Most states have corollary rules to Federal Rule of Civil Procedure Rule 11 modeled after the federal rules. In general, the reasonable pre-suit inquiry may not be limited to a conversation with the client. Where such preliminary investigation beyond a conversation with the client could have objectively established that the claim is not grounded in fact or law, the lack of appropriate research could result in sanctions. Plaintiff's counsel should, in all cases, attempt to confirm what the client said in fact occurred. This corroborative investigation must be objectively reasonable, and should proceed from the detailed interview of the client to a review of available documents, including those provided by the client at the outset, and those that are publicly available. In addition, there should generally be both an interview of witnesses identified by the client, and collection of pertinent documentation that is obtainable even if not in the client's possession. In addition, there are many circumstances when there are complexities, and consultation with an expert is needed.

Plaintiff's attorneys should be aware of particular state's requirements impacting the need for pre-suit expert consultation. For instance, since 2005, in Connecticut, medical malpractice plaintiffs are required to demonstrate a good faith belief that there has been medical negligence by filing with their pleading a written and signed opinion letter of a similar health care provider that there appears to have been negligence, including a detailed basis for the formation of that opinion. Other states have similar requirements affecting suits against professionals.

Beyond these ethical requirements, other up-front, fact gathering responsibilities particular to plaintiff's counsel include critical timing issues such as the expiration of statutes of limitations. Consideration of the applicable statute of limitations should be undertaken immediately and researched where necessary. By including this inquiry at the earliest interaction with the potential client, key facts can be gathered that might bear upon whether an extension of the statute of limitations exists because of, for instance, the "discovery rule," or where a wrongful death case brought late and dismissed because the decedent's personal representative was awaiting official appointment by a probate court is able to be reinstituted.

Attorneys for defendants also have "up front" work at the time of their engagement. Timely answering the pleading in an informed, accurate manner is, of course, on the list. Federal Rule of Civil Procedure Rule 11(b)(4) imposes on defense counsel a similar mandate to the rule relating to pre-suit factual investigation, that a responsive pleading containing denials of factual contentions have been signed by counsel of record who certifies by signing that the denials are reasonably believed to be warranted by the evidence. Such a certification can only be done accurately after having undertaken a reasonable investigation of the factual bases for the responses prior to serving the answer.

THE INITIAL INTERVIEW

Attorneys for either side are wise to initially conduct a detailed "what is this all about" inquiry with their client—some part of this process may be delegated to a paralegal, but our view is that discussions and assessments of the critical part of a claim or defense is best done, and perhaps only done, under the direction of an attorney. Generally, this preliminary fact-gathering inquiry will include an initial interview or interviews of the client or the involved people at the entity client. If the client is an individual, or you are meeting with a client representative who witnessed or was involved in the accident or performed the contract or was involved with the problem which generated the litigation, ideally, such interviews should be face-to-face. Undeniably, in these digital times, the frequency of in-person communication may be dwindling, but there is no more critically important relationship as that between an attorney and client. This is a relationship that cannot mature without in person interaction. Maybe subsequent discussions can be accomplished by other means, but at the outset of a matter, attorney and client should meet in person.

Depending on the sophistication of the client, and their familiarity with the legal process and working with attorneys, it will often be important to stress the strictly confidential nature of the discussions. Some clients need to be specifically told what a client tells to their attorney is completely private and confidential. The attorney should tell that person that what they say to the attorney cannot be revealed by the attorney unless the client agrees. Relating to or reminding a client of the confidential nature of the communications should help foster the kind of candor required for building an effective case or defense that will not later be debilitated by receipt of previously unknown contradictory facts or bad documents. If the person is the employee of the client, and this is true whether the employee is a low-level employee or the CEO, the person should be told that the client is the company, and *not* the individual you are speaking to.

Regardless of the client, it is important to demonstrate empathy to the client's circumstances. Although this may be obvious in the case of a client who is a victim of an accident, it is no less important with a corporate client or a physician or home health aide. When asked what they look for in an outside counsel, corporate clients often remark that they value (and return to) counsel who understand their business, care, and empathize with their legal situation.

During the interview, it is generally wise to ask open-ended questions to elicit the client's own explanation of the situation or occurrence. Seek clarification of anything unclear. This serves the dual purpose of eliminating later confusion and letting the client know you are listening and they have your attention.

Additionally, the attorney will want to stress to potential clients, whether defendants or plaintiffs, that they should bring or send all pertinent documents in advance of or, at the very least, at the initial interview so their significance can be reviewed and confirmed by counsel at the outset.

Get an understanding of the client's risk tolerance. What resolution does the client want for the dispute that has been brought to you? Is the goal to win big at all costs, or are there competing considerations such as maintaining a familial or business relationship in the future that might signal the need for a more nuanced approach?

If there is a lawsuit, then at its most basic and banal, there is a money dispute to be resolved. How would the client like it resolved? The presence of an insurer for part or the entire dispute will color that assessment. This is true for plaintiffs and for defendants for whom counsel may have a tripartite relationship between counsel, carrier, and client. What is the client willing to spend to get what result? These are all issues to be discussed early in the relationship. And issues must be revisited on "as events warrant" basis throughout the course of the litigation.

This sounds basic, and perhaps it is, but it bears repeating that you should make clear that your client and witnesses can call or e-mail you anytime about anything, as you do not want a communication failure. It is well-known that failures to communicate are at the center of many, if not most, attorney-client disputes.

We offer two other initial thoughts. You should ensure that you comply with your state's requirements, if any, about retainer letters. And you should make sure that the client understands about attorney's fees and how you expect to be paid, and when you expect to be paid. Fee disputes are another notorious cause of the breakdown of client relationships.

WHAT NEXT?

Having completed the initial interview, it is time to bring to bear your legal skills and analysis. There are many considerations at this point in the game, and they will be different for every matter. Always, however, the considerations deal with preparation, preparation, preparation!

This is part of the paradox of the practice at law. Lawyers do not want and do not like surprises. We do everything in our power to avoid surprises. At the same time, we know that, without fail, there will be surprises and we need to be prepared to deal with them as they arise. Trying to answer questions like the ones that follow are critical to providing good advice to the client. Proceed? Concede? Settle? Go for broke? Do not start the lawsuit?

- Is the claim good, or defense good, under prevailing law?
- Is there a good-faith reason for seeking an extension, expansion, or contraction of prevailing law?
- Is this a run-of-the-mill case (for you, not for the client—remember, it is almost never a run-of-the-mill matter for most clients)?
- What is it that you do not know that you need to know in order to properly advise your client?
- Where are the gaps in the elements of what is needed on those things where you have the burden of proof? A corollary is where is your evidence, while present, weak, and is there anything you can do to strengthen it?
- What can you do to try to fill those gaps before proceeding?
- What does a scene inspection tell you (and any expert you have retained at this point) about the plausibility of your client's story and the claims or defenses you are preparing to advance?
- What kind and manner of preliminary product inspection should be done prior to the litigation and what precautions should be put in place to avoid claims of destruction of evidence?
- Have necessary preservation letters or cautions gone to the clients to impress upon them the importance of maintaining evidence, whether it be safekeeping the subject lawnmower, or having an IT department adjust e-mail and document retention protocols?
- Is the evidence that you think that you have admissible?
- Do you need pre-action discovery before deciding whether to proceed?

- Do you have the documents you need, or do you need to get them?
- Do you know the client? If not, some vetting may be in order.
- Is the client litigious? What effect might that have on the case?
- Is this a high-profile case? Does the client want it to be? What can you do to affect that?
- Is it a bet the company or precedent setting matter in terms of either the law, or the alleged conduct of the defendant?
- Are there any statute of limitation issues?
- Conditions precedent to suit—such as requirement of notice of claim to municipality, or notice of breach in a breach of contract claim?
- Is there insurance for the claims being made?
  - If plaintiff, has the carrier been placed on notice?
  - If defendant, what coverage is implicated? Have the carrier(s) been placed on notice, including excess insurers, if applicable?
- Will a jury like the client?
- Will a jury like the narrative of the case? Can you change the narrative?

You now have had an initial assessment of your client, the case, and other considerations. The hard work begins—proving the case. How do you refine the narrative so the jury or judge will see things your way at the end of the case. There is no doubt these days that most cases are resolved by motion, settlement, or dismissal, and not by a jury or judge verdict. But, preparing the case from the outset, as if it is to be tried, is without doubt the best preparation for an early resolution.

Attempting a pre-suit resolution can be a cost-effective way to resolve a dispute. It is difficult to accomplish this without a thorough understanding of the strength of your legal position and factual posture. Equally important, you must understand the motivation and goals of your client *and* those of the other party. How personal is the dispute to your client, and to the other party? How do you move beyond the client's personal animus or other motivations to seek resolution of the lawsuit. How can you address the opposing party's animus in a constructive way that moves the matter closer to resolution?

Most times, at the end of the day, or the litigation, when the parties are spent emotionally and financially, the dispute moves (as Mike's wife and Jill's friend like to say) from the princi*ple* to the princi*pal*—from the "ple" to the "pal." It is at that point that many cases can be resolved. Consider what ways you can develop to move the dispute to the "pal" as early in the dispute resolution process as possible.

WORK-UP AND ANALYSIS

You now have a thorough understanding of the dispute's framework and many of the questions you need to deal with. Your job is to position the dispute in a way your client is in the best position to have the suit resolved in his/her/its favor. How do you get there?

A crucial first step, which is often overlooked—and this applies equally to the defense side of any dispute in the crush of daily practice—is to take a deep breath to consider what your theme of the case needs to be. Start to develop the story, which is the narrative that the case is about.

- "This is a case about a father and family devastated by a company hell-bent on selling a widget that it knew from many other cases can kill people, and did kill this man."
- "This case is about a company stealing its main competitor's confidential ideas and business strategies by hiring the person responsible for keeping that information."

What is the theme, and what are the claims and defenses? What tools do you have, or can you develop to best help your client sell that theme and those claims and defenses not only to the judge and jury but to the other side? Now, the story will evolve as the litigation proceeds, but start at the beginning so you can develop facts to prove your narrative. If you wait until the end and work with what has developed, you have lost the chance to influence the narrative.

No matter which side of the "v" you are on, there is work to be done. More work for the plaintiff side most likely, but if the defense side knows a suit is coming it can begin preparations as well—and in so doing, may be able to develop information to head off, or resolve, the dispute before slow, expensive, and inefficient litigation is initiated.

If your client has been involved in a similar dispute or litigation, you need to assess whether they have taken a contrary or inconsistent position to the one they wish to take in the new matter. This will be something an alert adversary will surely identify and employ to score points against you with the judge or jury. Depending on circumstances, you may want to collect prior pleadings, depositions, motions, orders, and so on.

To some extent, what we are talking about falls under the umbrella of avoiding surprises. As an example, we have a case where a plaintiff brought a product liability suit. Our investigation revealed he had a pending medical malpractice suit alleging the same injuries brought by a different plaintiff's counsel. At deposition, the product liability plaintiff counsel was surprised and had no idea that the medical malpractice suit was pending. We are sure that you have similar stories of surprising others and being surprised yourself. Other litigation involving your client can be a gold mine for enterprising counsel. A second issue that may need to be addressed from prior litigation is whether there is case law precedent involving your client that bears on the issues being brought to you in the new matter.

Both sides should be obtaining, reviewing, and considering any social media content created by their client or the other side. This should be a part of the standard investigatory and work-up phase of any case by any party. Both sides should caution their clients at the outset about commenting on the case, issues related to the case or themselves on social media.

Never say never and never say always, but there needs to be considerable caution on the social media front. Social media is fertile ground for obtaining information with which to surprise, and undermine, the other side's case. As an example, we defended a putative consumer fraud class action in which the proposed class representative had been a prolific contributor to social media sites of highly personal, unflattering content that showed her true colors and made her unfit to represent others. Confrontation of the proposed plaintiff at her deposition with just a fraction of the material (which was demonstrably at least tangentially relevant to issues in the case) spelled the beginning of the end of what otherwise might have been protracted, expensive litigation.

You will need to start the follow-up on your initial client meetings in terms of witnesses and documentary evidence to be pursued. The sooner you investigate these types of things, the sooner you can make an informed assessment of your liability posture, and of the value of the case.

With regard to document collection, the issue of electronically stored information (ESI) is typically always present. Litigation holds should be placed. Decisions as to the extent of data collection can be made at a later time, but once there is a reasonable likelihood of litigation—for both sides—litigation holds should be strongly considered. Extensive advice about ESI issues can be found elsewhere and are beyond the scope of this chapter. Dismissal of a defense or claim, or even an adverse inference resulting from a finding of spoliation, is not something you want to deal with. Litigation is hard enough.

In all but the most routine cases, customized and targeted discovery demands should be developed rather than reliance on boilerplate discovery. Propound early key requests tailored to fill information gaps in your theory or to eliminate issues. If you are waiting until depositions simply to gather facts as to more than a few core issues, you likely have missed the opportunity to use limited and expensive deposition time strategically for trial preparation.

Make a realistic assessment of the costs of prosecution or defense of the case, including expenses such as experts, records collection, travel, transcripts etc. You must also make a realistic assessment of the value of the case in the jurisdiction where it is to be brought.[1] Consider what the other side's costs and expenses may be. This is information you can use to assist your client in having realistic expectations as to what it may recover, and what it will cost to get there. Or, if on the defense side, you can provide the client with the tools to make a cost/benefit analysis of what it can expect to spend to defend a case with a given amount of financial exposure.

---

1. As a general matter, we begin to assess early on what we believe is the likely sustainable judgment value for a particular case in a given venue, based on an early assessment of the outcome of liability issues and an assessment of claimed damages.

Realistic and accurate estimates about litigation costs and case value are critical for all sides to make realistic assessments of what to expect out of the suit. Of course, as the case proceeds into litigation, these assessments need to be revisited and resolved on an "events warrant" basis. Regular review of the progress of the case in the context of the goals of the litigation will ensure that the expenses, risk, and exposure and potential recovery are aligned.

This brings us to the potential for pre-suit resolution. The goal of the investigation, work-up and analysis discussed previously is to collect enough information to allow for an informed judgment as to the potential value of the case, and likelihood of success. By definition, an initial assessment is one without complete information. There will likely be many situations where you make this assessment and can honestly say to your client—we do not know enough to make a decision to resolve the case. We need to move forward and collect more information—either through investigation, discovery or both—before we decide. There will also be situations where you believe that engaging in the discovery process will improve your negotiating position. Obviously, in those cases your advice should be to forge onward.

However, it is likely that there will be many cases, where if you have done your homework, and you can convince the other side that your narrative or theme of the case may prevail, and you have made an honest and *realistic* assessment of your potential risk or reward, there can be a meeting of the minds, and a resolution of the dispute. This assumes both sides are realistic, of course. But, being prepared and ready at this stage, even if you cannot resolve the case, will set the background and framework for your litigation, and for future case resolution efforts. It is not time wasted because everything you will have done is trial preparation. It is just being done at the beginning of the case instead of in the fervor of the months, days, or even moments before or during trial.

We have been involved with multiple matters in which the parties have attempted early mediation. This can be done pre-suit, under a tolling agreement, or shortly after the complaint, particularly where liability appears all but a foregone conclusion and the extent of damages is the central point of contention.

FOR THE PLAINTIFF'S SIDE

The first step is an obvious one. Thoroughly understand the elements of the causes of action you may assert, as well as the affirmative defenses you may face, especially those that may be a silver bullet—statute of limitations, contractual conditions precedent, arbitration, personal jurisdiction, and so on. Only once you understand what you must prove, and what affirmative defense obstacles you must dodge, will you have the roadmap for developing your litigation strategy and for developing responses to the key affirmative defenses you will face.

Investigation is necessary concerning the exercise of personal jurisdiction over desired defendants. Although you may have a clear view where you would like to bring a lawsuit, few things can cause more delay out of the gate than a lengthy, costly, and perhaps losing battle over jurisdictional issues. Where the target of your litigation is a corporation or L.L.C., research will be required into the nuances of determining citizenship of the company or the members of an L.L.C., who might not be required to be disclosed.

If venue selection is important, and it always is, consider the steps you can take, and investigation that may be needed, to appropriately get the right parties in the case, and to get the case into the court (state versus federal) and venue you want. While jury pools and tendencies may make it easy to see where you would like to proceed, it will be important to evaluate the likelihood you can maintain in your chosen venue. Thus, other considerations in choosing your venue should include the potential for removal or for transfer of the venue of your action. Should you have a strong preference for remaining in state court, or a particular state or venue, for instance, tactical decisions about who to join as defendants may have to be made to avoid providing your adversary with an easy opportunity to move or remove the case, and thereby obtain a home court advantage or the advantage of a federal court less favorable to the claims being advanced.

You should examine any relevant contract or customer agreement to determine if there is a mandatory arbitration or mediation agreement. To the extent there is one, detailed consideration should be given to whether it will be inefficient to sue anyway, when you may just be buying three or more months of procedural sparring over a motion to compel arbitration, when resources might be better spent researching favored mediators or positioning the case for the most favorable arbitration setting. In some instances, there may be viable arguments that an agreement cannot be enforced. There also may be ways around an arbitration agreement such as leaving off a defendant with whom your client has an arbitration clause in favor of other viable targets who would have no similar basis for avoiding ADR.

Another practical consideration for plaintiff's counsel is the need to investigate the financial viability of the target defendants. A pyrrhic victory will not serve your client's goals, and will likely raise the ire of your law partners. While risks cannot be eliminated entirely, undertaking pre-suit review of the potential defendant's assets, credit rating, and so on, to the extent possible, can avoid a difficult conversation with the client after a long litigation proves worthless because the defendant declares bankruptcy or is determined to be "judgment proof."

Another important area of investigation is prior litigation against your potential adverse parties. Such investigation can provide key clues to likely adversaries, potential litigation strategies, possible settlement values, and the like.

As discussed earlier, a plaintiff may need to retain experts to prove one or more of the elements of the cause of action—on liability and on damages. Early retention of experts will provide information for counsel (and, importantly, the client) as to the validity of the claims, anticipated defenses, and economic losses. This early expert information can be used to convince the other side (and/or its insurer if an insurance situation) as to the liability and damage exposures it will face. And, even if it does not convince them, they may understand you "mean business" because you have done your homework and invested in credible experts on issues important to the case.

Is this a case where you need preliminary relief like an injunction? You then are faced with a balancing decision of how quickly you need the injunction, and whether you have enough information to sustain your burden of proof to obtain it. In every jurisdiction with which we are familiar, injunctive relief is considered extraordinary relief—obtaining it may not be easy or cheap. If you decide to proceed seeking preliminary relief, be sure to be comfortable you have developed enough evidence to sustain that burden. Otherwise, it may be more prudent to "keep your powder dry" and wait until you have the elements of a more convincing presentation.

At the point where plaintiff's counsel feels there is enough information, and leverage in that information, to try to convince the other side to resolve the case, counsel might consider a detailed claim letter laying bare whatever they feel is appropriate given the stage of the case. There is no harm provided you do not disclose more than you are comfortable disclosing at that stage. If you are well prepared, and reasonable, you may find a willing listener on the other side of the letter. If you are not well prepared and/or are unreasonable, this approach is a waste of time, and may well have a negative effect and create unreasonable expectations on the part of your client. As we discuss elsewhere, managing client expectations is a crucial part of your counselling role as a counsellor at law.

FOR THE DEFENDANT'S SIDE

Understand each cause of action alleged, and its elements. Develop your responses and affirmative defenses to each cause of action. Develop an initial assessment of each, and develop a plan for dealing with each, and for those affirmative defenses for which you have the burden of proof, and begin to develop what you will need to prove it.

As a prompt and first step after analyzing the pleading, carefully consider the court and venue in which the action has been brought. Are you comfortable that the case has been brought there? If not, review all options including removability and possible fraudulent joinder of parties to improperly destroy diversity. Options will include an assessment of whether the case is in an improper venue and of the procedural tools that may be available to change venue.

If service of the summons and complaint is the first notice of the suit to a defendant, then all of the issues and strategies discussed earlier that apply when you become aware of a dispute involving a client apply—investigation, insurance notification (if applicable), interviews, document collection, litigation holds, early case liability and damage assessments, develop a litigation plan depending on the client's litigation goals, identify and develop a case theme, and so on.

In terms of litigation strategy:

- Is a counterclaim against the plaintiff in order?
- Are there non-parties who may owe your client either indemnity and/or a defense?
- Are there non-parties who should be made parties? Implead them, let plaintiff counsel know they should be joined as parties and let plaintiff add them or both?

Defense counsel needs to obtain all relevant contracts with the plaintiff and with others which bear upon the dispute that the lawsuit has been brought to resolve. The contracts need to be analyzed to assess how its provisions may affect one or more of a host of issues such as liability, quantification (or limitation) of damages, scope (or limitation) of duty owed, venue provisions, arbitration/mediation provisions, choice of law provisions, risk transfer issues, insurance procurement issues, warranty issues, requirements of notice of breach, and the like. No list of considerations can be exhaustive unless looking at a particular contract in a particular context of an individual suit. We offer these as examples of what you might be looking for.

Similarly, where appropriate, applicable insurance policies should be obtained and analyzed. In the event of a declination or reservation of rights by an insurer, then the potential need to address coverage issues, commence a declaratory judgment action, or retain coverage counsel may come into play. Ensure that notice is given to all potentially implicated insurers consistent with the terms of the insurance policies.

CONCLUSION

From the standpoint of initial case assessment, every dispute and lawsuit comes with issues and strategies unique to that fact pattern and the law that applies to that fact pattern. Every area of substantive law in which disputes and lawsuits arise has its own elements and defenses and quirks. It is impossible to create a one-size-fits-all approach for all kinds of cases and fact patterns. A dispute between two shareholders is different than one between shareholders and the company, which is different than a medical malpractice case, which is different than a nuisance claim in which a preliminary injunction is sought.

What we have tried to do here is develop a coherent package of litigation and dispute resolution principles (the "ple," not the "pal") that can be applied to many if not all such disputes. The concepts we offer are important for newer lawyers to come to understand sooner rather than later in their careers, and may serve as a reminder for more experienced counsel.

Dispute resolution principles are similar across cases—the scale and the tactics may differ, but the principles are the same. A reasoned and knowledgeable assessment of the risks and benefits of resolving a dispute versus the risks and benefits of proceeding with litigation occurs in every dispute, whether over $1,000 or $2 billion.

Good and effective attorney counseling is critical to helping mold and advance client goals, and in helping inform and manage client expectations. This cannot be accomplished without the use of the skills and tools we discuss herein. Using these tools, more often than not, will result in a satisfied client who will return to you to help resolve other disputes. An unsatisfied client will not do that.

In addition, unsatisfied clients will not recommend you to others, and you will not get that call that we described at the start of this chapter, as you are leaving the office to head for the beach.

When embarking on dispute resolution always prepare and understand what you need to know early, and plot a litigation course based on that early litigation assessment and investigation. This will provide you with the ability to leverage an early resolution (by motion or settlement), or prepare you for a successful trial outcome. Either way, the time spent is well worth the effort.

One last truism—failing to plan is planning to fail.

CHAPTER 8

Discovery Themes

Keeping It Simple, but Effective[1]

Sawnie A. McEntire

Most trials consist of three distinct opportunities when trial lawyers speak directly to the jury. Most state court jurisdictions allow trial lawyers to conduct voir dire, and many federal courts also permit some level of direct lawyer participation in jury selection. All jurisdictions allow opening statements and final argument. Each of these opportunities are critical stages in a trial, but, importantly, jury selection and the opening statement are perhaps most critical. This is when trial lawyers make *first* impressions, and when they first present their all-important trial themes to potential jurors, some of whom become actual jurors deciding the case.

There is substantial truth to the maxim that a lawyer wins or loses a case in the first days of a trial. There is also significant wisdom in Will Rogers' famous quote: "You'll never get a second chance to make a first impression." All trial lawyers intuitively know this, and they should take full advantage of these important opportunities to talk directly to jurors.

One way to make a *good* first impression is to present cogent, simple trial themes as you first introduce your case and client to the jury. This chapter focuses on effective techniques for presenting simple, understandable messages to the jury, and how and why this process begins well before the jury is in the box. It starts with basic discovery at the beginning of the case.

EFFECTIVE TRIAL THEMES

Good advocacy starts with the fundamentals, and the Greek philosopher, Aristotle, described these basics most effectively over 2,000 years ago. They consist of the three cornerstones of effective argument: *ethos*, *pathos*, and *logos*.

---

1. Certain portions of this chapter are derived from the author's book entitled *Mastering the Art of Depositions*, published by the American Bar Association © 2016, and such use is authorized by the American Bar Association.

- *Pathos* represents the emotional hook included within the storyteller's message to the intended audience—the jury. It is the emotional glue inviting the jury into the story. It is a story's appeal that attracts interest, empathy, or sympathy.
- *Logos* is the logic or reasoning of the lawyer's argument—that is, the facts, figures, and empirical observations from witnesses or other evidence. It is the reasoned, common sense used to persuade the jury to adopt a position.
- *Ethos* is the credibility and trustworthiness of the speaker (the trial lawyer), the client, and the witnesses in the case.

Every seasoned trial lawyer knows these three principals at an instinctive level; Aristotle simply gave these concepts names and explication. Every trial lawyer also should endeavor to package his or her case with these three principals as cornerstones, and then test his or her messages to the jury to make sure these elements are presented effectively. In that manner, the case is pre-packaged to win—a case that is credible, trustworthy, logical, appealing, and interesting.

The lawyer's messages in jury selection and opening statement should be simple, readily understandable, and internally consistent. They must make logical sense, they must be credible, and the case and client must be presented to the jury in an appealing and sympathetic manner. To achieve these goals, the trial lawyer's work begins well before first words are ever spoken to the jury. This means the path to a successful trial starts with a disciplined, well-conceived discovery plan.

Although discovery objectives evolve and change as factual issues are better defined, there is always a first step. By the time the venire panel enters the courtroom, the trial lawyer will have simplified months, and perhaps even years, of discovery into simple, logical, believable themes. There are several steps in this process.

DISCOVERY PLANS

Every case needs a discovery plan. The purpose of such a plan is to identify key legal principles at an early date, and then evaluate known facts within this legal context. The goal is to identify favorable facts, as well as negative facts. The lawyer then should identify strategies to neutralize the bad facts and accentuate the good. Several tools are available to get this job done.

Initial client and key witness interviews are critical. The lawyer must acquire a basic understanding of the claims and defenses rooted in both the law and the facts. Developing facts during discovery without legal context is a waste of time, and perhaps dangerous. The lawyer must develop a plan based upon a realistic appreciation of the factual needs for a successful case, that is, an accurate understanding of the legal and factual elements of the claims or defenses. Once initial interviews are completed, the lawyer is equipped to review and better understand the documents and other tangible evidence.

Chronologies and timelines are an excellent tool for organizing facts, and this is particularly important in large cases or document-intensive cases. Important information should be isolated and segregated from less important evidence. This is a sifting process. Key events are identified through initial witness interviews, and then supporting documents are identified to either confirm or negate witness recollections. The goal is to structure order out of chaos. Ultimately, the lawyer takes even the most complicated case and reduces it to a manageable number of simple, but critical, thematic principles. These are the lawyer's trial themes incorporating the pathos, logos, and ethos of the lawyer's argument. After further development during the life of the case, these now refined trial themes are what the jury hears when the lawyer first stands to speak.

Every case has a starting point and an end, and discovery plans and trial themes necessarily evolve as a case matures. Subtle issues may become more important. Issues with presumed importance at the outset may lose significance after more facts are established, and the parties' respective positions are better defined. Nevertheless, every lawyer must begin at the beginning, and every lawyer must initially try to identify the primary factual objectives for the case.

Multiple discovery mechanisms are available to achieve these objectives. Traditional discovery vehicles, of course, include interrogatories, requests for admission, inspections of tangible property, and document discovery. If possible, given the circumstances presented in each case, reasonably thorough written discovery should be completed before deposition discovery is initiated.

- Discrete surgical interrogatories ferret out important aspects of the opposing case and the opposition's factual positions;
- Carefully crafted requests for admission effectively limit an opposing party's flexibility and maneuverability as the case develops; and
- Both interrogatories and requests for admission help define the contours of the factual disputes.

Once the lawyer defines these contours, then the lawyer is ready to begin depositions. There should be no doubt that deposition discovery, including depositions of both lay witnesses and experts, ultimately defines the path to the courthouse.

Every Deposition Is a Trial Deposition

Every discovery plan should identify which witnesses should be deposed, and which witnesses should not. Sometimes, legitimate strategic reasons dictate that a particular witness should not be deposed. There should be an informed effort to select key witnesses who can best sponsor the trial themes. Witnesses with potentially harmful testimony, who reside outside the subpoena power of the court, are not likely candidates for the deposition wish list.

In addition, at this stage, it is critical to appreciate that every deposition is a trial deposition. That is, every deposition is an opportunity to narrow and limit the factual focus of the case; every deposition is an opportunity to advance favorable testimony; and, every deposition is an opportunity to neutralize or counter negative facts. Every deposition should be approached with heightened awareness of these truisms, and the lawyer should enter the deposition room fully prepared to achieve objectives. Every effective trial lawyer knows that what happens in the deposition room does not always stay in the deposition room. Thus, the trial lawyer should approach every deposition as if it is for jury consumption.

Keeping It Simple, Credible, Logical, and Appealing

As a rule, the attention span of the average American citizen is decreasing. This is also true for the average juror. As society becomes increasingly more dependent on "sound bite" technology, our society seeks information sources that are quickly accessible, and information that is rapidly digestible. This is how we receive the news. This is how we use our computers and the Internet.

The average attention span of a juror is short. The average juror's ability to focus on one fact is even lower—substantially lower—and measured in seconds. This reality has significant ramifications for the trial lawyer:

- complicated messages should be avoided;
- unnecessary, multiple messages should be avoided;
- short, concise, messages should be crafted;
- easily understood messages should be repeated, and then repeated again; and
- *all* messages should be appealing, logical and believable—the pathos, logos, and ethos of the advocate.

The goal is to reduce the complex to the simple, while giving the jury something interesting to consider, focusing its attention on believable facts that support a favorable verdict.

Simplicity is always good. Simple themes are easily repeated, and repeated themes are easily remembered. When lawyers repeat simple messages frequently, much like marketing soundbites or advertisements, the information is more likely to reside with the targeted audience. Complicated messages alienate the targeted listener; the listener's focus is invariably lost. Unnecessary messages also cloud and dilute what is important, and cause distraction. On the other hand, the jury more easily receives and processes simple messages.

SIMPLIFYING QUESTIONS DURING DEPOSITIONS

The best questions are also simple questions, and most seasoned trial lawyers already know this. An examining lawyer should avoid complicated, compound questions. Sometimes an examining lawyer gets lost in complex sentence structures with many moving parts. In those instances, the listener may get lost in the question. Complicated questions burdened with technical terms also risk losing the audience. Compound questions are often confusing, and the jury may not appreciate important answers. Complex questions are frequently boring, and lack the pathos of good advocacy. On the other hand, simple questions are more easily grasped, and shift the focus to the witness's answers.

If possible, examining lawyers should avoid technical terms; such terms are better defined by using commonly understood words and concepts, making it easier for lay jurors to track the witness's testimony. The jury can more easily track simple questions using common words rather than long sentences with complex, strange, or foreign terms. Simple questions also give an examination more "punch." Again, the goal is to avoid confusion and boredom by presenting captivating and dramatic testimony. Here are some brief examples of how to simplify and make questions more interesting:

Complicated v. Simple Questions

COMPLICATED, BORING QUESTION	SIMPLIFIED, INTERESTING QUESTION
Please describe the details of your company's document retention policy.	What steps did you take to prevent the destruction of important documents?
Did your company have established written rules to make sure that the risks of accidents on the premises are reduced?	Isn't it true you had no written policies to make sure my client did not get hurt?
What design protocols does your company follow to make sure that product designs are safe?	Tell the jury everything you did so your product didn't hurt people like it did my client.

ACTION WORDS: VERBS, ADJECTIVES, AND ADVERBS

Questions are more appealing and interesting to jurors if the lawyer uses "power" words or "punch" words. Although this technique is largely second nature to many talented trial veterans, it bears mentioning again because it is so important. Effective lawyers typically use action verbs. Easily understood adjectives and adverbs artfully inserted into questions can provide dramatic effect. Once again, the objective is to capture both the ethos and pathos of the witness and the testimony, using the witness to advance your case. This is accomplished by using questions that contain words conveying dramatic action or dramatic qualities. This helps simplify the message. Here are some additional examples of how to add punch to questions, and all lawyers should invest some time before a deposition examination in crafting such questions consistent with his or her style:

BLAND QUESTION	INTERESTING, DRAMATIC QUESTION
Do you agree that the merger clause under section 10 on page 5 of the agreement means that all prior discussions are superseded?	Isn't it true this contract is your *only* agreement as stated in section 10?
Does your company have a system for monitoring adverse reactions once the pharmaceutical is distributed into the marketplace?	What did you do to make sure your drug did not kill people after it was advertised to sick people, like my client?
Do you agree you only conducted limited due diligence before you bought the new company?	Isn't it true you failed to look at the books of the company before you paid a lot of money?

A single question with a single answer seldom wins or loses a case. However, effective questions are building blocks upon which success is achieved. By peppering questions with dramatic or "punchy" words, the jury's attention span is extended because the jury is more interested in the examination. If questions are long and complicated, the jury's focus will diminish quickly. If the questions are boring or disjointed, the jury's focus will stray. Thus, a time-tested principle comes into play—keep it *simple, simple, and simple*.

The examining lawyer will necessarily tailor questions to the specific type of case at issue. Thus, the words used in the examination logically change depending upon the legal and factual issues involved—whether it is a business tort case, a personal injury case, a contract case, or a simple negligence case. Deposition questions for each type of case involve different *buzzwords* because there will be different types of testimony sought. Creative, case-specific planning is therefore required. By doing this, the lawyer can develop a script that may be presented to the jury during final argument. If all goes as planned, the lawyer will have specific answers to specific questions that translate immediately into answers in the jury charge.

ASKING "DUTY" AND "NO LOSE" QUESTIONS

Another time-tested technique involves so-called duty and no lose questions. Both are equally effective at maintaining the jury's focus, and are used typically with adverse or hostile witnesses. These types of questions trigger helpful answers regardless of how the witness responds. These are "no lose" questions for the lawyer yielding "no win" answers from the witness.

These types of questions use common-sense notions that a reasonable witness must concede, and are frequently predicated on moral or ethical principles. If the witness resists the question, the witness invariably loses credibility with the jury. The ethos, or credibility, of the adverse witness is undermined. Because these types of questions reflect common sense and fairness, any attempt to avoid or debate the question is poorly perceived. Fighting or resisting common sense is alienating. Thus, the goal of the question is to place the reluctant witness in an awkward position where the basic common sense of the question must be conceded.

In similar fashion, "duty" questions incorporate concepts of duty, obligation, or responsibility as an operative premise. The lawyer can ask questions substituting nouns with verbs to create the same effect. Auxiliary verbs can communicate a sense of duty, such as "should," "must," "need," and "require," and may be used interchangeably with nouns like "responsibility," "obligation," and "duty" with the same forceful effect.

Again, the goal is to frame questions that include simple, powerful messages for later use at trial. Using concepts of "responsibility" with strategically placed adjectives and adverbs, powerful questions are crafted easily. Here are some specific examples of combining "power" words with "duty" words in "no lose" situations:

The "Duty" and "No Lose" Questions

Do you agree a company has an (***important***) **obligation** to provide a safe workplace?
Do you agree a company has a (***significant***) **responsibility** to provide a safe workplace?
Do you agree a company **must** (***always***) provide a safe workplace?
Do you agree a company has a **duty** to design products that do not **kill** people?
Do you agree a company **must warn** patients that the drugs could lead to **death**?
Do you agree that a company **should** (***always***) take steps to ensure a **safe** workplace?

USING DEMONSTRATIVE EXHIBITS TO SIMPLIFY MESSAGES

All lawyers should assume that every deposition (or at least excerpts from every deposition) will be read or shown to the jury. As such, a primary objective should be to capture the jury's attention and hold it. Using demonstrative exhibits during a videotaped deposition will enhance and magnify the lawyer's message for later jury consumption. The effective use of demonstrative exhibits can make a deposition come alive when it is later viewed by the jury.

Hand-drawn diagrams are traditional options, and usually effective. Any hand-drawn diagram may be shown real time in a video deposition and can underscore its credibility and authenticity. There is a sense of drama when a jury sees a lay witness drawing a diagram. The jury wants to see the picture or the drawing. For added effect, the examining lawyer should request the videographer to zoom in on the diagram to enlarge and magnify its impact with the jury. The examining lawyer should also make sure the witness signs the diagram and dates it. This adds further drama and authenticity to the exercise.

Using a photograph, the witness can identify relevant information by drawing circles or otherwise marking on the photograph with arrows, lines or other marks reflecting the testimony. Again, it is helpful to have the witness initial his or her name to the markings. Then, once again, for dramatic effect, the examining lawyer should request the videographer to zoom in on the photograph with the witness's personalized markings asking the witness to describe what the markings signify.

Witness charts are also simple, and highly effective, particularly with third-party witnesses. Using a large flip chart in a deposition where the witness draws a picture or writes key words will capture the jury's attention. The jury will be attracted by the witness's movement standing and moving toward the flip chart. Opposing counsel may object if you attempt this exercise with an opposing party. But, it is frequently used with independent witnesses. Having a large flip chart next to the witness seat, and directing the witness to stand and then draw pictures or list other information, fosters the impression the examining lawyer has complete control of the situation and the examination. It is also easy for the videographer to zoom in on the chart for the jury's later viewing. Again, the witness should initial the flip chart and date it. The examining lawyer should make sure it is marked as an exhibit for later use at trial.

Aerial photographs are also excellent ways to reinforce deposition testimony. One particularly useful approach is to magnetize a large (bigger than life) aerial photograph with hard-board backing. The process of making the board magnetic is important because magnetic props can be placed on the photograph and moved across the board to enhance testimony by allowing the witness to reinforce certain factual points. This could be a magnetized model car or truck, trees or roadway obstructions, flags, and so on. The witness can move magnetized vehicles across the photographic backdrop reinforcing the witness's testimony of what he or she saw as an automobile or truck accident unfolded. The lawyer also can direct the witness to use a dry marker to identify other relevant information on the photograph while the videographer is focusing on the witness's testimony and markings. Again, there is movement in the video capturing the jury's attention. The jury will be fascinated with the exercise as the underlying event comes to life. Here are some examples:

Aerial Photographs Deliver Simple Messages

In a multi-vehicle auto accident, the aerial photograph can depict the roadway system where the accident occurred. The witness can identify what he or she saw by placing marks on the aerial photograph of the relative positions of the implicated automobiles. Another option is to use toy cars, also magnetized, that the witness can place on the magnetized board demonstrating movement of the vehicles in real time.
In a real estate boundary dispute, the aerial photograph can be used to identify significant boundaries giving the jury an interesting perspective of the dispute.
In construction disputes, aerial photographs can be utilized to establish the stage and phases of a major construction project. Several aerial photographs of the same project, which are taken over time, can depict the progress or delays in construction over time.
In environmental disputes, the aerial photograph can be used to show the extent or radius of contamination or pollution.

In each instance, the lawyer's trial themes are bolstered by aerial photographs using the witness's real time explanations of an event. The effect is dramatic.

Another highly effective demonstrative exhibit in a consumer goods case or product liability case is to bring the product or consumer good into the deposition room as an exhibit during examination. This is useful with both lay witnesses and expert witnesses. The examining lawyer can ask the witness to stand and describe how the product failed, or how a piece of equipment failed. This can range from small consumer goods, industrial goods, and equipment such as valves or piping to even a chassis of an automobile. Indeed, there are no limitations on what types of real-life exhibits may be used except the size of the deposition room and the logistics of moving the exhibit to the deposition location. One's sense of creativity, imagination, and a flexible budget is all it takes.

Another highly effective demonstrative exhibit involves split screen video. One side of the screen depicts the witness, while the other side of the screen depicts an important document used in the examination. The video is jury friendly—the jury can see the witness responding to questions while simultaneously seeing pertinent excerpts from the document at issue. Using available software, the lawyer can easily pull, magnify, and highlight an excerpt from the document significant to the prosecution or defense of the case. The result is an enhancement of the witness's testimony. These types of split screen examinations may trigger an objection from opposing counsel. Thus, the procedural rules of each relevant jurisdiction must be consulted.

Another effective technique is the use of toys or models. This is particularly useful in automobile accidents to show how cars impacted in a multi-vehicle accident. A scale model of a train, boat, or plane are easily developed to give a witness's testimony added punch. The witness can be asked to show how cars collided, the boat flipped, the train derailed, or the plane crashed. Again, simple devices can carry powerful images leaving lasting impacts on a jury.

Topographical models also are useful, and are used frequently in automotive product liability litigation where environmental factors may be significant. Trees, roads, road shoulders, bridges, ramps, slopes, and hills can be modeled to show the different surfaces and terrains where an accident occurred. The model can be brought to the deposition room, and the witness asked to stand and describe what he or she saw using the model as a visual reference point. Again, this helps enhance simple messages that the lawyer wants to reinforce for later jury consumption. Simple messages take on the added power when visually reinforced.

In summary, the goal is to win, and winning a case means using logical, appealing, and credible arguments. What is true today has not changed since the days of Aristotle in Ancient Greece. Today's technology allows practicing lawyers to incorporate pathos, ethos and logos into a discovery plan at new, sophisticated levels through the effective use of demonstrative exhibits. The first step is to develop an effective discovery plan, and then implement that plan seeking simplicity and clarity along the way—that is the formula for success.

CHAPTER 9

Getting Organized

Preparing Timelines of Important Events and Documents

Robert L. Christie

The title of this chapter could be misinterpreted to imply there is a point in time in a case when you should "get organized" around key events and documents, and you should then sit down and prepare a master timeline. That is too difficult. Why not start out a case with a systematic approach to organizing key events and documents in a timeline so that when you get to the point of needing that information, it is ready to go?

Every case has a sequence of significant events and evidence connected with those events. Why not use simple technology to catalog this information when it comes into your office, and build on that structure as additional information is collected during investigation and discovery. Create this organized structure for every case and simply replicate the process beginning at the outset of a new matter.

This sounds straightforward, and it is. Start with digitalizing the case materials. Create a numbering protocol for all incoming documents and follow it with respect to everything that comes in on that case. Develop an electronic file structure that makes sense for your practice and routinely add new information to these folders. Working with digitally stored information creates tremendous flexibility in how you view, capture, and highlight key documents and key dates during the life of the case. By following a process of systematically adding to your digital file, an attorney can stay on top of a case as it unfolds, not be placed in the difficult and time-consuming position of organizing a file late in the life of the case.

Now that you have a digital filing system, either stored locally or in a cloud-based environment, you are ready to "get organized." Not to plug a particular piece of software or a particular software company, but every lawyer and every legal assistant has PowerPoint™ on their computer. When a new file comes into your office, create a new PowerPoint™. Call it your "case management PowerPoint™" if you are looking for a naming protocol. Just as you create form pleadings in word processing for use in every case, create a form PowerPoint™ and add it to your internal process of setting up a new file. Then, as you review materials on the case, start building slides. Create a slide for every key date, and add a text field to briefly summarize the significance of that date. Add to it an image of the first page of the key document associated with that date or event. Since you already have added control numbers to the documents, it will be easy for you or your assistant to locate the full document for future use in a deposition or otherwise. You can also easily add hyperlinks into the PowerPoint™ itself, so that a click on the link will take you to the full document stored elsewhere (click "Insert" from the menu bar, then select "Hyperlink").

This organizational system, with events and documents separated onto individual slides, provides complete flexibility in organizing the information chronologically for purposes of creating a timeline. Remember you can "move" the slides in a PowerPoint™ into any order at any time. You do not need to worry about whether you are reviewing documents in a chronological order. Feel at ease in reviewing case materials in the order in which they come into you through discovery or otherwise. Because you have created individual slides for each key date, event, or document, you can later place the slides in chronological order.

For document-intensive cases, not everything produced in discovery will be worthy of its own slide. You will likely have spreadsheet style indices of significant document productions, medical records, and the like. These may be produced through separate litigation management software, but review of those larger indices will reveal individual documents and key dates worth separating from the mass of information. Because you have created a separate system for capturing and organizing that information—your case management PowerPoint™—these new key documents can be instantly added to individual slides for later use.

Increasingly, many of our cases involve video media, either as part of discovery or because of the video depositions you have taken. Because of its flexibility, PowerPoint™ allows you to imbed this video media onto a slide just as you would a pdf or a jpeg. Depending on file size, you may add only a screen capture of the video itself, combining it with a hyperlink to the full video file.

I practice primarily in Washington state. Under our court rules, attorneys have the option, under Evidence Rule 904, to compile a list of certain types of documents that are typically admissible—medical treatment records, bills for treatment, bills for estimates of property damage, standard weather or traffic signal reports, to name a few. The rule permits each side to designate these documents in advance of trial. They are deemed admissible unless properly objected to in a specified time frame. The compilation of this list in the weeks approaching trial can present an organizational challenge unless you have anticipated its preparation during the life of the case. The case management PowerPoint™ discussed earlier can be part of that solution. During the life of a case, as we build our individual slides highlighting key documents, we will note on the slide itself which ones will be included in our ER 904 submission. Compiling that information for ER 904 purposes then becomes simply a matter of reviewing the case management PowerPoint™ and creating our list from what has already been selected.

A case management PowerPoint™ lends itself well, with appropriate modification, for use as (1) a case summary that can be viewed and supplemented by multiple attorneys and legal assistants working on a single matter; (2) a quick informational reference for answering client inquiries about aspects of the case; (3) a living "status report" that can be shared in whole or in part with a client or an insurer; (4) part of a presentation that might be made in a mock jury setting; and (5) part of a presentation that might be made to a mediator or settlement judge.

Figure 9.1   Samples of Individual Slides in a Case Management PowerPoint™

There are other tried and true methods of preparing chronologies and timelines that you may have developed and perfected. If you have a system that works for you, follow it. We all know that the "best timeline wins" at trial, and perhaps have experienced the joy of having the opposing attorney ask to use your visual timeline—prepared from your well-organized case management system—during the examination of a key witness. You do not want to be on the other side of that experience.

Figure 9.2 shows a timeline created for a case and designed around the minute hand on a clock. Built entirely in PowerPoint™, each progressive slide brought in the next sequential event, showing that key events happened in a matter of minutes. A large blow up of the complete timeline was used at trial with each witness to fill in the events.

There are other software solutions to presenting timelines at mock trials, mediation, summary judgment motion arguments, or trial itself. Another particularly effective program is Timeline 3D from BEEDOCS.com. It is a product designed to run on IOS software, so we use it both on a MAC laptop or an iPad. As described on the company website: "Present historical events with Timeline 3D to reveal connections and clarify relationships. Make timeline charts of world history, family

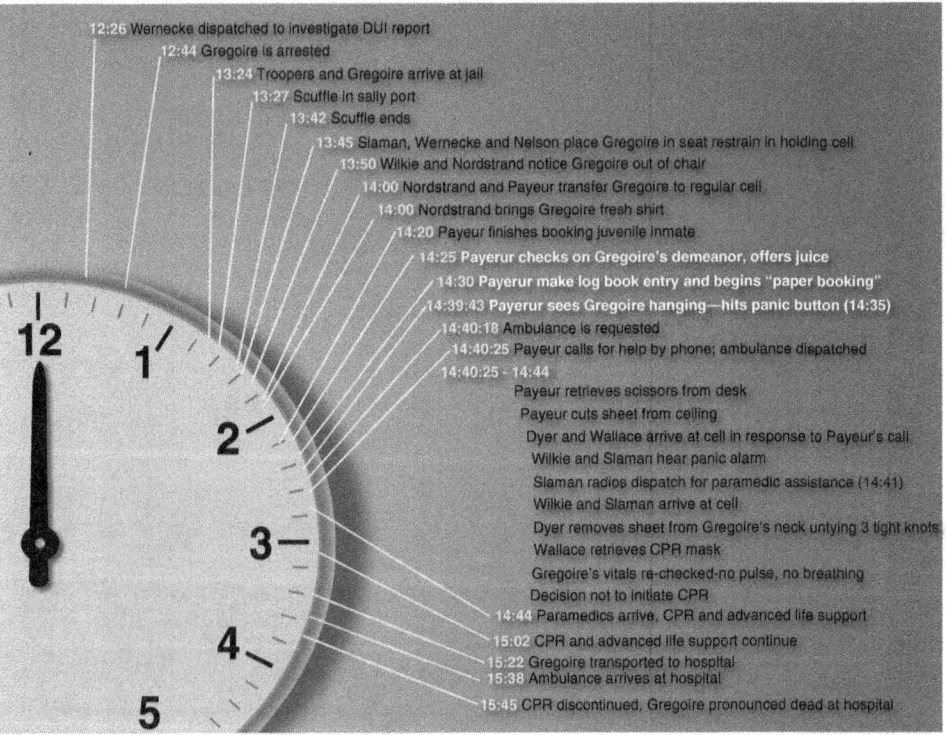

Figure 9.2   Timeline designed around minute hand on a clock.

trees, fictional stories or business deadlines. Timelines help you understand and present history with new perspective!"[1]

There are three features to this software that are particularly useful and persuasive. First, it is easy to use. As you create individual slides, all of which will have an assigned date, the software automatically places them in chronologic order. Second, you can imbed media in each slide, just as you would in PowerPoint™. Third, when the visual timeline is projected it lays out in a three-dimensional fashion (hence the name), with early events in large size at the left side of the screen and later events falling away toward a vanishing point on the right side of the screen. While it is old tech now, for readers of my generation, think of the awe you felt when you watched the opening scene of *Star Wars* as the story vanished in the distance. And the way that the software moves you from one event to the next is visually eye-catching and interesting.

In a recent bench trial where this software was used with a medical expert to explain the complicated history of when a plaintiff developed certain neurological symptoms, making the point that many of them were developed long before the traumatic event that was at issue in the lawsuit, worthy opponent counsel objected: "Your Honor, I object to this. He is showing you his entire theory of the case right there in that timeline." The judge responded: "That is exactly what he is doing, and I find it rather helpful. Objection overruled." You get the point. So check it out as another way to organize, compile, and present a timeline of events linked to key pieces of evidence.

One of the challenges of managing information in any case is separating what is important—what exhibits will influence the outcome of the case—from what does not matter. How many of you have been involved in trials where the pre-trial order that each side has participated in preparing designates hundreds of documents as potential trial exhibits, only to reach the end of trial and find that a fraction of them have been offered and admitted into evidence? My experience is that this is the rule, not the exception. This places a premium on an information management system that forces you to make ongoing decisions about what is important to the case and what is not. When opposing counsel submits a massive volume of potential trial exhibits, it is usually a strong tell that they have not taken the time to focus their case on what is important, but rather are covering themselves for trial. The best practice is to cull the herd of materials during the life of a case, refining and reinforcing your core theories as information is developed, demonstrating in your submissions that you know what events and documents are likely to be admitted into evidence and are likely to influence the decision makers.

The key to preparing effective timelines and chronologies of important documents and events is to develop a systematic approach to the process, which is then

---

1. https://www.beedocs.com/timeline3D/mac/.

followed during the life of the case as new information develops. Best practices dictate that this not be done late in the life of a matter, but started early and built over time. Find a system that works for you and follow it. Be open to using developing software products to assist you. As suggested here, consider starting with software that is already on every computer in your office. Remember that a simple solution is one likely followed.

Don't wait until final trial preparation to start this process. Organize your digital information at the outset and start building your virtual "storyboards" from the beginning of your case review process. Be creative and visual. Develop your timelines in more than one medium. Assemble and use timelines at key stages of case development. At trial, have witnesses fill in events by referencing your timeline. Some courts will admit the timelines into evidence so that the jury will be working from it when deciding the case. Connect events and evidence with something visual that your audience will remember. Make your presentation organized, simplified, and direct. You will strengthen the power of your story telling and enhance the stickiness of your client's message.

CHAPTER 10

Motion for Summary Judgment

Strategies and Timing

James Miller

The term *summary judgment* is a bit of a misnomer. While a successful motion will result in a judgment, there is typically nothing "summary" about the process. Motions for summary judgment are time-consuming and expensive. But, increasingly, summary judgment—not trial—is how cases are won or lost. So, too, discovery is generally conducted in order to set the stage for summary judgment motions to come.

Whether true or not, many accomplished trial lawyers will answer the questions, "when do you start thinking about opening statement," or "when do you start thinking about jury instructions," with "when I draft the complaint [or answer]." The start of the case is also when you need to start thinking about summary judgment and its basic standard—the absence of a genuine dispute as to any material fact and entitlement to judgment as a matter of law.

Motions for summary judgment are frequently used to "educate the judge," as an effective "discovery tool" to flush out the other side's evidence, or as pre-settlement posturing.[1] But the goal is judgment. Here is an eye-opening statistic:

---

1. None of these provide an appropriate basis for a motion, but once it is determined that there are good grounds to support a motion for summary judgment, these are worthy considerations in determining strategies including timing and content.

49 percent—nearly half—of all summary judgment motions made by defendants are granted either in full or in part according to a study by the Federal Judicial Center.[2] Although plaintiffs fare less well (29 percent to 36 percent success rate reported in Trends), it is obvious that judges are receptive, and there is evidence that they have grown more receptive over time.[3] Comparing these success rates with the fact that only 1 percent of cases now go to trial in federal court,[4] summary judgment must at least be considered in every case.

This chapter explores the strategies for seeking summary judgment and the timing of a motion, as well as the strategies for defeating summary judgment. To help with a better appreciation for strategic concerns, this chapter begins with a discussion of the federal summary judgment rule, Rule 56 of the Federal Rules of Civil Procedure,[5] the jurisprudence surrounding it, and some interesting (and surprising) empirical evidence concerning the use and effects of the summary judgment process.

Here is the executive summary in two words—simple and complicated. If you are moving for summary judgment, it must be simple. If you are opposing, it must be complicated.

SUMMARY JUDGMENT: WHAT IT IS AND WHAT IT ISN'T

Summary judgment is a judgment without trial. In essence, a motion for summary judgment tells the court there is nothing to be tried. Instead, there are a set of uncontroverted facts sufficient to establish a claim or defense as a matter of law. The summary judgment device gives any party, whether a claimant or one defending against a claim, the opportunity to convince a court that it should enter judgment in its favor without a trial. The standard for summary judgment is stated in one concise sentence of Rule 56(a): *"The court shall grant summary judgment if the movant shows that there is no genuine dispute as to any material fact and the movant is entitled to judgment as a matter of law."*[6]

---

2. Joe S. Cecil, Rebecca N. Eyre, D. Dean Miletich & David Rindskopf, *Trends in Summary Judgment Practice: 1975-2000*, FEDERAL JUDICIAL CENTER (Jan. 1, 2007), *available at* https://www.fjc.gov/content/trends-summary-judgment-practice-1975-2000-0 [hereinafter *Trends*].

3. See discussion *infra* at page 134 *et seq.*

4. United States Courts, *Judicial Facts and Figures 2016*, http://www.uscourts.gov/statistics-reports/analysis-reports/judicial-facts-and-figures. This same report shows that in 1990, 4.3 percent of cases went to trial.

5. This chapter is limited to Rule 56 motions for summary judgment and federal case law. Each of the 50 states has some form of summary judgment procedure, many modeled after Rule 56.

6. The entire text of Rule 56 is set out in the appendix at the end of this chapter. There is a good deal of meat on Rule 56, and the rule should be read and reread. In addition, the rule has a substantial history since its adoption in 1937, as reflected in the Advisory Committee Notes which contain a wealth of authoritative commentary (emphasis added).

In ruling on a motion, the court may not weigh the evidence or judge the credibility of the witnesses, and it must construe the evidence in a light most favorable to the nonmoving party, drawing all permissible inferences in its favor. Applying these standards, any substantial evidence in favor of the nonmoving party is sufficient to defeat the motion. These standards serve, in part, to insure that the jury function is not usurped.

The success of the motion will turn not simply on whether the party filing it has a very strong case, but on a clear presentation of the material facts which are uncontroverted, the absence of a genuine dispute, and the requirements of the applicable law. A good motion for summary judgment cuts through the pleadings and immaterial noise and shines a light on a compelling record that leads to no other conclusion than a judgment for the movant. A good opposition to a motion for summary judgment makes noise by demonstrating that there are genuine issues of material fact that should be resolved through trial.

Whether one or more motions for summary judgment are filed or not, the consideration of summary judgment is a major factor in discovery. In a survey of its members, the ABA Section of Litigation found that approximately half of all lawyers believe "discovery is used *more to develop evidence for summary judgment* than it is to understand the other party's claims and defenses for trial."[7]

A successful summary judgment motion will obviously save the time and expense of a trial and will expedite the conclusion of the case. Even when a summary judgment motion is not granted in full, it may result in streamlining the case for trial or having a positive effect on settlement.

That is what summary judgment is. What it is not is an uncomplicated and inexpensive procedure. It does not always save lawyer time, legal fees, or court time.[8] In most cases it does not eliminate the need for trial. It is not for every case. But, it should be seriously *considered* for every case, and its focus on a careful analysis of the material facts, what is really in dispute, and the applicable law, provides a useful discipline for good case assessment.

Summary Judgment Standard

No Genuine Dispute as to Any Material Fact

Summary judgment procedure seeks to separate the wheat from the chaff. Court files and even pleadings tend to accumulate a lot of chaff. Some of the chaff is necessary to create a narrative and establish winning themes for the case. But chaff does not

---

7. A.B.A. Sec. Litig. Member Survey on Civil Practice: Full Report 71, tbl. 6.11 (Dec. 11, 2009) (emphasis added).
8. D. Brock Hornby, *Summary Judgment without Illusions*, 13 Green Bag 2D, 273 (2010).

require a trial. And so for purposes of summary judgment, it is only *genuine* disputes of *material* facts which require trial and which preclude summary adjudication.

Genuine Dispute

A dispute is genuine when the evidence would permit a reasonable jury to find in favor of either party.[9] In making that determination the court must view the evidence "through the prism of the substantive evidentiary burden."[10] Thus, in the typical civil case in which the burden of proof is preponderance of the evidence, the court must determine that the evidence is sufficient for a reasonable jury to find, by a preponderance of the evidence, for either party. Also, in order to create a genuine issue for trial, the evidence must be believable. The principal authority for this is the Supreme Court's decision in *Scott v. Harris*,[11] in which eight members of the Court, on a de novo review of the police videotape of a high speed chase, found it to "closely resemble[] a Hollywood-style chase of the most frightening sort." The majority concluded that "no reasonable jury could conclude otherwise," disagreeing with both the trial judge and the Eleventh Circuit Court of Appeals and directing the entry of summary judgment in favor of the police officer who had been sued by the fleeing driver who had been rendered a paraplegic in the ensuing car crash. Justice Scalia, writing for the majority, described the "believability" standard:

> When opposing parties tell two different stories, one of which is blatantly contradicted by the record, so that no reasonable jury could believe it, a court should not adopt that version of the facts for purposes of ruling on a motion for summary judgment.
>
> That was the case here with regard to the factual issue whether respondent was driving in such fashion as to endanger human life. Respondent's version of events is so utterly discredited by the record that no reasonable jury could have believed him. The Court of Appeals should not have relied on such visible fiction; it should have viewed the facts in the light depicted by the videotape.[12]

Only Justice Stevens, like the trial judge and the circuit court judges, saw the videotape differently. In his lone dissenting opinion, Justice Stevens observed that

> eight of the jurors on this Court reach a verdict that differs from the views of the judges on both the District Court and the Court

---

9. Anderson v. Liberty Lobby, Inc., 477 U.S. 242, 250, 106 S. Ct. 2505, 91 L. Ed. 2d 202 (1986).
10. 477 U.S. at 252, 253.
11. Scott v. Harris, 550 U.S. 372, 378–80, 127 S. Ct. 1769, 167 L. Ed. 2d 686 (2007).
12. 127 S. Ct. at 1776.

of Appeals who are surely more familiar with the hazards of driving on Georgia roads than we are.[13]

This "blatant contradiction" exception to the rule that the court should accept the nonmovant's version of the facts is sparingly used.[14] However, it has been used a number of times based on videotapes,[15] and in today's world where there is a video camera on every corner and in many commercial and residential properties, it would seem that the "blatant contradiction" exception and the *Scott* case will have continued relevance.

Desperate times call for desperate measures, and on occasion, a party, typically the nonmovant, will principally rely on an uncorroborated affidavit or deposition testimony of some key person. Such testimony or affidavit are targets for the "blatant contradiction" exception. Thus, "a party's uncorroborated self-serving testimony cannot prevent summary judgment, particularly if the overwhelming documentary evidence supports the opposite scenario."[16]

Material Facts

A fact is "material" if it might affect the outcome of the case under the governing substantive law.[17] Conversely, disputes over immaterial facts will not preclude summary judgment.[18]

The only facts that may affect the outcome of the case—and thus are material—are those that tend to prove or disprove the "legal elements" of the claim or defense.[19] In a simple breach of contract case, the elements are the existence of a contract,

---

13. *Id.* at 1781.

14. E.g., Robinson v. Pezzat, 818 F.3d 1, 10–11 (D.C. Cir. 2016) (evidence satisfying this standard "rarely exists").

15. E.g., Williams v. Brooks, 809 F.3d 936, 942 (7th Cir. 2016); Marvin v. City of Taylor, 509 F.3d 234, 245–51 (6th Cir. 2007).

16. Vinewood Capital, LLC v. Dar Al-Maal Al-Islami Tr., 541 F. App'x 443, 447 (5th Cir. 2013) (deposition testimony and declaration not enough to establish genuine issue of fact when contract language and previous contract drafts belied contentions in declaration); *see also* Villiarimo v. Aloha Island Air, Inc., 281 F.3d 1054, 1061 (9th Cir. 2002); Johnson v. Washington Metro. Transit Auth., 883 F.2d 125, 128 (D.C. Cir.1989) ("The removal of a factual question from the jury is most likely when a plaintiff's claim is supported solely by the plaintiff's own self-serving testimony, unsupported by corroborating evidence, and undermined either by other credible evidence, physical impossibility or other persuasive evidence that the plaintiff has deliberately committed perjury."). However, a "court should not disregard self-serving statements made in sworn testimony simply because they are self-serving at the summary judgment stage," Murray v. Birmingham Bd. of Educ., 172 F. Supp. 3d 1225, 1237 (N.D. Ala. 2016) (citing Feliciano v. City of Miami Beach, 707 F.3d 1244, 1252 (11th Cir. 2013)).

17. *Anderson*, 477 U.S. at 248 (actual malice a material fact in public figure defamation action).

18. *E.g.*, Fenster v. Tepfer & Spitz, 301 F.3d 851, 856 (7th Cir. 2002) (when loan program initiated and by whom immaterial when absence of signature rendered it invalid in any event); Miller v. Blattner, 676 F. Supp. 2d 485, 497 (E.D. La. 2009) (plaintiff's subjective expectation of privacy concerning immaterial emails in light of employer's policy prohibiting personal use of office computers).

19. *Anderson*, 477 U.S at 248.

breach of the contract, and resultant damages. Facts that tend to prove or disprove these elements are material. Everything else, such as the defendant's intentions in breaching, is immaterial. An excellent place to look when preparing for summary judgment, as in drafting pleadings, is the pattern jury instructions. The jury instructions are what will tell the trier of fact how to decide, and they provide the target to aim for when building the record. Although jury instructions are too often one of the last things a lawyer drafts in a case, they are one of the first things that should be consulted when starting out.

Materiality is determined not only by the law, but also by the pleadings.[20] The potential for summary judgment is one of the considerations in drafting the complaint. In general, the fewer the causes of action alleged and the fewer the facts, the easier it will be to move for summary judgment.[21]

THE TRILOGY

It is generally accepted that the use of summary judgment was greatly expanded by the Supreme Court's 1986 famous "trilogy" of decisions approving its use.[22] Some understanding of these cases is essential to summary judgment practice, and seeing how they have been applied (or not) by lower courts is instructive for developing strategies in advancing or opposing summary judgment. In the first, *Matsushita Elec. Indus. Co. v. Zenith Radio Corp.*,[23] the Court held that an antitrust plaintiff with an inherently implausible claim was subject to dismissal on summary judgment, showing that summary judgment was available in complex cases, and even those involving state of mind. Next, in *Anderson v. Liberty Lobby, Inc.*,[24] the Court heightened the standard of proof in opposing a motion for summary judgment to "substantial evidence," the same as in a motion for judgment as a matter of law.[25] Finally, in *Celotex Corp. v. Catrett*,[26] the Court sought to clarify the shifting allocations of burdens of production, persuasion, and proof at summary judgment.

According to Moore's Federal Practice, "the trilogy engendered a stronger and more aggressive approach to summary judgment practice that reduced the movant's

---

20. Fed. R. Civ. P. 8(a).
21. However, the pleader must steer between the "short and plain statement" required by Rule 8(a) and the plausibility standard of Bell Atlantic Corp. v. Twombly, 550 U.S. 544, 127 S. Ct. 1955, 167 L. Ed. 2d 929 (2007), and Ashcroft v. Iqbal, 556 U.S. 662, 129 S. Ct. 1937, 173 L. Ed. 2d 868 (2009).
22. Seventh Circuit Court of Appeals Judge Diane Wood refers to these three cases as the "Revolution." Diane P. Wood, *Summary Judgment and the Law of Unintended Consequences*, 36 OKLA. CITY U. L. REV. 231 (2011).
23. Matsushita Elec. Indus. Co. v. Zenith Radio Corp., 475 U.S. 574, 106 S. Ct. 1348, 89 L. Ed. 2d 538, (1986).
24. Anderson v. Liberty Lobby, Inc., 477 U.S. 242 (1986).
25. But the *Anderson* Court also ruled that the evidence must be construed in the light most favorable to the non-moving party and all reasonable inferences must be drawn in its favor.
26. Celotex Corp. v. Catrett, 477 U.S. 317, 106 S. Ct. 2548, 91 L. Ed. 2d 265 (1986).

burden, increased the nonmovant's burden, and generally expanded the circum-stances under which summary judgment could be granted."[27] The trilogy cases were widely reported and discussed in legal publications. *Liberty Lobby* and *Celotex* remain the two most frequently cited cases in reported federal decisions, while *Matsushita* comes in at number five.[28] These cases were widely viewed as signaling to federal judges that it was appropriate to grant summary judgment, and they should get over their reluctance to do so.[29] Everyone expected a surge in motions filed and granted.

However, studies by the Federal Judicial Center[30] show that was not the case. In examining summary judgment data in 15,000 docket sheets from a random sam-pling of terminated cases in six district courts, the researchers found that the filing of at least one motion for summary judgment increased *before* the Supreme Court trilogy from approximately 12 percent in 1975 to 17 percent in 1986 and then remained fairly constant at approximately 19 percent since then. This data led the researchers to question the actual impact of the trilogy and to conclude that increased summary judgment practice was more the product of rules changes over the years that encouraged more active case management practices.[31]

If the trilogy has not had the expected impact on summary judgment practices, have they at least changed the way such motions are resolved by judges? One would expect so. In particular, the several opinions in *Celotex* contain a labyrinthine dis-cussion of the shifting burdens of production, persuasion, and proof.[32] The follow-ing chart summarizes how this is supposed to work:[33]

---

27. 11 Moore's Federal Practice, § 56.50, at 56–120.2 (3d ed.).

28. Adam Steinman, *Ever Wonder Which SCOTUS Cases Have Been Cited the Most?*, Civil Procedure & Federal Courts Blog (Sept. 21, 2016), http://lawprofessors.typepad.com/civpro/2016/09/ever-wonder-which-scotus-cases-have-been-cited-the-most.html. The top five, in order, with the number of reported citations are: Anderson v. Liberty Lobby, Inc., 477 U.S. 242 (1986) (195,159); Celotex Corp. v. Catrett, 477 U.S. 317 (1986) (183,365); Bell Atl. Corp. v. Twombly, 550 U.S. 544 (2007) (127,521); Ashcroft v. Iqbal, 556 U.S. 662 (2009) (104,712); Matsushita Elec. Indus. Co. v. Zenith Radio Corp., 475 U.S. 574 (1986) (94,229). It is interesting to note that the top five also include Twombly and Iqbal, cases on the plausibility standard in pleading, and thus all five of the most cited Supreme Court decisions concern methods for disposing of cases.

29. That reluctance is demonstrated in, e.g., Douglas v. Anderson, 656 F.2d 528, 535 (9th Cir. 1981) ("It is true that courts are generally reluctant to grant summary judgment in a case in which motivation and intent of a party are at issue."); Conrad v. Delta Airlines, 494 F.2d 914, 918 (7th Cir. 1974) (questions of intent or motive are particularly ill suited for disposition on summary judgment).

30. The Federal Judicial Center is the research and education agency of the judicial branch of the U.S. govern-ment. The center was established by Congress in 1967 (28 U.S.C. §§ 620–629).

31. *Trends, supra* note 2, at 23, 24.

32. It has been argued that by making the requirements of summary judgment for both the movant and non-movant to correspond to each other's ultimate burdens at trial, *Celotex* effectively completed the transforma-tion of summary judgment from a plaintiff's tool prior to the promulgation of the Rules of Civil Procedure in 1938 to more of a defendant's motion. Samuel Issacharoff & George Loewenstein, *Second Thoughts About Summary Judgment*, 100 Yale L.J. 73, 83 (1990).

33. This chart is reproduced from Linda S. Mullenix, *Summary Judgment: Taming the Beast of Burdens*, 10 Am. J. Trial Advoc. 433, 464 (1987).

Burdens of Production and Persuasion on Summary Judgment

1. Party Moving for Summary Judgment: Initial Burden of Proof:

Movant carries burden
of persuasion at trial
Must show:
(1) Credible evidence to support
negating directed verdict at trial

Nonmovant carries burden
of persuasion at trial
Must show:
(1) Affirmative evidence essential
(2) Nonmoving party's evidence
is absent or insufficient to establish essential element of nonmoving party's claim

2. Party Opposing Summary Judgment: Shifted Burden of Production
(Rule 56(e))

Movant carries burden
of persuasion at trial
Must show:
(1) Evidentiary materials
demonstrating existence of
genuine issue for trial

Nonmovant carries burden
of persuasion at trial
Must show:
(1) Sufficient evidence to make
out existence of genuine issue
for trial claim, or
(2) Affidavit requesting
additional time for discovery
(Rule 56(f))

3. Party Moving for Summary Judgment: Ultimate Burden of Persuasion

Evaluate:
(a) Entire setting of case; entire record and summary judgment
materials
(b) Whether it is clear that trial is unnecessary
(c) Whether there is any doubt as to existence of genuine issue for
trial[34]

Curious to learn if federal judges were having greater success than law profes-
sors in applying the *Celotex* burden-shifting analysis, Professor Mullenix set out to
study all published and unpublished Circuit Court of Appeals decisions in 2010,
a surprisingly low 222 cases. What she found was that *Celotex* was cited only a
little more than a fourth of the time and, even when it was cited, the courts rarely
applied the burden-shifting analysis correctly, but only "partially or haphazardly."[35]
Her conclusion is that in a great number of cases courts appear to decide summary

---

34. It appears Professor Mullenix's chart faithfully follows the Celotex opinions. As she states, "[t]eaching Celotex, then, is not for the faint-hearted civil procedure professor." Linda S. Mullenix, *The 25th Anniversary of
the Summary Judgment Trilogy: Much Ado About Very Little*, 43 Loy. U. Chi. L.J. 561, 564 (2012).
35. *Id.* at 573.

judgment motions using a "gestalt," "seat of the pants," or "I know it when I see it" approach.[36] Her advice to the practicing lawyer? There is no need to "overly fret over shifting burdens of production, persuasion, and proof."[37] As one Circuit Court has put it, the movant only needs to "put the ball in play."[38]

However, practicing lawyers have seen it all, and they understand the most obvious conclusion from this study—it depends on the judge. Even Professor Mullenix acknowledges that "some erudite judges on the federal bench may justifiably take pride in wending their way through a recitation and application of the Celotex standards"[39] The lawyer moving for or opposing summary judgment needs to know the practices and record of his or her judge and be familiar with the opinions of the circuit court having jurisdiction. The lawyer needs to know the shifting allocations of burdens of production, persuasion, and proof applicable to the motion and cite to *Celotex* as used and applied in the published opinions of the particular circuit and district courts.

TO FILE OR NOT TO FILE

The first strategic issue is whether or not the case is suitable for summary judgment. The lawyer and her client should first conclude that the chances of success are better than 50 percent. That is because, in addition to time and expense, the cost of the motion is giving the adversary a preview of the movant's evidence and arguments for trial. If the movant is simply taking "a shot," it is probably wiser to save the "thunder" and keep the opponent guessing. Importantly, a loss on summary judgment is deflating to the movant, encouraging to the nonmovant, and may provide the nonmovant with a "settlement premium."[40] Any notion the movant had that there is nothing to be tried is now gone; the case is going to trial, and it is going to cost.

Cost is a big factor. Consider what is at stake. A case may be worth litigating over $100,000, but unless it is a clear-cut winner on a statute of limitations defense or the like, it probably makes more sense to hurry the case to an early trial. What will it cost? The typical summary judgment motion requires a memorandum of law in support along with a statement of facts as to which there is no dispute, a memorandum of law in opposition along with a statement of genuine fact issues requiring

---

36. *Id.* at 573, 574.
37. *Id.* at 584.
38. Evans Cabinet Corp. v. Kitchen Int'l. Inc., 593 F.3d 135. 140 (1st Cir. 2010) (stating that the moving party must "put the ball in play," and the nonmoving party must then "come forward with competent evidence to rebut the assertion of the moving party").
39. Mullenix, *supra* note 34, at 584, 585.
40. See Edward Brunet, Essay, *The Efficiency of Summary Judgment*, 43 Loy. U. Chi. L.J. 689 (2012), proposing that among the efficient effects of summary judgment motions, are clarification of the facts and legal issues, early case assessment, judicial engagement, and the "settlement premium."

trial, a reply memorandum, appendices containing record evidence, and all the legal research and analysis to produce that work product. Then there may be a hearing along with the attendant preparation. It is not unusual to spend $100,000 or more in the process. Too often these legal fees get lumped in with an initial estimate or budget without a separate assessment of all that goes into a motion for summary judgment. For this and substantive and ethical reasons, the client should be closely consulted before filing a motion for summary judgment.

Another early consideration is the court. The data show that there is great variation across courts.[41] Within a jurisdiction there are even differences among the judges. A lawyer must know the requirements of the local rules of the court, any individual practices of the judge, and general trends within the court. As examples, the authors of the Federal Judicial Center's report, *Trends*, attribute a relatively low incidence of summary judgment motions in the Southern District of New York and the Northern District of Illinois to stringent procedural requirements in both courts, including a common practice in the Southern District of requiring a pre-filing conference with the judge and the incidence of Rule 11 sanctions against meritless motions for summary judgment in the Northern District of Illinois.

TIMING

Rule 56(b) addresses the timing for filing a motion: "Unless a different time is set by local rule or the court orders otherwise, a party may file a motion for summary judgment at any time until 30 days after the close of all discovery." While there is little ambiguity in "any time," the Advisory Committee Notes to the 2009 amendment clarifies that a motion may be filed "as early as the commencement of the action." However, most motions for summary judgment are filed after the completion of discovery or at least after the opportunity to conduct some discovery. The federal rules afford liberal discovery, and courts are reluctant to grant summary judgment against a party who complains that it has not had an opportunity to conduct discovery.[42] Rule 56(d) provides remedies for a nonmovant who demonstrates by affidavit that it is unable to present facts essential to its opposition to summary judgment, including deferring or even denying the motion. In most cases, at least the depositions of the parties and key witnesses should be taken before a motion is filed in order to commit them to their version of the events.

---

41. *Trends, supra* note 2, at 9.
42. "Only in the rarest of cases may summary judgment be granted against a plaintiff who has not been afforded the opportunity to conduct discovery." Hellstrom v. United States Dep't of Veterans' Affairs, 201 F.3d 94, 97 (2d Cir. 2000). *But, cf.,* Burgess v. Fairport Cent. Sch. Dist., 2010 U.S. App. LEXIS 6426, at *3–4 (2d Cir. Mar. 29, 2010) (no abuse of discretion in denying request for discovery before grant of summary judgment where no basis for belief that discovery would have produced relevant facts).

However, there are some cases where an earlier motion might be appropriate, and courts have held that Rule 56 "does not require trial courts to allow parties to conduct discovery before entering summary judgment."[43]

An early motion for summary judgment on a dispositive issue may even be *required* in order to avoid unnecessary further litigation. In *Cordoba v. Dillard's, Inc.*,[44] the court reversed a substantial award of attorneys' fees where those fees could have been avoided by raising the dispositive issue in an earlier motion for summary judgment. The court rejected the argument that the defendant had pursued discovery on all issues because it wanted to move for summary judgment on all available grounds, and "'you only get to do one motion for summary judgment.'"[45] In rejecting the "one bite at the apple" argument, the court noted:

> [T]here is no reason to assume that a district judge will stubbornly refuse to rule on a motion for summary judgment at an early stage of the litigation if the moving party clearly apprises the court that a prompt decision will likely avoid significant unnecessary discovery. *In fact, we expect that district judges will be open to such motions.*[46]

Settlement, and settlement timing, are important considerations in when to file a motion for summary judgment. A strong motion that is pending at the time of a mediation can provide momentum for settlement and ammunition for an effective mediator. Whatever the likely outcome of the motion, it certainly "ups the ante."

MOVING FOR SUMMARY JUDGMENT: KEEP IT SIMPLE

To begin with, here are words or terms that should be used in a motion for summary judgment:

Simple
Clear
Ordinary
Clean
Straight-forward

---

43. Humphreys v. Roche Biomedical Labs., Inc., 990 F.2d 1078, 1081 (8th Cir. 1993) (claim on its face is time-barred and plaintiff failed to specify how additional discovery might unveil information that could overcome that bar). *Accord* Brown v. Chaffee, 612 F.2d 497, 504 (10th Cir.1979).
44. Cordoba v. Dillard's, Inc., 419 F.3d 1169, 1188 (11th Cir. 2005).
45. *Id.*
46. *Id.* (emphasis added).

Uncontested
Well-established

Here are the impressions the movant wants to avoid making:

Innovative
Creative
Cutting-edge
Novel
Complex
Intriguing
Visionary

If a motion cannot include some or all of the words listed above or, if, upon reading a draft, it leaves any of the impressions listed, it should probably not be filed. The motion should never stray far from this mantra: *There is no genuine issue of material fact, and movant is entitled to judgment as a matter of law.* It is a simple standard, and simple wins summary judgment.[47]

Effective summary judgment practice requires great discipline. Avoid the temptation to win on all claims or defenses when one is strong and sufficient. The odds of success are greatly increased by narrowly tailoring the issues to focus on the most essential elements of the case.

Most local rules and judges allow 20 pages for a memorandum of law in support of a motion for summary judgment. Consequently, most supporting memoranda are 20 pages. Start with this proposition: Do not file a motion for leave to exceed the page limitation. If a memorandum of law in support of a motion for summary judgment requires more than 20 pages, the motion should probably not be filed. In a motion for summary judgment, brevity speaks volumes. At an ABA Litigation Section Conference several years ago, a federal district judge said in a panel discussion that the best summary judgment motion he had ever seen was a five-page motion filed by Houston, Texas trial lawyer, Steve Susman, in a large antitrust case. The motion got right to the point, focused on the dispositive, material facts that were not in dispute and the governing law that allowed for judgment. The motion was granted.[48]

Many, if not most, district court local rules require the filing of "point/counterpoint" statements of material facts as to which there is no genuine issue (movant)

---

47. Judges grant motions for summary judgment in cases that they see as being clear and straightforward. *See, e.g.*, First United Mortg. Co., Inc. v. Chaucer Holdings PLC, Civil No. 2:08-2754, 2010 WL 3283525, at *1 (D.N.J. Aug. 17, 2010) ("This matter is a straight forward coverage dispute rooted in the language of the policy agreement, and for the reasons which will be elaborated below, the Court will GRANT Defendant's Motion for Summary Judgment. . . .").

48. The author e-mailed Mr. Susman to ask for a cite to the case and for his permission to tell the story. He could not cite the case but said that it "sounds like me," and he graciously allowed me to use the example.

and statement of material facts as to which genuine issue remain for trial (opponent). These are extremely important and, when well done, are perhaps more effective in advocating for granting or denying than all of the arguments in briefs. Even more than the motion itself, the movant's statement of undisputed material facts should be as short and to-the-point as possible. A ten-page statement with multiple "material facts" screams out, "genuine issues remaining to be tried!" Sometimes it cannot be avoided, but the movant's statement should be as short as possible. The lawyer must ask himself, "Do I need to prove this to win?"

In jurisdictions that do not require the filing of such "point/counterpoint" statements, the lawyer should seek leave to file one or work it into an early section of the motion. This is the crux of summary judgment, and the judge should not have to keep track of the material facts without some kind of scorecard.

Rule 56(c) requires pinpoint citations to those portions of the record that support a material fact (or remaining issue). This subsection was added in 2010, and the Advisory Committee Notes suggest the filing of an appendix to assist the court in locating materials. This is a no-brainer. Although the court "may consider other materials in the record," under Rule 56(c)(3) it "need consider only the cited materials." Do not make the court search. The materials cited should be placed in an appendix, complete with index, and the motion should cite to the item and its location in the appendix. If there is one, dispositive document, it may be more convenient to attach it to the motion as an exhibit, but if there is more than one, create an appendix.

How Judges Decide Summary Judgment Motions

There is a reason why judges may often decide summary judgment motions based on some sort of "gestalt" rather than a close reading of *Celotex*, as Professor Mullenix posits. They are human. Although they endeavor to "call balls and strikes," judges see the curveballs and knuckleballs we throw through human eyes. On a motion for summary judgment, the order "stat[ing] on the record the reasons for granting or denying the motion"[49] is preceded by the judge's decision on who should win and who should lose. Judges are not immune to the concept that there are good guys and bad guys, guys who should win and guys who should lose based on a sense of fairness and simple common sense.

The curtain on how judges actually decide was lifted back quite a bit in Judge Richard Posner's book, *How Judges Think* (2010). In it, Judge Posner states that in deciding cases judges rely less on what we regard as formal legal analysis but, rather,

---

49. Rule 56(a).

like the normal layperson, depend on their ideology, common sense, and human emotions. Imagine that! Judge Posner's candor was on display in his opinion for the court in *Wallace v. SMC Pneumatics, Inc.*,[50] affirming on other grounds the grant of summary judgment in an employment discrimination complaint.

> The expanding federal caseload has contributed to a drift in many areas of federal litigation toward substituting summary judgment for trial. [Citations omitted.] The drift is understandable, given caseload pressures that in combination with the Speedy Trial Act sometimes make it difficult to find time for civil trials in the busier federal districts. But it must be resisted unless and until Rule 56 is modified (so far as the Seventh Amendment permits) to bring federal practice closer to the practice in the legal systems of Continental Europe, where there is no hard and fast line between pretrial and trial and where procedure is more summary and informal than in the United States.[51]

This is an astonishing acknowledgment by a leading jurist and scholar that courts are "substituting summary judgment for trial" because of judicial economics, i.e., it saves time. Equally astonishing is that he seems to suggest that American rules be modified (to the extent that the Constitutional right to trial by jury permits) to allow judges greater flexibility in deciding summary judgment motions.

In finding it "highly unlikely" that the plaintiff in *Wallace* had been discriminated against, Judge Posner observed that "[a] little *common sense* is not amiss in a discrimination case. (The Supreme Court in Matsushita deemed the fact that the plaintiffs' claim was 'implausible' a basis for granting summary judgment for the defendants. [Citation omitted; emphasis added])"[52]

Every trial lawyer has experienced firsthand the caseload pressures and economic concerns facing judges. A lawyer who wastes time with repetitive questioning is soon admonished by the judge that juror time is expensive and only so many days can be devoted to this trial. Trials are also a lot of work. While a federal judge can rely a great deal on law clerks to assist with the research and writing that go into a summary judgment order, the law clerks are of limited help at trial.

The message here is that judges are receptive to motions for summary judgment, and they should be pursued when the merits and economics allow. But being receptive is one thing; being persuaded is another. Judges are well aware of the rigors of Rule 56 and *Celotex*, and they work hard to get it right, but they must also be persuaded that granting summary judgment is the *right thing to do* and that it comports with their sense of fairness and everyday common sense. While exercising

---

50. Wallace v. SMC Pneumatics, Inc., 103 F.3d 1394 (1997).

51. *Id.* at 1397.

52. *Id.* at 1400.

care not to create fact issues that could preclude summary judgment, the movant needs to create a narrative, one or two themes, just like at a jury trial, that explain why it is right and just that the movant wins.

MOTION FOR PARTIAL SUMMARY JUDGMENT AND ORDERS ESTABLISHING FACTS FOR THE CASE

Rule 56 provides that any "party may move for summary judgment, identifying each claim or defense—or the part of each claim or defense—on which summary judgment is sought." This first sentence of Rule 56(a) was added by the 2010 amendments to "make clear at the beginning that summary judgment may be requested not only as to an entire case but also to a claim, defense, or part of a claim or defense."[53] In addition, the heading of subsection (a) was amended to read "Motion for Summary Judgment or Partial Summary Judgment," "adopt[ing] the common phrase 'partial summary judgment' to describe disposition of less than the whole action, whether or not the order grants all of the relief requested by the motion."[54] Note that there are two aspects to the rule on partial summary judgments. First, in actions involving multiple claims or defenses, a summary judgment motion may be directed to only one or some of the claims or defenses. Thus, in a contract case in which the complaint also includes business tort claims such as tortious interference or breach of fiduciary duty, the plaintiff may file a motion for summary judgment only on the contract claim. Second, the rule allows for a motion that addresses only a "part" of a claim or defense. In the same contract case, a motion could be made on only the existence of the contract, leaving for trial the issues of breach and damages. A motion for summary judgment can be made as to liability only, leaving the issue of damages for trial.[55]

One court has described partial summary judgment as serving a "useful brush-clearing function."[56] It can be hard to resist a motion for partial summary judgment on weak claims or defenses. But, in a case in which trial seems to be inevitable, a good trial lawyer can use the other side's weakest claims or defenses to paint with a

---

53. Advisory Committee Notes on Rules—2010 Amendment.

54. *Id.*

55. Even before the 2010 amendments many courts allowed motions for partial summary judgment (e.g., Barker v. Norman, 651 F.2d 1107, 1123 (5th Cir. 1981) ("In cases that involve complicated fact patterns and multiple causes of action, summary judgment may be proper as to some causes of action but not as to others, as to some issues but not as to others, or as to some parties but not as to others."). Also, the text of the 2007 version of Rule 56 provided in subsection (d)(2) that "[a]n interlocutory summary judgment may be rendered on liability alone, even if there is a genuine issue on the amount of damages." However, prior to the 2010 amendments there were a number of reported decisions holding that summary judgment could not be used as to a part of a claim or defense. (E.g., SEC v. Thrasher, 152 F. Supp. 2d 291, 295 (S.D.N.Y. 2001); Antenor v. D & S Farms, 39 F. Supp. 2d 1372, 1375 n.4 (S.D. Fla. 1999).) Those cases are no longer good law.

56. Hotel 71 Mezz Lender LLC v. Nat'l Retirement Fund, 778 F.3d 593, 606 (7th Cir. 2015).

broad brush and discredit the opponent's entire case. Think twice before knocking out "easy ones" on a motion for partial summary judgment.

Even if the court denies a motion for summary judgment or for partial summary judgment, it can enter an order limiting the issues for trial. Rule 56(g) provides a mechanism for courts to narrow the issues to be tried in the case where summary judgment has been denied by the court. The court may enter an order "stating any material fact—including an item of damages or other relief—that is not genuinely in dispute *and treating the fact as established in the case.*"[57] The courts view this as providing an opportunity to "salvage" something constructive from all of the legal and judicial effort that goes into the summary judgment process and to narrow the issues remaining for trial.[58] In order to rule that a material fact is established for the case, the court must apply the same strict summary judgment standard as applies to a motion for summary judgment.[59] The determination that a material fact is established for the case is discretionary with the court, with courts looking to whether such a finding is practical and economical compared to leaving it for trial.[60] Although such a ruling is interlocutory and may be changed by the court, such a determination is not lightly disturbed, and the parties have a right to rely on it and must be given notice and opportunity to be heard if the ruling is to be changed.[61]

OPPOSING SUMMARY JUDGMENT: IT'S NOT SO SIMPLE

Of course, if you are opposing a motion for summary judgment, you should try to paint a different picture. Your case is very complicated, with many factual twists and turns.[62]

When responding substantively to the motion, the nonmovant should seek to clarify, in light of pertinent legal principles, what material factual issues are in dispute and the evidentiary support for that position. If additional discovery is needed in order to respond to a summary judgment motion, Rule 56(d) allows for a motion

---

57. This must be distinguished from a ruling that a fact is established only for purposes of the motion which may occur, for example, if a material fact is not properly contested in the summary judgment papers (emphasis added).

58. *See, e.g.,* Geneva Int'l Corp. v. Pegrof, Spol. S.R.O., 608. F. Supp. 2d 993, 1004–05 (N.D. Ill. 2009); McCollough v. Johnson, Rodenberg & Lauinger, 587 F. Supp. 2d 1170, 1177 (D. Mont. 2008).

59. *See, e.g.,* Global Crossing Bandwidth, Inc. v. Locus Communication, Inc., 632 F. Supp. 2d 224, 238 (W.D.N.Y 2009).

60. Advisory Committee Note to 2010 Amendment.

61. *See, e.g.,* Leddy v. Standard Dry Wall, Inc., 875 F.2d 383, 386 (2d Cir. 1989).

62. *See, e.g.,* Star Spa Servs. Inc. v. Robert G. Turano Ins. Agency, Inc., 595 F. Supp. 2d 519, 529 (M.D. Pa. 2009) ("The court concludes that this complicated factual situation would be best resolved by a jury and will deny summary judgment on this point.").

to extend discovery before responding. Such a motion must be supported by an affidavit or declaration citing specific reasons.

The party opposing summary judgment needs to remind the court of the rigorous standards applicable to summary judgment. In particular, the court may NOT: (1) weigh the evidence, (2) make credibility determinations, or (3) decide between reasonable inferences, and the court MUST: (1) view the evidence in the light most favorable to the nonmovant and (2) indulge all reasonable inferences in favor of the nonmovant.[63] While string citations are generally to be avoided, here the nonmovant needs to load up its brief in opposition with the leading cases from the controlling jurisdictions and some great language can be found.[64]

Conflicting deposition testimony is compelling evidence that a case is not suitable for summary judgment. It can be very effective to set forth conflicting deposition testimony in quoted, Q&A form.

As with the arguments in support of summary judgment, the arguments in opposition must persuade and provide a narrative that is the other side to "two sides of the story." The papers opposing summary judgment should always use the word "error." It would not only be *wrong* to grant summary judgment, it would be *error*. Judges hate to make error. Error results in reversal. If a jury trial has been requested, the argument should be made that the judge should not "take the case away from the jury" and "invading the province of the jury." That is a sobering reminder to any judge that there are basic constitutional rights involved.[65]

SHOULD YOU REQUEST A HEARING?

Rule 56 does not require or even make reference to a hearing. Instead, a hearing must be scheduled by the judge, whether by sua sponte order or on motion, and, like almost everything else, it depends on the judge. This is an area where the lawyer needs to know the judge and her preferences. It also depends on lawyer preference. In general, if one side has an advantage on the papers, that is, one side writes much better than the other, the better writer should think twice before requesting a hearing.

---

63. Anderson v. Liberty Lobby, 477 U.S. 242, 255 (1986).
64. E.g., Gossett v. Oklahoma ex rel. Bd. of Regents for Langston Univ., 245 F.3d 1172, 1175 (10th Cir. 2001) (court "must disregard all evidence favorable to the moving party that the jury is not required to believe").
65. Although the Supreme Court has never directly ruled on the issue, many courts have rejected the argument that summary judgment violates the Seventh Amendment and cite to Fidelity & Deposit Co. v. United States, 187 U.S. 315, 319–21, 23 S. Ct. 120, 47 L. Ed. 194 (1902) as the authority. At least one court has sanctioned counsel for advancing such a "discredited theory." Macklin v. City of New Orleans, 300 F.3d 552, 553–54 (5th Cir. 2002).

CONCLUSION

Moving for summary judgment is a strategic consideration, not a reflex. When the material facts are indisputable and the law is on your side on the case or on key issues, there is no need to risk trial. But not every case is a summary judgment case. The summary judgment process is time-consuming and costly. That time and money are well-spent in those cases in which the facts, the law, and the economics support it.

APPENDIX A

Rule 56—Summary Judgment

(a) **Motion for Summary Judgment or Partial Summary Judgment.** A party may move for summary judgment, identifying each claim or defense—or the part of each claim or defense—on which summary judgment is sought. The court shall grant summary judgment if the movant shows that there is no genuine dispute as to any material fact and the movant is entitled to judgment as a matter of law. The court should state on the record the reasons for granting or denying the motion.

(b) **Time to File a Motion.** Unless a different time is set by local rule or the court orders otherwise, a party may file a motion for summary judgment at any time until 30 days after the close of all discovery.

(c) **Procedures.**

(1) *Supporting Factual Positions.* A party asserting that a fact cannot be or is genuinely disputed must support the assertion by:

(A) citing to particular parts of materials in the record, including depositions, documents, electronically stored information, affidavits or declarations, stipulations (including those made for purposes of the motion only), admissions, interrogatory answers, or other materials; or

(B) showing that the materials cited do not establish the absence or presence of a genuine dispute, or that an adverse party cannot produce admissible evidence to support the fact.

(2) *Objection That a Fact Is Not Supported by Admissible Evidence.* A party may object that the material cited to support or dispute a fact cannot be presented in a form that would be admissible in evidence.

(3) *Materials Not Cited.* The court need consider only the cited materials, but it may consider other materials in the record.

(4) *Affidavits or Declarations.* An affidavit or declaration used to support or oppose a motion must be made on personal knowledge, set out facts that would be admissible in evidence, and show that the affiant or declarant is competent to testify on the matters stated.

(d) **When Facts Are Unavailable to the Nonmovant.** If a nonmovant shows by affidavit or declaration that, for specified reasons, it cannot present facts essential to justify its opposition, the court may:

(1) defer considering the motion or deny it;

(2) allow time to obtain affidavits or declarations or to take discovery; or

(3) issue any other appropriate order.

(e) **Failing to Properly Support or Address a Fact.** If a party fails to properly support an assertion of fact or fails to properly address another party's assertion of fact as required by Rule 56(c), the court may:

(1) give an opportunity to properly support or address the fact;

(2) consider the fact undisputed for purposes of the motion;

(3) grant summary judgment if the motion and supporting materials—including the facts considered undisputed—show that the movant is entitled to it; or

(4) issue any other appropriate order.

(f) **Judgment Independent of the Motion.** After giving notice and a reasonable time to respond, the court may:

(1) grant summary judgment for a nonmovant;

(2) grant the motion on grounds not raised by a party; or

(3) consider summary judgment on its own after identifying for the parties material facts that may not be genuinely in dispute.

(g) **Failing to Grant All the Requested Relief.** If the court does not grant all the relief requested by the motion, it may enter an order stating any material fact—including an item of damages or other relief—that is not genuinely in dispute and treating the fact as established in the case.

(h) **Affidavit or Declaration Submitted in Bad Faith.** If satisfied that an affidavit or declaration under this rule is submitted in bad faith or solely for delay, the court—after notice and a reasonable time to respond—may order the submitting party to pay the other party the reasonable expenses, including attorney's fees, it incurred as a result. An offending party or attorney may also be held in contempt or subjected to other appropriate sanctions.

(As amended Dec. 27, 1946, eff. Mar. 19, 1948; Jan. 21, 1963, eff. July 1, 1963; Mar. 2, 1987, eff. Aug. 1, 1987; Apr. 30, 2007, eff. Dec. 1, 2007; Mar. 26, 2009, eff. Dec. 1, 2009; Apr. 28, 2010, eff. Dec. 1, 2010.)

CHAPTER 11

Shifting Risk with Offers

Alexandra W. Wahl[1]

There is more than one way to balance the litigation playing field. Thorough preparations, effective advocacy, favorable venue selection and carefully crafted voir dire are all critical ingredients for success. But exploiting procedures for allocating risks of cost and expense can also provide leverage to force an opposing party to stop, pause, and consider the benefits of settlement. These cost-shifting mechanisms expose one of the parties, frequently a plaintiff, to unexpected risks. Most notably, the looming potential for an award of significant costs and, possibly, attorney's fees—which could outweigh a "winning" judgment—can cause even a gambler to get more realistic.

This chapter analyzes various procedural rules available to shift the risks of litigation costs and, therefore, change the risk-benefit calculus for the opposing party. These rules encourage settlement, with the effect of punishing an offeree who fails to accept a reasonable offer. Because state court jurisdictions lack uniformity in how they approach this issue, and some differ significantly from federal practice, lawyers should consult the procedural rules in their relevant jurisdictions in appropriate cases. These shifting devices are useful in particular cases where an opposing side greatly overestimates its chances of success.

1. The author wishes to acknowledge the substantial contributions and efforts of Farshad Marzban, an attorney with Parsons McEntire McCleary PLLC in Dallas, Texas.

FEDERAL RULES OF CIVIL PROCEDURE RULE 68

Federal Rules of Civil Procedure Rule 68 "Offer of Judgment" states in full:

> **(a) Making an Offer; Judgment on an Accepted Offer.** At least 14 days before the date set for trial, a party defending against a claim may serve on an opposing party an offer to allow judgment on specified terms, with the costs then accrued. If, within 14 days after being served, the opposing party serves written notice accepting the offer, either party may then file the offer and notice of acceptance, plus proof of service. The clerk must then enter judgment.
>
> **(b) Unaccepted Offer.** An unaccepted offer is considered withdrawn, but it does not preclude a later offer. Evidence of an unaccepted offer is not admissible except in a proceeding to determine costs.
>
> **(c) Offer After Liability Is Determined.** When one party's liability to another has been determined but the extent of liability remains to be determined by further proceedings, the party held liable may make an offer of judgment. It must be served within a reasonable time—but at least 14 days—before the date set for a hearing to determine the extent of liability.
>
> **(d) Paying Costs After an Unaccepted Offer.** If the judgment that the offeree finally obtains is not more favorable than the unaccepted offer, the offeree must pay the costs incurred after the offer was made.[2]

This rule is "one of the most powerful pieces of leverage" for a defendant in federal court, but is largely underutilized.[3] It is a "hybrid between a settlement and a decision on the merits."[4] Under Rule 68, at any time after the lawsuit is filed, but at least 14 days before trial, a defendant may make an offer including a "judgment on specified terms, with the costs then accrued."[5] After service, the plaintiff has 14 days to serve a written acceptance.[6] The offer remains irrevocable during this 14-day period. Thereafter, an unaccepted offer is deemed withdrawn.[7] Still, this does not preclude a defendant from submitting subsequent proposals. If accepted, either side may file the offer, the notice of acceptance, and proof of service, prompting the

---

2. FED. R. CIV. P. 68
3. Darren Nicholson & Mark Strachan, *Turning the Tables—Offers of Judgment Under Federal Rule 68*, DALLAS BAR ASS'N (Aug. 24, 2015).
4. W. David Paxton & Michael J. Finney, *Rule 68 Offers of Judgment—A Useful Defense Tool*, XXIV-4 J. CIV. LITIGS 533, 533 (Winter 2012–13).
5. FED. R. CIV. P. 68(a).
6. Rule 68 does not contemplate offers made by plaintiffs.
7. FED. R. CIV. P. 68(b).

clerk to automatically enter a public judgment against the defendant in accordance with the terms of the offer, without a trial.[8]

The purpose of Rule 68 is to encourage settlement and avoid litigation and the associated costs by prompting "both parties to a suit to evaluate the risks and costs of litigation, and to balance them against the likelihood of success upon trial on the merits."[9] In furtherance of this purpose, the offer of judgment must specify a definite sum or other relief for the judgment to be entered and must be unconditional.[10] This allows the plaintiff to have clarity concerning what is being offered.[11]

As encouragement, the rule effectively provides a penalty if the offeree fails to obtain a judgment "more favorable" than the extended offer. If the plaintiff prevails at trial, but receives a judgment *less favorable* than the rejected offer, the plaintiff "must pay the costs incurred [by the defendant] after the offer was made."[12] Moreover, because the plaintiff won the case but lost the Rule 68 battle, the plaintiff will be deprived of its post-offer costs as a prevailing party. As a result, a plaintiff who refuses a reasonable Rule 68 offer can experience a dual penalty.[13] By this framework, defendants are "motivated to make well-grounded offers of judgment, and plaintiffs are incentivized to carefully consider such offers."[14] Since the "offer of judgment shifts liability for costs to the plaintiff as of the date on which it is extended, it is advantageous to the offeror to extend the offer as early in litigation as possible."[15]

REQUISITES AND SUFFICIENCY OF THE OFFER

An effective Rule 68 offer does not require a specific refence to "costs." However, a failure to do so creates peril for the defendant (offeror). Defendants must draft "clear and unambiguous offers of judgment"—meaning, effective drafting may determine whether an offer is enforceable.[16] Since the terms of the offer are strictly construed, poor drafting may lead to unintended consequences.

In *Marek v. Chesny*, the Supreme Court held the Rule 68 offer need not recite that costs are included, specify the amount defendant is allowing for costs, or refer to costs at all. The Supreme Court reasoned,

---

8. The offer must allow judgment against the defendant, but does not require admission of liability. *See* Simmons v. United Mortg. & Loan Inv., LLC, 634 F.3d 754, 764 n.6 (4th Cir. 2011).

9. Marek v. Chesny, 473 U.S. 1, 5 (1985).

10. WRIGHT, MILLER & MARCUS, FEDERAL PRACTICE AND PROCEDURE, CIVIL 2d § 3002 (1997).

11. Arkla Energy Res. v. Roe Realty & Developing, Inc., 9 F.3d 855, 867 (10th Cir. 1993).

12. FED. R. CIV. P. 68(d).

13. Posting of Caitlin Hawks to SAVITT BRUCE & WILLEY, LLP "Duty and the Breach" blog, *Rule 68 Offers of Judgment,* http://www.sbwllp.com/rule-68-offers-of-judgment/.

14. Paxton & Finney, *supra* note 4, at 535.

15. Posting of Caitlin Hawks to SAVITT BRUCE & WILLEY, LLP "Duty and the Breach" blog, *Rule 68 Offers of Judgment,* http://www.sbwllp.com/rule-68-offers-of-judgment/.

16. Jim Steele, *Litigation: Rule 68 offers of judgment—A matter of clarity,* LAW.COM (May 9, 2013).

if the offer does not state that costs are included and an amount for costs is not specified, the court will be obliged by the terms of the Rule to include in its judgment an additional amount which in its discretion . . . it determines to be sufficient to cover the costs.[17]

Although the offer is technically still valid, the defendant may risk an additional award against it for the additional costs.

Citing *Marek*, when defendants offered a judgment of $30,000 "as full and complete satisfaction," the Fourth Circuit effectively determined that the offer was silent as to "costs."[18] Even though defendants argued their offer included costs, the District Court awarded the plaintiff $66,463.80 in costs *in addition* to the $30,000 judgment. In its reasoning, the Fourth Circuit noted the offer places the plaintiff at a difficult choice: either accept on defendant's terms or proceed to trial, running the risk of attaining a judgment less than the offer and paying defendant's post-offer costs.[19] Because a Rule 68 offer may have consequences for a plaintiff either way, the court "construe[d] the offer's terms strictly, and ambiguities in the offer are to be resolved against the offeror."[20]

Because a Rule 68 offer cannot be modified or revoked during the 14-day consideration period, a defendant must be careful to precisely convey its intended terms. In a First Circuit case, *LaPierre v. City of Lawrence*, a defendant submitted an offer of judgment for $300,000, which was otherwise silent as to costs. Realizing this mistake, the defendant immediately attempted to revoke the offer and, the next day, attempted to send clarification that the offer was inclusive of all costs. Notwithstanding this attempt, the court held the plaintiff could accept the original offer.[21] The court noted the original offer was "unambiguously exclusive of both costs and, as a subset of costs, attorneys' fees."[22] Relying on *Marek*, the court awarded plaintiff (appellant) an additional amount for the pre-offer costs incurred, as well as costs on appeal.

In contrast, in *Radecki v. Amoco Oil Co.*, a defendant offered judgment for $525,000 "including costs now accrued."[23] The Eighth Circuit held the original offer "subsum[ed] within the amount offered any liability for 'costs.'"[24] Because the underlying statute did not define "attorney's fees" as part of "costs," the court found the original offer was not clear as to whether it was intended to include attorney's fees.[25] For that reason, the Eighth Circuit concluded a pre-acceptance clarification

---

17. *Marek*, 473 U.S. at 6.
18. Bosley v. Mineral Cnty. Comm'n, 650 F.3d 408, 414 (4th Cir. 2011).
19. *Id.*
20. *Id.*
21. LaPierre v. City of Lawrence, 819 F.3d 558, 565 (1st Cir. Mass. 2016).
22. *Id.*
23. Radecki v. Amoco Oil Co., 858 F.2d 397, 399 (8th Cir. 1988).
24. *Id.* at 400.
25. *Id.*

was valid and operative, and the court would consider extrinsic evidence to determine whether the defendant intended the offer to be inclusive of attorney's fees.[26]

The Rule 68 offer also may not impose any additional obligations on the plaintiff which could not otherwise be obtained from a judgment in a trial on the merits.[27] For example, the Fourth Circuit found a defendant's offer was not a valid "Rule 68 offer" where the written offer provided only five days for acceptance (instead of the mandatory 14 days), required the plaintiff to produce affidavits, required a settlement agreement instead of a judgment, and required plaintiff to keep the settlement and the terms of the settlement confidential.[28] The lessons here are clear. As a defendant, make sure to get your offer right the first time, or, as a plaintiff, be able to spot an invalid offer or any omissions to your advantage!

Are Attorney's Fees Included in "Costs"?

The *Marek* court also opined that "costs" under Rule 68 do not include attorney's fees unless the underlying statute for the plaintiff's cause of action includes attorney's fees within the definition for recoverable "costs."[29] For example, federal courts have held that statutory "costs" encompass attorney's fees in Title VII cases,[30] but do not under the Age Discrimination in Employment Act, the Fair Labor Standards Act (FLSA), and the Americans with Disabilities Act, where attorney's fees are defined or referenced separately.[31] Of course, where attorney's fees are within the definition of recoverable "costs," this can exponentially increase the stakes for a plaintiff by potentially extinguishing the plaintiff's right to recover fees following a rejected offer.

Be careful. If the underlying statute allows recovery for attorney's fees as a separate claim, recovery of attorney's fees may remain possible even after a less favorable judgment.[32] For example, in *Fegley v. Higgins*, a plaintiff brought a cause of action under the FLSA and obtained a nominal damages award less than defendant's Rule 68 offer of judgment. But, FLSA does not include the award of attorney's fees as

---

26. *Id.*
27. *See* McCauley v. Trans Union, 402 F.3d 340, 342 (2d Cir. 2005) (plaintiff is not obligated to accept a Rule 68 offer of judgment conditioned on settlement being kept confidential and judgment under seal; party engaged in litigation is not entitled to confidentiality); Wright, Miller & Marcus, Federal Practice and Procedure, Civil 2d § 3002 (2d ed. Supp. 2010) (offer of judgment requiring confidential settlement rather than court judgment seeks something not authorized by Rule 68).
28. Simmons v. United Mortg. & Loan Inv., LLC, 634 F.3d 754, 764–66 (4th Cir. 2011).
29. *Marek*, 473 U.S. at 5.
30. Because Title VII allows recovery plaintiff's attorney's fees "as part of the costs," if a Title VII defendant makes an offer determined to be more favorable than the ultimate judgment, attorney's fees that may otherwise be included "can be avoided by the defendant." Marryshow v. Flynn, 986 F.2d 689, 692 (4th Cir. 1993).
31. William J. Wortel, *Reducing Exposure to Attorneys' Fees Awards Through Use of Rule 68 Offers of Judgment*, Lexology (Apr. 12, 2017).
32. Fegley v. Higgins, 19 F.3d 1126, 1135 (6th Cir. 1994).

recoverable "costs." Rather, under the statute, "attorney's fees" are addressed *separately and apart from* "the costs of the action." Therefore, a Rule 68 offer does not affect the trial court's award of attorney fees under the FLSA.[33] The Sixth Circuit upheld the district court's award for $40,000 in attorney's fees to the plaintiff as the prevailing party and granted discretion to the district court to increase for the additional effort of the appeal.

FAVORABILITY OF OFFER COMPARED TO THE JUDGMENT

The burden to prove an unaccepted offer was more favorable than the ultimate judgment lies with the defendant.[34] Typically, this calculation will be straightforward. The "judgment finally obtained" includes the jury verdict plus costs "actually awarded by the court for the period that preceded the offer."[35] However, different fact patterns may complicate the analysis.

For instance, a plaintiff may seek equitable, injunctive, or declaratory relief which may obscure the valuation of the judgment which is finally obtained. For example, in a copyright suit in which the plaintiff "prevailed" but was awarded no damages, the final judgment was not deemed less favorable than defendant's offer of judgment of $250; vindication of plaintiff's copyright was deemed more favorable than payment of $250.[36] Also, in an employment suit, the plaintiff rejected the employer's offer of judgment of $20,001 and won a mere $10,000 at trial. However, because the plaintiff/employee also obtained equitable relief, including reinstatement to a c-suite position, which also meant his return to a corner office and senior executive compensation, the verdict was considered more favorable and he was still entitled to recover attorney's fees and costs.[37] It is undoubtedly difficult to compare monetary and non-monetary relief. In considering whether the judgment is more or less "favorable," the courts must use a realistic assessment and "must try to compare apples to oranges as best they can."[38]

---

33. *Id.*; *See Marek*, 473 U.S. at 13, 43–44 (Brennan, J., dissenting) (noting that for "[s]*tatutes that do not refer to attorney's fees as part of the costs* [such as the FLSA] [...] where an action otherwise is governed by Rule 68, attorney's fees that are potentially awardable under these statutes are *not* subject to Rule 68 and instead are to be evaluated solely under the reasonableness standard").

34. Ibe v. Nat'l Football League, No. 3:11-CV-0248-M-BK, 2015 WL 11110850, at *3 (N.D. Tex. Dec. 3, 2015).

35. *Marryshow*, 986 F.2d at 692; J.P. ex rel. Peterson v. Cnty. Sch. Bd. of Hanover Cnty., V.A., 641 F. Supp. 2d 499,507–09 (E.D. Va. 2009) (In order for a lump-sum offer of judgment to be "more favorable" than the final judgment in an IDEA action, so as to prohibit the award of attorney fees and related costs for services performed subsequent to the offer, the offer must be greater than the sum of the actual damages and the pre-offer attorney fees and litigation costs.).

36. Lish v. Harper's Magazine Found., 148 F.R.D. 516, 520 (S.D.N.Y. 1993).

37. Reiter v. MTA New York Transit Authority, 457 F.3d 224, 232 (2d Cir. 2006).

38. Paxton & Finney, *supra* note 4, at 541 (citing WRIGHT, MILLER & MARCUS, FEDERAL PRACTICE AND PROCEDURE, CIVIL 2d § 3006.1).

USING OFFERS FOR JUDGMENT STRATEGICALLY

Tactically, a defendant invoking Rule 68 will want to make a Rule 68 offer (1) sufficiently enticing to be accepted or (2) low enough for the plaintiff to reject and high enough to exceed a potential judgment. Courts interpret Rule 68 offers using general contract formation principles.[39] It is important to balance the amount of possible damages at trial against plaintiff's reasonable attorney's fees at the time of the offer. If the plaintiff has a statutory entitlement to reasonable attorney's fees with a successful verdict, the plaintiff has a stronger incentive to litigate a viable claim through trial.

Rule 68 offers can sometimes be used to "moot a plaintiff's claim entirely by divesting the court of subject matter jurisdiction under Rule 12(b)(1) of the Federal Rules of Civil Procedure."[40] Unlike a settlement offer, a Rule 68 offer is for a judgment against the defendant. If the Rule 68 offer "unequivocally offers a plaintiff all of the relief she sought to obtain, the offer renders the plaintiff's action moot."[41] This presents an interesting defense strategy for making an early offer where plaintiff could recover attorney's fees at trial, thereby effectively terminating the accrual of further attorney's fees and extinguishing any incentive to continue prosecution of the case.

When considering defendant's Rule 68 offer, a plaintiff is wise to first review the offer against the corresponding statute to determine the offer's validity. If the offer is invalid, the plaintiff has a perfectly good reason for rejection. Second, look for ambiguities and omissions. This will dictate whether plaintiff was "reasonable" in rejecting the original offer. If the offer is silent as to attorney's fees or costs, the plaintiff may accept and file the offer for the judgment, still asserting entitlement to the additional amounts. Where the offer is unclear, a plaintiff should demand clarification. The plaintiff's demand may itself serve as evidence the offer was insufficient or ambiguous. Remember, the law permits a full, irrevocable 14-day period to review the offer.

STATE RULES AND STATUTES

The various state jurisdictions employ a variety of approaches. Here are some examples.

Many states, such as Mississippi, provide an offer of judgment rule or statute patterned after Federal Rule 68.[42] This allows for docket clearing and penalizes

---

39. Torres v. Empire Envtl. Grp., LLC, No. 3:13-CV-0723-G BN, 2013 WL 6231400, at *5 (N.D. Tex. Dec. 2, 2013).
40. Paxton & Finney, supra note 4, at 542.
41. Warren v. Sessoms & Rogers, P.A., 676 F.3d 365, 371 (4th Cir. 2012).
42. *See* Miss. R. Civ. P. 68.

unreasonable or frivolous litigants. As in federal court, an offer is generally not admissible as evidence and other settlement offers are not impacted.

Notably, many states allow either party a choice of offering judgment (enforceable as a court order and including all relief that might be awarded in a final judgment, i.e., prejudgment interest, taxable costs, attorney's fees, and punitive damages) or settlement (which is not enforceable as a judgment but may become a breach of contract action).[43] The penalties vary by state, but usually include a combination of attorney's fees, costs, and interest accumulated after the offer is made or rejected. The most significant differences and difficulties arise with (1) timing limitations; (2) construction and interpretation of terms; and (3) allowance and determination of attorney's fees.

TIME LIMITATIONS

Most state statutes contain express timing provisions, generally within a designated number of days before trial and holding the offer of judgment terminates on the commencement of trial.[44] Consequently, courts have examined when "trial begins" to determine whether an offer was timely, resulting in vastly different views.[45] Another timing consideration is whether the time to respond to an offer of judgment can be tolled. Some courts allow tolling dependent on the circumstances and corresponding statute.[46] For instance, an Arizona court found a trial court could extend the time to respond to an offer of judgment allowed under the rules.[47]

Most courts have determined offers are irrevocable during the statute's specified acceptance period; others, however, have adhered to general contract principles to allow revocation before acceptance.[48] Nevertheless, the offeree needs to be given the requisite amount of time provided under the statute to consider the offer; otherwise, the offer may be considered fatally defective.

---

43. *See Annot., Application and Construction of State Offer of Judgment Rule Determining Whether Offeror Is Entitled to Award* (2005) 2 A.L.R. 6th 279.
44. Tucker v. Benevolent & Protective Order of Elks Lodge #417, 6 P.3d 1082, 1084–87 (Okla. Civ. App. 2000) (holding that, where defendant made an offer of judgment prior to a trial and verdict favoring defendant, plaintiff could not then accept offer of judgment after verdict.)
45. *See Annot., Application and Construction of State Offer of Judgment Rule, supra* note 43.
46. *Id.*
47. Digirolamo v. Superior Court in and for Cnty. of Mohave, 173 Ariz. 7, 839 P.2d 427 (Ct. App. Div. 1 1991).
48. *See Annot., Application and Construction of State Offer of Judgment Rule, supra* note 43.

CONSTRUCTION AND INTERPRETATION OF TERMS

In determining whether an offer is valid, courts will consider whether the offer complies with the relevant statute, whether the offer is made in good faith, whether it resolves the litigation, whether it contains vague or non-specific terms, and whether it attempts to obtain more relief than is available upon final judgment.[49] As with Rule 68, the burden is on the offeror to comply with the offer of judgment rules with any ambiguity construed against the drafter.

Consequently, it is the offeror's obligation to draft well-defined terms allowing the offeree to understand and properly evaluate the offer. For example, in a multiple party context, offers should be made separately to each party[50] and each should clearly state the authority of the offeror(s) (which parties are making the offer), the offeree(s) (who is the offer extended to), and any proposed apportionment. The drafter should include the applicable statute, claims to be resolved, any relevant conditions identified with particularity, any non-monetary terms, detailed proposed releases, any punitive damages, whether attorney's fees are included, and the total amount of the proposal.

ALLOWANCE AND DETERMINATION OF ATTORNEY'S FEES

Clarity in drafting is particularly important with the inclusion, or exclusion, of attorney's fees as "costs." Because most states do not have express provisions addressing attorney's fees, courts frequently examine this issue, that is, whether an offeree can seek fees when the offer is otherwise silent.[51] Some courts have denied recovery of attorney's fees when they are not specifically addressed in the offer, reasoning the parties did not explicitly contract for them, but others have awarded such fees where a statute taxes attorney's fees as "costs" in the underlying action.[52] The courts must address whether the fees are recoverable as "costs," whether an award is justifiable, and what amount is appropriate.[53] By way of further example, the Florida Supreme Court denied the use of a multiplier in awarding attorney's fees under the offer of judgment statute, reasoning that a multiplier promotes litigation in contrast to the statute itself.[54] The drafter is cautioned to specifically include (or exclude) attorney's fees, as well as special costs, to avoid uncertainty.

---

49. *Id.*
50. Service upon all parties is usually not required.
51. *See Annot., Application and Construction of State Offer of Judgment Rule, supra* note 43.
52. *Id.*
53. *Id.*
54. Sarkis v. Allstate Ins. Co., 863 So. 2d 210, 223 (Fla. 2003).

EXEMPLARY ANALYSIS OF TEXAS RULES OF CIVIL PROCEDURE 167

Texas Rules of Civil Procedure Rule 167 is an excellent case study for statutory offers of judgment. The underlying policy is similar to the federal policy: "to encourage early resolution of cases and to punish those who reject fair settlement offers."[55] It encourages pre-trial settlements "by minimizing risks to the party making the offer, and increasing risks to the offeree" and awarding some litigation costs against the party who rejects the settlement offer.[56] Thus, Rule 167 is a two-way street—which can be invoked by either party. The Texas rule also expressly contemplates an award of attorney's fees "thereby giving a party the ability to shift significantly more risk."[57]

Rule 167 awards litigation costs "against a party who rejects an offer made substantially in accordance with this rule to settle a claim for monetary damages."[58] The rule explicitly includes counterclaims, cross-claims, and third-party claims.[59] However, the law does not apply to class actions, shareholder's derivation actions, actions by or against the State, or suits brought under certain Texas statutes.[60] The rule generally applies to all other monetary claims, *but only* monetary claims.[61]

Notably, the defendant must file a declaration invoking the rule prior to the offer, no later than 45 days before the case is set for trial.[62] Texas also imposes a number of time restrictions. The offer cannot be served within 60 days after the appearance in the case of the offeror or offeree, whichever is later, or within 14 days before the case is set for trial (except a counteroffer may be made within seven days of a prior offer).[63] The offer must be served in writing, cite the statute, identify the party making the offer and to whom the offer is made, include specific settlement terms, and a "state a deadline—no sooner than 14 days after the offer is served—by which the offer must be accepted."[64] An offeror can place reasonable conditions on the offer and the offeree can object to such conditions before the offer's deadline.[65] Failure to object to a condition waives any objection that the offer is unreasonable.[66] "Rejection of an offer made subject to a condition determined by the trial

---

55. *Offers of Settlement and Shifting of Litigation Costs in Texas*, J.R. JONES LAW (Mar. 17, 2013), https://jrjoneslaw .wordpress.com/2013/03/17/offers-of-settlement-and-shifting-of-litigation-costs-in-texas/.

56. J. Allen Smith & Katherine L. Killingsworth, *Rule 167 Offers: Encouraging Early Settlement*, SETTLEPOU (Nov. 30, 2009), http://blog.settlepou.com/rule-167-offers-encouraging-early-settlement/.

57. *Shifting Litigation Risk by Offer of Settlement*, PASSMAN & JONES, http://www.passmanjones.com/passmanjones /media/Images/documents/westberg.pdf.

58. TEX. R. CIV. P. 167.1.

59. *Id.*

60. *Id.*

61. TEX. R. CIV. P. 167.2(d).

62. TEX. R. CIV. P. 167.2(a).

63. TEX. R. CIV. P. 167.2(e).

64. TEX. R. CIV. P. 167.2(b).

65. TEX. R. CIV. P. 167.2(c).

66. *Id.*

court to have been unreasonable cannot be the basis for an award of litigation costs under this rule."[67] Successive offers may be made at any time by any party, even after having made or rejected a prior offer.[68] A rejection of an offer is subject to the imposition of litigation costs "only if the offer is more favorable to the offeree than any prior offer."[69]

To be considered more "favorable" than the offer, Texas Rule 167 requires the judgment be more than 80 percent of the offer, where Florida and Georgia each find an "unfavorable" judgment to be less than 75 percent.[70] However, the Georgia rule only applies to tort claims.[71] If a significantly less favorable verdict is found, the prevailing party may bifurcate and determine frivolity, as defined by statute. Like Georgia, Florida, and Texas, many states are adopting similar statutes to punish those who bring frivolous cases.[72]

CONCLUSION

The use of offers of judgment in federal court can be a game changer, especially if "costs" are significant. The same is true for similar state court procedures, especially where attorney's fees and costs are both recoverable. Courts interpret offers using general contract formation principles. Practitioners should be mindful of certain guidelines in drafting or evaluating such offers. Plaintiffs suing under certain statutes may lose the ability to recover attorney fees if they reject a reasonable offer. In making your irrevocable offer as a defendant, strict construction of the operative statutes, timely service, and careful drafting is imperative for enforceability. Most importantly, always consider the possibility your offer may be accepted and transformed into a judgment against you.

---

67. *Id.*
68. Tex. R. Civ. P. 167.2(f).
69. *Id.*
70. *Cf.* Tex. R. Civ. P. 167; Fla. Stat. § 768.79; Official Code of Georgia Annotated § 9-11-68 (2015).
71. See Georgia Civ. Prac. Act § 9-11-68.
72. Richard J. Plezia, *Offer of Judgment, Settlement, or You Pay My Costs, Please*, The Advocate (Texas) (Summer 2006).

CHAPTER 12

Designing and Executing a Critical Witness Deposition

Raymond C. Lewis and John Jerry Glas

The most dangerous day for any trial lawyer is the day of a critical witness (discovery or trial perpetuation) deposition. You have not ramped-up for the deposition the way you would for trial. You have not combed through every medical record. You do not have the benefit of an opinion from your own expert. You do not have the benefit of a judge or jury to "feel" how the questioning is going. And, there's nobody there to help you. The partner you are working "with" either does not have time to help you or would laugh you out of the office if you asked for help with "depo prep."

No worries. We have been there. Truth be told, we are still there, learning more every day about designing and executing the perfect strategy for a critical witness deposition. But, what we have developed through deposition-and-error is a series of steps and decisions every lawyer should consider when deposing a critical witness. Right or wrong, it is our approach and it may help you.

First and foremost, do not sit down and start trying to compose the "perfect question" on the most important issue. Days will pass, seasons will change, and if, by some miracle, you word it perfectly, you are still not going to get the answer you want. Most deponents, especially expert witnesses, can see the "killer question" coming a mile away. So, save that step for last.

Pan back to the big picture. There is a finite number of "points" that the critical witness can make during the deposition, and you have to design and execute an effective strategy for addressing those points. Here are ten steps to complete when designing your overall deposition strategy:

1. *Deponent Points.* Make a list of every favorable and unfavorable fact, observation, memory, and opinion ("deponent points") the critical witness could offer at trial.
2. *Definitions.* Determine whether any deponent point or rebuttal point involves a key word that needs defining (especially for expert witnesses).
3. *Assumptions.* Determine whether a deponent point is based on an assumption and whether opposing counsel instructed the deponent to make that assumption.
4. *Admissions.* Identify every admission that the deponent must make based on the circumstances, the records, and prior statements by the deponent. When deposing an expert witness, always get the expert to admit they lack certain credentials and qualifications your expert possesses.
5. *Rebuttal Points.* Identify every fact or opinion you would want the jury to know about each favorable and unfavorable deponent point ("rebuttal points"). If necessary, add a column and write down every likely response or explanation ("responses") the deponent may offer to defend his or her original point, along with any rebuttal points you could use to combat those responses ("sur-rebuttal points").
6. *Deposition Exhibits.* Identify and make hard copies of every exhibit you would have to show the witness to support every favorable point, to establish every rebuttal point, and to counter likely responses. Decide the best way to present each exhibit during the deposition.
7. *Demonstrative Exhibits.* Prepare every demonstrative exhibits (timelines, charts, Styrofoam heads, models, etc.) that you will need to help jurors visualize favorable deponent points and rebuttal points.

Take a deep breath and clear your head. Now, get a soft drink, walk outside, call your mom, spouse, or significant other. Then, take the next three steps, which are the toughest.

8. *Forks in the Road.* Identify "forks in the road" where the witness could give one of two answers that would completely change your line of questioning. Be prepared for both answers in terms of deposition exhibits.

9. *Decision Time*. Decide whether to "raise or save" every rebuttal point during the deposition. Decide whether to "show or save" every document that undermines or rebuts the deponent's testimony. This is the eternal question of whether to show your hand during the deposition or wait for trial.

10. *Make It Good TV.* Decide whether to video the deposition and capture everything in real time. Decide how to make the deposition more entertaining and more memorable.

When we complete these steps, we may prepare a chart to remind us of the specific definitions, assumptions, admissions, rebuttal points, and exhibits to explore with the witness for each deponent point. For example, if an orthopedic surgeon opined that a motor vehicle accident (MVA) on January 2, 2017, caused the plaintiff's herniated disc and lower back pain (LBP), a single row of a critical witness chart may look like this:

DEPONENT POINTS	DEFINITIONS	ASSUMPTIONS	ADMISSIONS	REBUTTAL POINTS	EXHIBITS
1-2-17 MVA Likely Caused Herniated Disc at L5-S1 & LBP	(1) Herniated; (2) Bulging; (3) Likely; (4) Reasonable Degree of Medical Certainty	(1) No LBP before MVA; (2) Immediate LBP after MVA; (3) MRI shows a herniated disc	(1) Did not examine plaintiff before MVA; (2) Did not review ER records; (3) Not aware of any MRIs prior to MVA	(1) Plaintiff went to chiro for LBP month before MVA; (2) No LBP noted at ER; (3) Identical MRI in 2016; (4) Defense expert says only bulging	(1) Chiro record for 12-1-17; (2) ER records; (3) 2016 MRI image; (4) Defense expert report

When you finish these ten steps, you will be ready to start typing (or dictating, writing, chiseling in stone) your questions. And, yes, that is much easier said than done. Which is why the rest of this chapter is dedicated to explaining some of the more difficult steps, and to identifying some of the best tricks we have used or seen during critical witness depositions.

DEMAND DEFINITIONS FROM LAY AND EXPERT WITNESSES

There are many reasons to start a critical deposition by asking a witness, especially an expert witness, to define their terms. Start by asking a lay witness "what do you mean by . . ." or "what do you consider . . . ." Start by asking an expert witness to close their file and answer some "basic" or "general" questions. If this is your first time deposing the expert, or if the expert is affable, consider saying, "let's start by defining certain key terms for the jury," or "may I begin by asking you to explain what you mean by . . . ." And if you are already familiar with the expert, or the situation is already confrontational, consider skipping the pleasantries and diving straight into the first question. Nothing rattles an expert like a lawyer who begins a deposition with "what is *your* definition of . . . ."

Use Definitions to Attack the Credibility of Experts

The best way to undermine an expert's credibility, and to challenge whether they are qualified to offer an expert opinion, is to test that expert's ability to define basic terms or concepts. Nothing knocks experts off their expert pedestal faster than watching them struggle to define terms, and nothing destroys the "wow" factor like watching them become defensive and difficult.

In preparation for a 2010 wrongful death (product liability) jury trial, we deposed the elected coroner, who was eager to offer his opinion on whether a conducted electrical weapon could directly induce ventricular fibrillation, even though he had no expertise in the field of cardiac electrophysiology. Rather than asking "are you an expert in cardiac electrophysiology," we started his videotaped deposition by asking basic electrical questions. The elected coroner quickly became frustrated and defensive, as the following excerpts from the first 18 pages confirm:

Q. Am I correct in saying that you cannot define ampere for us?
A. No.
Q. Okay. What is your definition of ampere?
A. I don't have one. I'm not going to try to do that.
Q. What is your definition of coulomb?
A. I'm not going to try to define—to give you a definition of coulomb either.
Q. What is your definition of ohm?
A. I'm not going to do that.
Q. What is Ohm's law?
A. I'm not prepared to answer electrical engineering questions.
Q. I mean, do you know what Ohm's law is?
A. No, I do not.
* * *
Q. Okay. What is your definition of electricity?
A. It's a—I don't—I don't have a specific definition of my own of electricity.
Q. One volt represents the amount of force required to do what?
A. I—I—I'm not competent to answer that question for you.

The coroner's inability to define basic electrical concepts was so pronounced that the Louisiana Second Circuit Court of Appeal limited his testimony in the parallel (manslaughter) prosecution, and the district attorney chose not to call him during the criminal trial, which resulted in a jury verdict of "not guilty."

Nail Down Definitions Underlying Expert Opinions

Many experts are moving targets, and definitions are the best way to nail down their opinions. Ask the orthopedic surgeon to define "herniated disc" and "bulging disc" before you let them open their file and see what the MRI or CT scan of this particular plaintiff showed. We have had an orthopedic surgeon define a "herniated disc" as a bulging disc that causes pain and base his diagnosis on the plaintiff's saying the pain started after the accident. We also have had mechanical engineers define "unreasonably dangerous" as a product capable of causing injury. Remember that an incorrect, inappropriate, or circular definition may not result in an expert's exclusion, but it can cause the jury to ignore the expert's testimony.

Do not just limit your questioning to medical or scientific terms. Ask an expert to define key legal terms of art. Always do a deep-dive on what an expert meant when they included in their report the phrase "reasonable medical certainty" or "reasonable professional certainty." What is their definition of "reasonable medical certainty"? What is their definition of "more likely than not"?

With regard to certainty, always request that the expert identify a percentage and a rate of error. For example, studies show that only 15 percent of women with metastatic breast cancer live five or more years after diagnosis, so a medical expert could testify "with a reasonable degree of medical certainty" that a patient with metastatic cancer (sadly) will "more likely than not" die within five years. If pressed, that same medical expert could testify that there is an 85 percent likelihood that a patient diagnosed with metastatic cancer will die within five years, and could point you to the specific studies for the rate of error identified by those studies. Determine whether the expert in your case can say with *the same* medical certainty that a plaintiff's neck stiffness yesterday was "more likely than not" caused by a car accident seven years ago. Require the expert to give you a percentage and demand that the expert tell you the source for that percentage.

During a 2006 judge trial, a medical expert testified during direct-examination that the detention center "more likely than not" could have stopped the spread of Group F Streptococcus (which caused an induced coma and amputation) by starting antibiotics by a certain date. During cross-examination, we insisted on a percentage and the expert gave a different percentage than he provided during his deposition. When pressed, the expert changed his percentage again (on the stand) before finally admitting that he could cite no source for any of the percentages he offered. The trial court promptly excluded his testimony regarding percentages and later found the detention center was not negligent. On appeal, the appellate court affirmed the zero verdict, noting:

> Dr. [Redacted] went on to testify in his deposition that he thought starting antibiotics between the 15th and the 28th when swelling showed up would have prevented progression of the infection beyond the sinuses. He stated that one can say that antibiotics on the 20th perhaps would give him a better than 50% chance of

containing the organism or avoiding the complications. Then he said, probably, antibiotics some time between the 15th and the 25th, more likely than not, would have prevented his complications on the 26th. Dr. [Redacted] then followed with, "He would have had a better chance if he had been started on antibiotics on the 26th but I'm less comfortable with that as being a time that antibiotics and decongestants or whatever, would have worked." Dr. [Redacted] changed his testimony at trial, and his percentages were ultimately rejected by the trial court.[1]

Of course, an expert may refuse to give a percentage to support his opinion that something is "more likely than not," and an expert may default to testifying that his opinion is based solely only on personal experience. But, that type of admission can be half the battle. Telling the jury that an issue has not been studied well enough—or the case is so unusual—that an expert cannot provide a percentage may tell the jury all it needs to know.

Hold Experts Accountable for Changing a Definition

Definitions are forever. An expert may tacitly or expressly define a term in their report and offer a slightly different definition when asked during the deposition. Make sure your deposition outline identifies any previous attempts the expert has made to define a term.

Start a database of expert depositions at your firm, and track whether an expert's definition changes over time. Picture an orthopedic surgeon defining a "herniated disc" as a disc that extends more than 2 mm beyond the margin of an adjacent vertebral body, and then changing that definition to 1.5 mm in 2018 where (in a remarkable coincidence) the plaintiff's disc extended only 1.5 mm beyond the margin. Picture an orthopedic surgeon defining a "herniated disc" as requiring compression or impingement in 2017, but dropping that requirement in 2018 where (in a remarkable coincidence) the plaintiff's MRI does not show compression or impingement.

Transform a Definition into a Visual Target for Your Expert

Collecting expert definitions is not enough. Always think of ways to turn a pivotal definition into a visual target that your expert can attack during direct-examination. During a videotaped trial deposition, consider placing a flip chart next to the

---

1. Cole v. Acadia Par. Sheriff's Dep't, 2007-1386 (La. App. 3d Cir. 11/5/08); 998 So. 2d 212, 219, *writ denied*, 2008-2875 (La. 2/6/09); 999 So. 2d 784.

expert and writing down the key definition so you can flip to that page during the direct-examination of your expert at trial. If the deposition is not videotaped, consider writing down (or having the expert write down) the definition on a piece of paper. Mark that piece of paper as an exhibit to the deposition; include the marked exhibit in your list of trial exhibits; and blow-up that marked exhibit for trial. Picture yourself putting the blown-up (hard backed) definition on an easel like a bulls-eye target in front of your expert and asking your expert to take his or her best shot: "Do you agree with *this* definition?"

IDENTIFY EVERY ASSUMPTION MADE BY AN EXPERT WITNESS

Many expert opinions are based on key factual assumptions. Some factual assumptions are based on the evidence. Some factual assumptions are based on logical extrapolation. And, sometimes, counsel will instruct their expert to make certain factual assumptions. Make certain you identify and uncover every factual assumption the expert made, the source of that assumption, and what would happen if that assumption was wrong. Confirm that each of the expert's conclusions are based on those factual assumptions *and* get the expert to agree that the accuracy of those conclusions depends on the accuracy of the assumptions. Garbage in . . . garbage out.

Economists and accountants are perfect examples of how identifying assumptions can be used to undermine an expert's ultimate opinion. When opining on lost future wages, an economic loss expert must rely on multiple factors or factual assumptions, including base salary, future work expectancy, and projected salary increases. When deposing an economist, identify and fully explore each factual assumption and how modifying each assumption would change the final number. In recent years, we have developed a series of questions that solicit the testimony we need to paint that expert as nothing more than a calculator at trial, as demonstrated by the following excerpt:

Q. And you're not verifying or approving the accuracy of the information given to you by plaintiff's counsel?
A. Correct.
Q. Your role is to take the information that you were given and your methodology is essentially like a *calculator*, you take all of that information, and you get to an end result figure, is that correct?
A. That's right . . .
Q. So if another expert or another individual were to give you different information or different numbers, does your methodology change?
A. No, sir.

This line of questioning prevents and protects the jury from thinking that the economist personally concluded that opposing counsel was "right" to ask him to assume that base salary. Or, that the accountant independently confirmed the plaintiff would work through the age of retirement and earn annual raises. In many instances, exploring the expert's assumptions reveals that the expert's opinion is not much more than a precariously balanced house of cards.

COLLECT FACTUAL ADMISSIONS FROM LAY WITNESSES

Every prosecutor knows what it is like to conduct a "flying blind" cross-examination of a criminal defendant who takes the stand without being deposed or interviewed. That is why, prior to trial, a good prosecutor sits down and prepares a list of facts that a defendant must admit. No, the defendant is not going to admit to stabbing the victim (that only happens in old movies and television shows). But, the defendant may admit to the fact his wife was cheating (motive), to being alone in the same house with his wife that night (opportunity), and to fighting loud enough for the neighbors to hear. Collect enough admissions, and the jury will not listen to the (inevitable) denial.

Similarly, in a civil case, scour the records and prepare a list of admissions you can collect during the deposition of a critical lay witness. Unless it is a videotaped trial deposition, err on the side of caution and ask as many factual questions as possible. Unless you have a crystal ball, you never know which question will resonate with jurors, and the fact you think is irrelevant may be the fact that sways an entire jury.

In a 2017 wrongful-death case involving an industrial catastrophe, liability hinged on the testimony of an eye witness, who we knew was unreliable. The plaintiffs claimed our client's welding crew caused an explosion at a chemical plant during unsafe hot-tapping work. Their case was based on the testimony of a lay witness who claimed she saw the crew working minutes before the explosion. In reality, our crew stopped work an hour and a half before the explosion.

During her critical deposition, she was questioned in depth about that day, and we were able to harvest from that deposition transcript a number of admissions that destroyed her credibility. Prior to mediation, we prepared the following chart of admissions which we could have filled out during cross-examination at trial:

IS THE EYE WITNESS'S ACCOUNT CREDIBLE?	
Could she recall what the weather was like that day?	"No"
Could she recall if she was wearing a hard-hat and other PPE?	"No"
Had she been at the facility prior to the date of the explosion?	"No"

Was she familiar with the layout and configuration of the facility?	"No"
Was she familiar with the equipment being used by the work crew?	"No"
Did she know if that portion of the facility was actually operating on the day of the explosion?	"No"
Did she know if any safety protection systems were in place during the work?	"No"
Did she know if any hot-tapping or welding work was being performed?	"No"
Did she know what "hot-tapping" was?	"No"
Could she recall how many individuals were performing the work?	"No"
Could she recall if there were any individuals actually performing work at the time of the explosion?	"No"
Could she recall if she was facing the direction of the explosion?	"No"
Was she looking directly at the scaffolding at the time of the explosion?	"No"
Could she say where the explosion came from?	"No"
Could she recall if any sirens went off?	"No"

Instead of waiting for trial, we decided to place the chart "center stage" during the opening caucus of the mediation. The admissions became a prime topic of discussion and ultimately contributed to a successful mediation for our client.

It does not matter what kind of witness you are deposing, you should be able to easily identify from your list of deponent points and rebuttal points for that witness what kinds of questions would be ideal for these kinds of comparison charts and factual lists. If done right, these questions and the deposition responses become the groundwork for everything that follows the deposition (i.e., mediation, opening statement, cross-examination, and closing argument).

CREATE A CHART COMPARING THE QUALIFICATIONS OF CONFLICTING EXPERTS

Nothing is more effective during a jury trial than filling out a chart comparing your expert's qualifications with their expert's (lack of) qualifications. Before a critical deposition, meet with your expert and identify 10 to 20 credentials, qualifications, jobs, or experiences your expert has that their expert lacks. Make absolutely certain your expert can answer "yes" to the *exact* same question, and do your best to verify that their expert must answer "no." Comb through old curriculum vitae and depositions of their expert. When you are ready, prepare a simple (no frills) comparison chart. Hours or days later, jurors may not recall what each row said, but they will remember *seeing* a column of "yes" for your expert and *seeing* a column of "no" for theirs.

Remember to use leading questions and to only solicit a "yes" or "no." Never ask during the critical deposition "why" they did not obtain a credential or engage in a specific activity. Never ask the expert "why" they did not get an advanced degree or "why" they do not treat patients anymore. Even the most novice of expert witness can steal your thunder by droning on about why they are qualified and the credential or experience they lack is irrelevant. Deny them that opportunity. Just get the "no" and go!

Try not to sound judgmental. Do not betray your contempt for the expert's lack of qualifications with your tone or with unnecessary words (i.e., "you didn't even get your doctorate in . . ." or "you never even treated a patient with . . ."). Resist the temptation to scoff or shake your head as you write "no." Just get the answer on the chart. You can stress the importance of each qualification with *your* expert (i.e., why did you feel it was important to get a doctorate . . ." or "what have you learned by actually treating patients with . . ."). Just get the "no" and go!

In a 2017 jury trial in the Eastern District of Louisiana, a complex breach of contract case involving a failed oil and gas directional drilling prospect in Southeast Louisiana was going to be decided based on which of the competing petroleum engineers the jury believed. Because the experts' ultimate opinions on what occurred during the drilling operations, and who was to blame, were so diametrically opposed to one another, the jury was presented with an all-or-nothing choice.

During the critical deposition of their expert, we went through 50 or more questions regarding their expert's qualifications, work experience, and professional achievements. At trial, the jury watched us start our cross-examination of their expert by writing "no" in every row. Then, we started our direct examination of our expert by writing "yes" in every row of our expert's column. The completed chart looked like this:

QUALIFICATIONS AND CREDIBILITY		DR.
Masters and Doctorate Degrees	No	Yes
Registered Petroleum Engineer in Louisiana and Texas	No	Yes
Professor of Petroleum Engineering	No	Yes
Associate Dean of the College of Engineering at Louisiana State University	No	Yes
Taught Undergraduate and Graduate Courses in Drilling	No	Yes
Taught Graduate Courses in Directional Drilling	No	Yes

Taught Graduate Courses in Petroleum Engineering	No	Yes
Publishes Extensively in Journals and Books	No	Yes
Prepared a Directional Drilling Plan for a Drilling Project	No	Yes
Work Experience as Directional Driller	No	Yes
Actually Worked on Drilling Projects in Louisiana	No	Yes

During closing argument, we displayed the completed chart and told the jury "it all came down to which expert they believed." The jury returned a zero verdict, and jurors told us that the comparison chart convinced them that our expert knew what he was doing. They were particularly struck by the fact that plaintiff's expert never worked on a drilling project in Louisiana.

THINK BEFORE YOU REVEAL OR IMPEACH

Always be prepared for the possibility that, during the deposition, a critical witness will miss a key fact, testify inconsistently about a key issue, fail to review a key document, or outright lie under oath. What will you do? Will you reveal the un-obtained or overlooked document? Will you call their attention to the missed fact, the misquoted record, or the misinterpreted statement? Will you impeach them with their own report or deposition in a prior case? Or, will you wait for trial? To reveal or not to reveal—that is the question.

Ask a hundred trial lawyers and you may get a hundred different answers. "Trust your instincts," some might say. "Never educate a critical witness," others may say. "Wait until trial," still others may insist. The truth is that the right answer will always depend on the specific circumstances of the case, and anyone who gives you a general or blanket rule probably has not experienced enough depositions, mediations, and trials.

But, we may be able to help you decide whether to reveal or impeach during the deposition of a critical witness by suggesting that you develop your own "automatic" reveal checklists. For example, when it comes to a key document, ask yourself:

- Do you need the witness to authenticate the document?
- Do you need the witness to lay the proper foundation for the admissibility of the document?
- Do you need to file and rely on the document during motion practice?

- Do you need to nail down the witness's memory regarding the document?
- Do you need to nail down the witness's opinion regarding the document?
- Do you need to obtain additional information from the witness about the document to identify/subpoena additional records or witnesses?
- Do your experts need to know more about the document before issuing their expert reports?
- Is there any chance the witness will not be available for trial?

If the answers to every question on your reveal checklist is "no," feel free to trust your instincts and decide whether to save the document for impeachment at trial.

There are times that you should absolutely save a document or an argument for trial. In preparation for a recent jury trial, opposing counsel took a trial perpetuation of a psychiatrist, who relied on the fact that the plaintiff's treating neurologist diagnosed a concussion during his second examination (less than five months after an accident). During the videotaped trial perpetuation deposition, plaintiff's counsel attached a copy of the exam note for the second visit, which included the diagnosis "post-concussive syndrome." After that deposition, we discovered that our copy of the same exam note did not contain the diagnosis of "post-concussive syndrome," and that, years later (possibly very close to trial), the treating neurologist had gone back and added that diagnosis to his second exam note.

Under the circumstances, we chose to wait for trial and not call the *switcheroo* to the attention of plaintiffs' counsel. Instead, during opening statement, we circled the date and warned the jury that plaintiffs would "literally try to rewrite history." We kept that promise by proving the note was "doctored" and by showing plaintiffs had included the "doctored" exam note (not the original) in their exhibit book. The jury got the picture and, instead of awarding the $18.5 million plaintiffs' counsel argued during closing argument, the jury awarded only $1.5 million. Thus, in retrospect, even if we had discovered the *switcheroo* prior to the videotaped deposition, we should have remained silent and waited in the tall grass.

MAKE GOOD TELEVISION

Merriam-Webster dictionary defines "strategic" as "necessary to or important in the initiation, conduct, or completion of a strategic plan" and "of great importance within an integrated whole or to a planned effect." If the witness sitting across from you at the deposition comes close to fitting either of these definitions, you should be videotaping the deposition. While video depositions are most often played because the witness is not available for trial, they also can be used for impeachment, during direct or cross-examination, or during opening and closing argument. For these uses, video deposition testimony is a better, more trusted presentation of the evidence for jurors. Watching the witness's testimony and making exhibits come alive in the courtroom as opposed to a cold reading of the testimony is critical if you want it remembered.

Trials are not high school debates. Nobody cares if you win the trial on your legal pad. Many brilliant lawyers have (in monotone voice) covered every point on their legal pads, only to look up and realize that they lost the jury. So, remember that the first rule of designing and executing a critical witness deposition is: make good TV!

Be Consistent in How You Portray the Deponent

Every good TV show is built on the backs of memorable characters, for example, Lucy Ricardo, Hawkeye Pierce, George Jefferson, Frazier Crane, and so on. You have to identify what "character" you need the deponent to play at trial and highlight that throughout the deposition. Is the deponent the jack-of-all-trades expert, the hired gun, a professional witness, an independent fact witness, or the trusted, home-town medical doctor? Choose whatever character you need them to play and make that a consistent theme throughout the deposition.

In a 2012 trial involving the tragic wrongful death of a child at school, the plaintiff retained the former assistant coroner who performed the autopsy. The pivotal issue at trial was whether the child died from cardiac arrest due to stress or an abnormal heart disease, known as Arrhythmogenic Right Ventricular Dysplasia (ARVD). When we discovered that plaintiff's expert referred to herself as "Dr. Death," and had starred in a reality special (The M.E.) focusing on her unusual case work, she became "Dr. Death" or the "Reality TV Doc." In contrast, our forensic pathologist was a board certified pediatric pathologist and medical director of the pathology department at a local hospital.

Figure Out How the Witness Fits into Your Story

Most writers for television shows develop plots and storylines, and every character has a role to play in that plot or storyline. Similarly, most trial attorneys have a story to tell the jury, and it is important to identify the roles the witness will play in your story at trial. Answer all of the following questions and decide how the witness fits into your storyline, before you decide on a strategy for your critical witness deposition:

- Will you need the testimony for trial perpetuation?
- Do your experts need certain facts or assumptions this witness can offer?
- Is your goal to get the witness to commit to certain definitions, sequence of events, or expert opinion(s)?
- Do you need the testimony to build trial mock-up or demonstrative exhibits that will help the jury understand your case?
- Do I need the testimony to authenticate key documents and exhibits?

- Do I need the testimony for motion practice?
- Do you confront them with your impeachment or big reveal evidence?
- Do I need video of the impeachment for trial?
- Do you opt for an organized ramp up of the topics and questions?
- Or do you ask the pivotal question everyone wants answered seconds after introducing yourself to the deponent?

Stage the Deposition Properly

Most lawyers take the setting and backdrop of a video deposition for granted, and their presentation of the testimony and evidence suffers for it. The setting of a video deposition will never be as iconic as the bar in *Cheers*, the swamp in M*A*S*H, or Monk's Café in *Seinfeld*. But how the deposition is staged can make a difference in how closely the jury pays attention and how they perceive the witness.

Make certain the first image gives the right first impression. If you are taking the videotaped trial perpetuation of your expert, abandon the standard backdrop for something visually more natural and engaging. Take the deposition with your expert sitting in their office and behind their desk, with a backdrop of bookcases, diplomas, accolades, and family photos. Consider whether you want your medical expert in coat and tie (because he is professional), green surgical scrubs (because he saves lives and is being dragged out of surgery), or in a white lab coat (because he is a brilliant researcher).

At trial, jurors expect expert witnesses to show up clean-cut, dressed nicely, and on their best behavior. A video deposition should be no different. Prepare your witness accordingly. Instruct your witness to pretend the jury is seated behind the camera—or, better yet, that their grandmother is standing behind the videographer. Make certain their cell phone and any office phone is off.

Pay attention to detail and what is going on in the shot. Always ask the videographer to see the frame or field of view before the deposition begins. If you did not hire the videographer, instruct him (on the record) to notify you if he changes the frame or zooms in at any point during the deposition. If your witness is being deposed, remove all clutter and unnecessary items in the frame. A 64-ounce big gulp cup or an iced coffee is an eyesore. Remove any item on the deposition table that would not be with the witness if he or she was going to take the stand at trial. Make sure your witness is not at a bad angle or the frame is zoomed in for a less than a flattering close-up. Call for a break if your expert starts fidgeting with a pen or paper clip. And, last but not least, keep yourself out of the frame. You should be heard but not seen.

If your opponent's witness is the one before the camera, ignore all of the preceding advice. Let them use the dark gray pop-open backdrop. Let the expert haphazardly scatter papers all over table and in the frame. Offer him a cup of water or an iced coffee and leave it in (maybe he will knock it over or nervously drink from it during the deposition). Bring peanuts or hard candy in a noisy plastic wrapper and offer them to the expert before the deposition begins (maybe he will leave it on the table or play with the wrapper during the deposition).

But, make certain you stay out of the frame and on your best behavior. Remember that tone and behavior cannot be edited out of the video. If the video tape catches you in an ill-mannered way or behaving badly with the witness, that segment could be played in the courtroom and the jury will see you differently. Pretend the judge and jury is in the room—because they are.

Use Props and Visuals

There is a reason "show and tell" is a student's favorite day of the week. A proven way to keep your audience engaged is to give them movement and visual reinforcement. Do not be satisfied with having your expert explain what was tested—*show* them. If your expert analyzed a histology slide, let the jury *see* your witness "expertly" place that slide under a portable microscope, and *hear* your witness "expertly" describe the steps involved in their analysis. Do not be satisfied with asking your witness to describe the cervical spine, let your medical expert teach them with a three-dimensional model of the spine.

Never have the witness look down at exhibits where no juror can see what is going on. Set up a monitor next to the witness and facing the videographer. Have the witness use and engage with the exhibits so the jury can see it all. If you need the witness to do math, let the jury see him performing the needed calculations. If you need the witness to mark on a photograph the exact location or distance, make certain the jury can watch the witness draw every line and write every note. And, if you need to play favorable video evidence for the witness, let the jury watch the video on the monitor next to the witness *and* watch the witness's reaction to the video. Nothing makes better television than watching a witness dispute or try to "explain away" what the jury can clearly see on film.

In a products liability case involving a catastrophic failure at an oil refinery, we had Tulane University's School of Architecture create scaled 3-D models of the 4-foot industrial nozzle that failed and the 2-part liner inserted inside the steel casing so we could use them during the video depositions of the corporate representatives and employees of the company that fitted and assembled the 2-part liner into the nozzle. As suspected, the corporate representative described the installation process differently from the company employees, providing us with the option of showing (split-screen) the very different steps they described. Further, to everyone's surprise, the corporate representative *broke* the 3-D model while trying to show how his company installed the liners into the steel casing. In a moment of video deposition gold, the critical witness could be seen holding a broken model in his hands and apologizing on the record to the people at Tulane for breaking the model.

Use the Timeline That You Will Use at Trial

Remember that timelines are not just for trial anymore. If you are going to show the jury a timeline at trial, and you need the witness to help you fill in that timeline, do not be satisfied asking questions about the timeline. Let the jury see your witness mark on the timeline.

During a 2017 jury trial in state court in Shreveport, plaintiffs claimed that an accident caused a traumatic brain injury that was not diagnosed for more than eight months, but years later somehow caused severe psychiatric consequences that required 24-hour care for life. During opening statement, we showed the jury a "neurological timeline." During cross-examination of plaintiff's expert, we forced him to admit that the word "concussion" did not appear in any record during the first eight-month period and physically wrote "no" in red next to each date. We solicited similar admissions from other experts regarding negative diagnostic testing (MRI, CT scan, EEG), the absence of abnormal cranial nerve exams, and the absence of neurological deficits (Figure 12.1).

However, if any of the experts needed for our "neurological timeline" had not been available for trial, we would have presented the same blown-up timeline during their videotaped trial perpetuation deposition, solicited the same responses, and let the jury watch us write "no" in the same colors and in all the same places as we did at trial. One way or the other, we would have made certain the jury saw a seven-month timeline of "no."

End the Deposition with a Bang!

Every cross-examination and every direct-examination in every courtroom drama ends with a bang! Jurors expect you to end on a high note, and jurors will remember your last line of questioning. Never make the mistake of trying to push the envelope with the final questions of a critical witness deposition. Nothing is worse than having the court subsequently sustain opposing counsel's objection, and realizing (after that question is edited out) that your cross-examination will end with a whimper.

Sit down and identify a line of unobjectionable questioning that supports or makes a strong rebuttal point. When in doubt, end by soliciting a series of (undeniable) factual admissions.

    Q. You never treated the plaintiff before the accident?
    Q. You did not examine the plaintiff until one year after the accident?
    Q. You examined the plaintiff once?
    Q. You have not seen or heard from the plaintiff for the past two years?

Make sure you know *exactly* how your critical deposition will end before you ask your first question. That way, at any point during the deposition, you can decide to end with a bang!

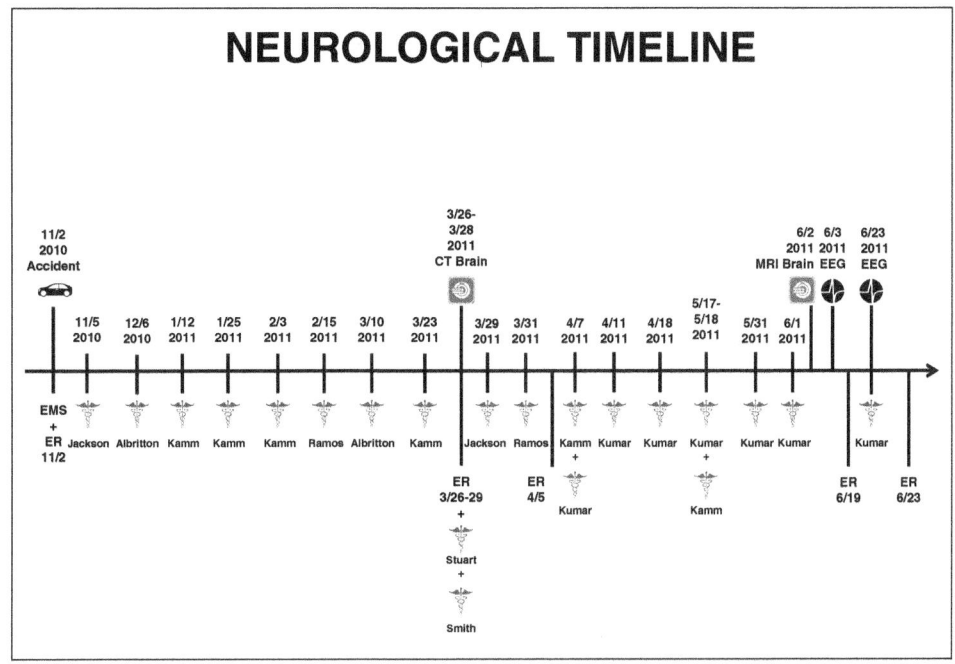

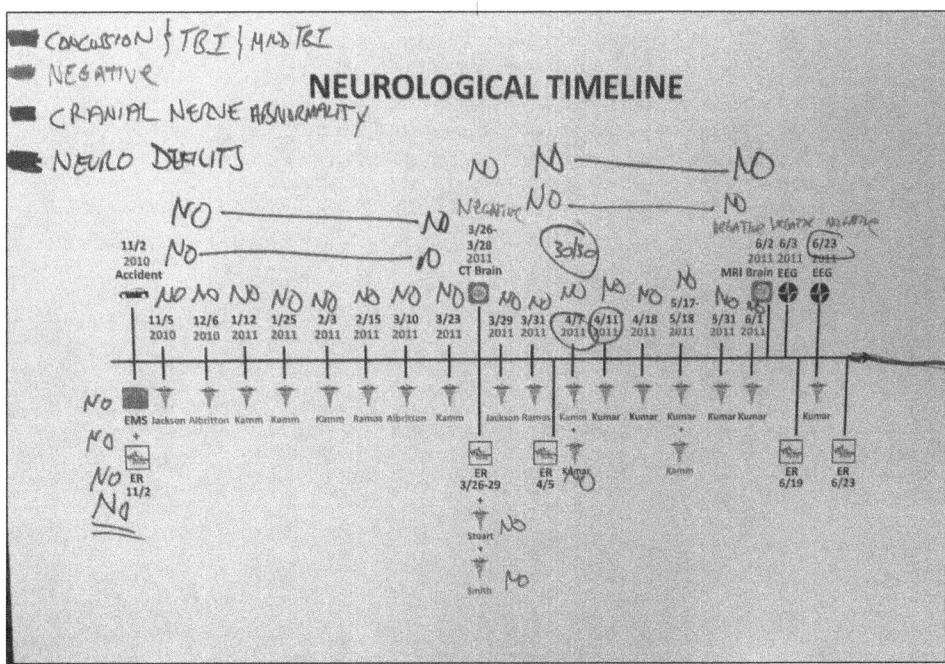

Figure 12.1 Neurological timeline.

CHAPTER 13

Making the Kitchen Hotter

Effective Use of Motions to Compel

David R. Pruet III

Harry S. Truman reportedly coined the old adage, "if you can't stand the heat, get out of the kitchen." Unfortunately for lawyers, though, getting out of "the kitchen" is rarely an option. Lawyers are therefore well advised to carefully consider their options before turning up the heat by filing a motion to compel discovery.

There is little wonder why discovery motions tend to turn up the heat. By definition, the motion's outcome determines what information a party is able to obtain and ultimately present at trial. While an adverse ruling on a discovery motion might not in and of itself preclude counsel from pursuing a particular argument or line of questions at trial, the prospect of doing either without having first obtained discovery from the opposing side can be risky and is certainly not appealing.

Raising the stakes even higher, discovery motions typically involve a court's first opportunity to decide a contested issue and often involve a court's first substantive exposure to a lawsuit on any level. By the same token, discovery motions afford counsel with an opportunity to educate a court about what a case is about—usually without making formal submissions of evidence. These first impressions about the merits of a lawsuit, and the reasonableness of the parties' positions, can set the stage for later rulings directed to the merits of claims and defenses.

Compounding matters, judges seem to have a near universal disdain for discovery disputes, and for good reason. Practically speaking, the resources and support staff necessary to adjudicate tedious discovery disputes are often unavailable. Setting these practical considerations aside, though, many discovery motions must appear, at least on the surface, to involve trivial issues that should be susceptible to resolution without court intervention. And, all too often, in order to decide a discovery motion, the court must sift through layers upon layers of supposed misdeeds bandied back and forth between counsel.

Yet, this understandable judicial predisposition against discovery motions does not necessarily tip the scales in favor of the party pursuing or the party resisting the motion to compel. Frequently, these judicial-oriented considerations simply result in a discovery motion remaining under submission for a lengthy period of time until a court has the time and inclination to reach the motion or until the parties are able to resolve the motion on their own.

The rub is that close judicial scrutiny is often precisely what is required to ensure the fair and appropriate exchange of information, particularly in complex litigation. This is because the significance of the information being sought in a discovery motion is not always apparent from the pleadings, particularly in the early stages of a lawsuit. In other situations, a party's failure to produce the type of information being requested, or the insufficiency of the information already produced, may be undetectable without examining individual discovery responses or document productions.

On the other hand, even where the discoverability of the information in question seems clear, other considerations can come into play, such as the potential consequences, favorable or not, that may result from a motion to compel. In other situations, there may be alternatives to pursuing a discovery motion that serve the same end without raising the stakes.

The lesson, then, is that counsel should be careful to avoid "making the kitchen hotter" by filing a motion to compel without good reason for doing so. Having said that, the most experienced, and well-intentioned counsel can disagree about the proper scope of discovery, and, in those situations, a motion to compel provides an indispensable tool for securing critical information. To be effective, though, counsel must carefully frame and present the motion so the court will recognize the significance of the discovery being sought and the necessity of the court's intervention.

SETTING THE TABLE: DEVELOPING THE RECORD

Developing a record to support a motion to compel involves consideration of all types of information and evidence that may eventually be submitted to the court when it decides the motion. Thus, the record embraces everything from discussions between counsel, to witness testimony, to the discovery requests themselves. Throughout the process of developing that record, the goal is to establish both the importance of the information being sought and the reasonableness of counsel's efforts to secure the information before filing a motion to compel.

Pre-Discovery Conferences

In some situations, where an area of contested discovery is foreseeable from the outset, counsel can begin to develop a record before a discovery request is even served. Particularly if the relevance of the contested discovery may not be readily apparent to the court, counsel should consider raising the potential discovery issue during the parties' planning meeting or during an initial scheduling conference.

The idea here is not necessarily to begin debating the relevance of the discovery before the dispute is ripe. Rather, the point is simply to call the potential issue to everyone's attention and to inform the court that counsel will continue to discuss the issue in an effort to avoid having to seek relief from the court. The court therefore receives a brief preview of the issue, which may help lay the foundation for a more robust argument down the road. More importantly, though, counsel has signaled to the court that the issue is important while at the same time demonstrating counsel's commitment to avoid filing a discovery motion unless necessary.

As an additional benefit, after being alerted to the potential discovery issue, opposing counsel may elect to avoid the discovery dispute altogether by agreeing to produce the information, or opposing counsel may begin the process of addressing the discovery issue with their client before discovery requests are even served. At a minimum, the parties are afforded additional time to discuss and potentially resolve the issue.

Unfortunately, more times than not, the areas of contested discovery are either unforeseeable during the early stages of a lawsuit or they are simply too nebulous to address with opposing counsel or the court until a lawsuit has begun to unfold. There are still important steps that can be taken to develop a proper record once a contested area of discovery emerges.

Preparing Discovery Requests

If a discovery motion becomes necessary, the content of the discovery request can be just as important as the opposing party's response to that request. After all, it is difficult to persuade a court to grant a motion to compel if the information being sought was not clearly requested in the first place. In fact, some jurisdictions require that any motion to compel quote the requests and responses at issue verbatim. It is therefore important to closely consider the terms and scope of a discovery request before serving it.

As a threshold matter, if a dispute evolves concerning an opposing party's response to a discovery request, it needs to be clear to the court that the disputed information was encompassed by the terms of the request. The discovery request should therefore plainly define and identify the information being sought.

Sometimes, of course, the precise types of information an opposing party possesses are not known, and it is difficult to predict how an opposing party, particularly a corporate party, characterizes or internally labels its information. In these situations, the best practice is to focus less on the labels that a party may use to describe the information and focus more on the content actually being sought. At the same time, it is always a good idea to include examples of the types of documents that may contain the desired content.

Of course, if counsel is aware of the specific type of document or information in the opposing party's possession, then counsel's discovery requests should clearly describe that document or information. In other words, counsel should never propound a deliberately vague or ambiguous request with the goal of "springing" a motion to compel on the opposing party in the event the document or information is not produced. This sort of contrived dispute only fuels judicial predisposition against discovery motions and is certainly not an effective form of advocacy.

It is also important that the request does not appear unreasonable in scope or in terms of the effort that would be required to respond. Indeed, in litigating a motion to compel, it is equally important for counsel defending the motion to avoid leaving the impression they have unreasonably withheld pertinent information as it is for counsel pursuing the motion to avoid leaving the impression they have overreached in seeking immaterial information.

Needless to say, counsel should tailor discovery requests as much as possible to the individual allegations and issues of each particular case. However, in some instances, the information being sought may be relevant to a position the opposing party has taken, but on the surface, the information may not appear to be directly tied to an underlying claim or defense. One effective approach in these situations is to include a reference to the position taken by the opposing party in the discovery request, and, if possible, even cite the page of the brief or transcript in which the opposing party took the position that created the need for the information being sought.

Preparing Discovery Responses

When developing a record to support a motion to compel, it is also important to avoid responding to discovery in a manner that could be viewed as being inconsistent with the forthcoming motion. For example, if counsel anticipates seeking to compel the production of information concerning some particular topic, then counsel should have a plan for addressing that corresponding topic if and when opposing counsel propounds discovery pertaining to it. Sometimes this means that counsel must weigh the pros and cons of propounding discovery that counsel's own client would find objectionable if the roles were reversed.

Of course, all situations are different, and there may be a sound rationale for reconciling an apparent inconsistency in discovery positions. After all, just because some type of information is relevant to the position taken by one party does not necessarily mean the information will be relevant to all parties. Further, if a good explanation exists for the ostensibly inconsistent position, then counsel may consider briefly referencing that explanation in the discovery responses—to avoid providing counsel with an unhelpful "sound bite" that might be referenced in response to a discovery motion.

Establishing Relevance

Relevance, of course, is derived from the causes of action and the defenses that have been pleaded in a lawsuit. In some situations, particularly where notice pleading is involved, the relevance of information underlying a cause of action or defense may not be readily apparent. In these situations, there are a variety of approaches to creating a record that will help establish the relevance of the contested area of discovery.

One option is to serve an interrogatory or a request for admission framed in such a way as to cause the opposing party to acknowledge the contention or position that creates the need for obtaining the underlying contested type of discovery. For example, requests for admission or interrogatories can be used to require an opposing party to explain the basis for some claim or to explain the circumstances surrounding some event. Those explanations can then be used to supply the foundation needed to establish the relevance of the underlying area or discovery.

Of course, depositions are useful tools for establishing an opposing party's contentions and for correctly framing the issues surrounding a particular claim. Counsel might also consider obtaining an affidavit from an expert witness in which the expert attests to the importance of the contested information to a particular issue in a lawsuit. The expert may even explain why the information must be made available in order to arrive at certain opinions concerning the lawsuit. On the other hand, in proffering this sort of affidavit, counsel should consider the implications on the expert's credibility in the event the discovery is not permitted or if it turns out that the information being sought does not exist.

Another less direct approach to establishing relevance of a contested area of discovery is to file a motion in limine seeking to preclude the opposing party from introducing any evidence in support of the position or contention that is creating the need for counsel to pursue the contested area of discovery. For example, if a party is resisting discovery concerning its financial condition despite pursuing claims for financial damages, then counsel may consider filing a motion in limine to preclude the party from introducing evidence of those damages. While the motion in limine may not be granted, it should at least have the effect of illustrating the necessity of the contested area of discovery.

These options for establishing relevance all have one thing in common: they are time-consuming and, therefore, require advance planning. In weighing these options, then, it is important to keep in mind the deadlines or other time constraints that may limit their availability. Some courts, for example, will not entertain a motion to compel if it is filed too close to the close of discovery or if it appears counsel waited too long before calling the issue to the court's attention.

Sometimes these situations can be mitigated by creating a record of communications with the opposing counsel reflecting that the issue is clearly being preserved. However, if there is a real risk that the court may deflect hearing a discovery motion based on a perceived delay in filing the motion, then the best course is to file the discovery motion as soon as the record is complete or to seek advance relief from the court's schedule.

Meet and Confer

Most, if not all, jurisdictions require that counsel attempt to resolve a dispute informally before filing a discovery motion, and this requirement is critically important in terms of establishing a record to support such a motion. Simply put, if the dispute is worthy of a court's attention, then it should be worthy of counsel's genuine effort to resolve the dispute before filing a motion.

In many instances, this requirement is satisfied merely through the exchange of correspondence between counsel. In other jurisdictions, counsel may be required to schedule a conference with the judge to discuss a discovery dispute before a discovery motion can be filed.

Regardless what "meet and confer" requirements may exist in any given jurisdiction, the best practice is to discuss the dispute directly with counsel to ensure that the parties' respective positions are clearly understood and explored. This type of deliberation can often avoid the necessity of a motion to compel and can also help keep the "heat in the kitchen" to a tolerable level for everyone. Moreover, the lengths that counsel goes to in order to informally secure contested information can help illustrate to the court the importance of the information being sought.

As a corollary to this proposition, though, counsel should be equally conscious to avoid creating a record beset with inflammatory accusations directed against counsel or the opposing party. Such vitriolic exchanges are rarely justified and are even less rarely effective—and they have the unfortunate by-product of fueling our courts' predisposition against discovery disputes. The best practice is to keep these exchanges respectful and professional, which can easily be accomplished without sacrificing advocacy in the least bit.

Of course, time constraints do not always allow for extensive informal discussions between counsel, and in other situations, it may be patently clear that further efforts at resolution would be futile or could be used to create prejudicial delays. In those situations, counsel should not hesitate to file a discovery motion once the jurisdiction's "meet and confer" requirement is satisfied.

You Can Dish It Out, but Can You Take It?

Even in situations where a record supporting a motion to compel has been fully developed, there are other factors that should be considered before deciding whether to file the motion. Indeed, part of the reason discovery motions tend to turn up the heat in a lawsuit is that they frequently result in a corresponding discovery motion being filed by opposing counsel. Therefore, before filing a discovery motion, counsel should carefully consider the state of their own discovery responses and document production to ensure that both counsel and client are comfortable with inviting the scrutiny from opposing counsel that a discovery motion will likely bring.

Further, in contemplating a discovery motion, it is important to consider whether the motion might highlight or open the door to some area of discovery not previously explored by opposing counsel. To pile on another adage—and this time, one that is certainly invoked more frequently by lawyers than any chef—"what is good for the goose is good for the gander." That adage will certainly hold true if counsel uses a discovery motion to pursue a line of discovery equally material to counsel's own client.

Another consideration, of course, involves the consequences if the court denies the motion to compel or fails to rule on the motion. It is always worth assessing whether the lack of a ruling on a particular area of discovery may be more attractive than risking that the particular area of discovery, or even worse, a particular area of evidence at trial, is rendered completely unavailable by an adverse ruling on a motion to compel.

Similarly, in situations where a discovery motion may not attract the court's immediate attention or where the motion may remain pending for an extended period of time, counsel should consider the risk that the existence of the unresolved motion may cause the opposing party to become even more entrenched on the matters embraced by the motion, thereby creating substantial delays that otherwise could be avoided by reaching a compromise.

In deciding whether these considerations weigh in favor or against pursuing a motion to compel, it is critical to understand the procedural rules that will govern the dispute. This is because some jurisdictions, including federal courts, have adopted a "self-executing" discovery rule that may provide an adequate alternative to filing a motion to compel.

Specifically, Federal Rule of Civil Procedure 37(c)(1) calls for the exclusion of information or documents that are not properly disclosed—even if no motion to compel was ever filed. The rule provides in pertinent part as follows:

> If a party fails to provide information or identify a witness as required by Rule 26(a) or (e), the party is not allowed to use that information or witness to supply evidence on a motion, at a hearing, or at a trial, unless the failure was substantially justified or is harmless. In addition to or instead of this sanction, the court, on motion and after affording an opportunity to be heard: (A) may order payment of the reasonable expenses, including attorney's fees, caused by the failure; (B) may inform the jury of the party's failure; (C) may impose other appropriate sanctions . . . .[1]

Of course, because this type of self-executing rule is only effective in situations where the party withholding the contested information subsequently seeks to rely on that same information, it does not provide protection in all types of discovery disputes. Further, even in situations where the opposing party subsequently seeks to rely on the contested information, the court has discretion in assessing whether the failure to disclose was "substantially justified" or "harmless." Nevertheless, when an opposing party fails to provide information that is clearly necessary to a claim or defense, self-executing rules such as this one may provide an alternative to filing a motion to compel. Counsel is well advised, then, to carefully consider the short- and long-term consequences of filing a discovery motion before invoking the court's assistance in resolving a discovery dispute.

FROM THE SKILLET INTO THE FRYING PAN: CREATING WIN/WIN SCENARIOS

In addition to considering potential adverse consequences of a motion to compel, it is also important to evaluate the existence of potential collateral *advantages* to pursuing a motion to compel. Once these advantages are identified and understood, counsel is in a position to frame a potential motion to compel in a manner to achieve the best possible result—which, in some instances, can involve an even more meaningful outcome than the production of contested information or documents.

These scenarios often arise when a motion to compel is used to expose a suspected or apparent absence of evidence supporting a key claim or defense being advanced by the opposing party. Typically, the underlying discovery dispute is triggered when the opposing party is reluctant to unambiguously state whether it is in possession of information or documents that support the key claim or defense.

---

1. Fed. R. Civ. P. 37(c)(1).

More times than not, the opposing party's reluctance to provide an unambiguous response is driven by the fact that the party does not possess, and is not aware of, any such information or documents.

When these situations arise, a motion to compel can serve two important purposes. First, the motion to compel serves to avoid a "trial by ambush." If the opposing party possesses information or documents supporting a claim or defense, then it is critical to obtain that information so it can be vetted and fully understood well before trial. Second, as the briefing and argument on the motion to compel unfolds, the court may begin to question whether the contested information even exists. The onset of this type of judicial skepticism can create a foundation for a forthcoming dispositive motion directed to the underlying claim or defense.

These types of scenarios may become less common with the introduction of the 2015 amendment to Federal Rule of Civil Procedure 34. That amendment was adopted "to require that objections to Rule 34 requests be stated with specificity."[2] In addition, the 2015 amendment requires that a party responding to a Rule 34 request "must state whether any responsive materials are being withheld on the basis of [an] objection."[3] While these requirements should reduce the quantity of ambiguous responses served under Rule 34, it may nevertheless still be necessary for counsel to pursue a discovery motion to obtain a response in compliance with the amended rule.

Another type of win/win scenario comes into play when an opposing party is so reluctant to produce relevant information that the party ultimately concedes a claim or a defense to avoid the entry of an order granting a motion to compel. For example, where a party intends to rely on an advice of counsel defense, the party may choose to forgo that defense in lieu of producing discovery reflecting the advice on which the party relied. In other cases, where a party is pursuing a claim that places its sophistication or personal finances at issue, the party may choose to withdraw the claim to avoid close scrutiny of those types of matters.

As discussed earlier, these types of situations—that is, wherein a party withholds information that it intends to rely upon at trial—can also trigger Rule 37(c)(1)'s self-executing exclusionary rule, even if a motion to compel is not filed. The proper recourse therefore may be to file a motion in limine or a motion to strike once the opposing party seeks to rely on the previously withheld information.

Overall, though, when a motion to compel is necessary, counsel should be conscious of any potential collateral advantages that might be generated by the motion. If those advantages are not identified before filing the motion, counsel may miss an opportunity to achieve an even more meaningful result for the client.

---

2. 2015 Advisory Committee Notes, Fed. R. Civ. P. 34.
3. Fed. R. Civ. P. 34(b)(2)(C).

SMALL POTATOES: HANDLING FAILURES TO RESPOND

While involving far fewer strategic considerations, it is also important to appropriately address an opposing party's failure to serve timely responses to discovery. This is not to suggest that a motion to compel discovery should be filed the moment that an opposing party misses a deadline for responding to a discovery request. However, it is important to have a plan for obtaining the responses within a workable timetable and, in an ideal situation, the opposing party should commit to comply with that timetable.

In those situations where an opposing party fails to comply with an agreed timetable or fails to respond when contacted about that timetable, it is usually necessary to file a motion to compel. But the motion need not be lengthy, and it need not contain inflammatory accusations either. The point is to simply inform the court of the situation, so the court may establish a deadline by which the responses will be served. Most of the time, this court-ordered deadline can be established without a hearing or any meaningful briefing; it is usually appropriate to expressly inform the court that no hearing is even sought.

Of course, when addressing these types of situations, counsel should continue to monitor the deadlines governing the completion of discovery and, to the extent possible, ensure that sufficient time is allowed for pursuing the motion to compel and obtaining the subject discovery responses.

THE PROOF IS IN THE PUDDING: BRIEFING AND ARGUING THE MOTION TO COMPEL

Once the record is appropriately developed and all potential collateral effects of a motion to compel have been fully considered, counsel is then in a position to present the dispute to the court. In presenting the dispute, whether in the motion itself or in-person at a hearing, counsel must do so in a way to receive the benefit of the effort and considerations that went into the decision to file the motion.

Preparing the Motion

As with any motion, the overarching goal is to keep it simple. No matter how complex the subject matter may be, counsel must recognize the limitations on the court's resources and the other demands on the court's time. The motion should therefore get straight to the point and immediately make a compelling case for why the subject information is critical to the prosecution or defense of the action.

In some situations, this can be accomplished by letting the contested discovery requests and responses speak for themselves. If, for example, an opposing party has objected to a request seeking documents supporting a statement that a party made in a deposition or at hearing, then counsel should fully quote the request and the response in the motion itself. Or, if the contested response is ambiguous, then counsel should quote the response in the motion, so the court can appreciate the ambiguity itself.

It is also important to submit evidentiary exhibits along with the motion to help establish the significance of the contested information. For example, if the opposing party's response to a prior discovery request opened up the door to a contested area of discovery, then counsel should attach an excerpt of that prior response as an exhibit to the motion. Other potential exhibits can consist of documents produced by the opposing counsel, deposition transcripts, hearing transcripts, or affidavits. The goal is to provide the court with evidence, and not just argument, as to why the contested information should be produced.

The motion also presents an appropriate time to inform the court of contradictory positions taken by the opposing party in terms of the contested area of discovery. For example, if the opposing party has served and received responses to similar types of discovery requests, then counsel should inform the court of that fact in the motion.

Also, because discovery disputes are often quite case specific, it is easy to forget that other courts may have issued opinions granting the type of relief that is at issue. Counsel should fully understand that precedent, particularly any binding precedent, and include appropriate citations in the motion to compel. This sort of precedent always adds credibility to a discovery motion and makes the motion more of a dispute about the application of law, and less of a dispute about differing viewpoints on what is or is not reasonable.

The motion should also recount the efforts that counsel undertook to resolve the discovery dispute. This is important because most jurisdictions' rules of procedure require that a motion include a statement to this effect. For example, the Federal Rules of Civil Procedure mandate that a motion to compel "must include a certification that the movant has in good faith conferred or attempted to confer with the person or party failing to make disclosure or discovery in an effort to obtain it without court action."[4]

In order to be persuasive, though, counsel should not merely recite the required certification in the motion to compel. Where circumstances have permitted extensive discussions, counsel should briefly recite the steps taken to avoid court action, including telephone calls, face-to-face meetings, and correspondence. The goal here is not to malign opposing counsel with accusations of unreasonableness;

---

4. Fed. R. Civ. P. 37(a)(1).

rather, the goal is to illustrate how genuinely important the contested discovery is to the lawsuit.

To that point, the motion certainly should not play into the negative stereotypes that many courts have come to expect with discovery motions. That is to say, the motion should avoid personal attacks on opposing counsel and avoid inflammatory remarks directed to the opposing party's perceived motives. Rather, the motion should "stick to the facts," which usually does not require the sort of colorful commentary that tends to distract and turn off most audiences.

Most critically, the motion should emphasize the prejudice that will result in the event that the contested information is not produced. In many cases, this prejudice involves a risk that the opposing party will surprise counsel at trial by referencing previously undisclosed information. This is a powerful form of prejudice given that most contemporary rules of discovery are designed to prevent "trial by ambush." In other situations, the prejudice may take the form of an inability to challenge a position being taken by an opposing party or an inability to secure information about assumptions underpinning an opposing party's or expert's claims. Whatever form of prejudice is in play, it should be highlighted to appeal to the court's fundamental sense of fairness.

Arguing the Motion

The same general rules for drafting the motion also apply when arguing the motion, but there are some relatively simple approaches that can make the hearing more productive and increase the chances of a favorable outcome.

One effective approach when there are numerous discovery issues in play is to bring a short itemized summary of the pending issues to the hearing. The thought here is to reduce all of the pending issues to a list in which each issue is identified by: (1) the subject discovery request number, and (2) two or three words describing the subject matter of the request. Then, during the argument of the motion, that list can serve as a reference source for the court and all counsel.

Not only does this approach facilitate a more organized oral argument, it also provides the court with a document on which it can potentially note its ruling as to each of the requests. By adopting a clear organization to the argument and at the same time lessening the burden on the court in fashioning its ruling, counsel may very well increase the chances of a favorable *and prompt* ruling on the discovery motion.

Also, if there are key evidentiary exhibits or case law, counsel should bring extra copies to the hearing in case an opportunity arises to emphasize their importance. This is also a prudent practice because in many situations courts do not have sufficient time prior to a hearing to review all of the parties' submissions. Therefore, the hearing itself presents an excellent opportunity to ensure that the court actually sees and appreciates the key pieces of evidence.

Depending on the court, counsel also should consider bringing a proposed order to the hearing, particularly if the issue is straightforward, so it can be resolved without much deliberation. Of course, counsel should be mindful not to be presumptive, but if the court's decision seems clear, subsequent delays can potentially be avoided by inquiring whether the court would consider a proposed order.

Along the same lines, in the event a court has not ruled on a motion for an extended period of time after a hearing, then counsel should again consider whether to inquire about the submittal of a proposed order. Other potential approaches are to submit a copy of the parties' prior briefing or a copy of any hearing transcript to remind the court of the pending dispute and ensure that the court appreciates that the dispute has not been informally resolved.

You Just Laid an Egg: Salvaging Victory from Defeat

The availability of appellate review for an adverse ruling on a motion to compel varies from jurisdiction to jurisdiction. It is safe to say that the scope of that review, if it is available at all, will be limited, given the latitude in terms of discretion that most trial courts are afforded on discovery decisions. This is yet another reason why the stakes are high in a discovery motion.

Having said that, though, all is not necessarily lost if a trial court denies a motion to compel. Indeed, the good news is that if the information is truly relevant, then its significance will eventually become apparent to everyone as the case continues to unfold.

Moreover, rulings on discovery motions are typically interlocutory in nature and are therefore subject to reconsideration by the court as additional information becomes available. While counsel should certainly be reticent about raising the same issue with the court more than once, this does not mean that counsel cannot continue to develop the record necessary to support the motion. After the record has been more fully developed, a motion to reconsider may well be appropriate.

On the other hand, there are other options short of filing a formal motion reconsideration. In this regard, status conferences present excellent opportunities for counsel to update the court on additional information that has become available after entry of the adverse ruling. During these discussions, counsel also may be able to gauge the court's receptiveness to reconsideration of its ruling. In some cases, counsel may be pleasantly surprised to learn that the court's ruling was a "close call" that could be subject to reversal as additional information is developed.

* * *

Given the long-range implications of a ruling on a motion to compel, and considering most courts' predisposition against discovery disputes, counsel should always seek to resolve a discovery dispute before filing a motion to compel. Even when an out-of-court resolution is unattainable, counsel should carefully consider the potential consequences, both positive and negative, of filing such a motion. When appropriate care is taken, though, discovery motions continue to serve an indispensable tool for a litigant to secure the information needed to prosecute or defend a civil lawsuit.

CHAPTER 14

Another Perspective

Jury Consultants, Focus Groups, and Mock Trials[1]

Sawnie A. McEntire

No lawyer can guarantee a jury verdict against all odds. No responsible trial lawyer should provide a client with absolute assurances of victory. Regardless of skill and preparation, all trial lawyers face uncertainties at trial. The unexpected is always just around the corner, and veteran practitioners know this well. Juries are frequently unpredictable in how they react to the courtroom, the judge, the evidence, the witnesses, and even the trial lawyers. The only thing certain about a jury trial is uncertainty.

With that said, a lawyer can (and should) make educated, informed predictions based upon experience, the venue, the facts, and the law. Properly evaluating (and handicapping) trial risks is one of the trial lawyer's most important functions and a critical service provided to any client. It is frequently the lawyer's final advice that dictates whether the case "goes to the jury" or settles.

One tool for risk management is effective jury selection. Picking a good jury, and knowing how this goal is achieved, is an important skill. Another is making informed decisions concerning what evidence works and what evidence does not work. Yet another is understanding which trial themes are effective and which are not. Each of these variables are managed through honed instinct and experience. But, even then, these variables can be independently validated or, at least evaluated, through the use of professional trial consultants. In the right case, the use of

---

1. Certain portions of this chapter are derived from the author's chapter entitled "Winning Strategies During Voir Dire" as published in *From the Trenches*, published by the American Bar Association © 2015, and such use is approved and authorized by the American Bar Association.

such consultants can provide objective insights, improved strategies, and substantial comfort to the client.

Selecting a good jury begins before voir dire starts. Every successful trial lawyer invests energy and time to understanding and identifying the characteristics of the ideal juror. Equally important is the identification of the characteristics of a less preferred juror. And, these qualities will certainly change from case to case. These evaluations should be educated, informed decisions, and *not* rushed or ad hoc.

Judgments about potentially good or bad jurors are frequently intuitive, and based upon years of courtroom experience. Lawyers should certainly trust their instincts and experience; but, in complex cases involving significant financial stakes or important issues, a lawyer's intuition can be tested through mock trials, jury experiments, and focus groups. These studies, properly implemented, will yield empirical validation of the lawyer's pre-trial assumptions. If those assumptions are incorrect, then it is better to make this determination before trial begins.

Clients frequently ask their trial lawyers to predict jury outcomes. Some litigation-savvy clients use formulas for this purpose, and many lawyers also have developed techniques for handicapping verdicts. In larger cases, where budgets are more flexible, both the client and the trial lawyer are well advised to consider obtaining independent feedback from jury consultants to confirm these trial risks. Consultants can help judge the facts and other intangibles that may impact the trial outcome. They also help identify good and potentially dangerous jurors, refine trial themes, and prepare witnesses. Ultimately, feedback from jury consultants is useful to inform the lawyer and the client concerning the wisdom of settlement or "going to verdict."

The role of a jury consultant will vary from case to case depending on the unique concerns presented in each case, and the client's tolerance for expense. Consultants may be retained to provide only high-level advice concerning trial strategy and assistance in identifying evidence strengths and weaknesses. But, they are frequently used to help in jury selection, witness preparation, and demonstrative exhibit preparation.

Jury consultants are found in every major metropolitan area, and many travel cross-country to provide their consulting services. Most jury consultants are degreed psychologists or individuals with sociology backgrounds equipped to better understand and predict the dynamics of human decision making based upon controlled information. A simple Internet search for "jury consultants" yields dozens of websites throughout the country. In fact, there is now a national association serving as a forum and marketing platform for jury consulting companies across the nation. There is no shortage of professional consultants capable of handling the smallest to the most complex cases. The cost will vary depending upon the company, the issues tested, and the methods used.

FOCUS GROUPS

Focus groups are an excellent device to identify specific weaknesses and strengths in either the evidence or thematic approaches to a case. By their very nature, such groups "focus" on trial themes and the factual strengths or weaknesses supporting these themes. Akin to a marketing firm who markets consumer products, a jury consultant is used to gauge what works and what does not work with the target audience—*the jury*. The focus group is a proxy for the jury.

Focus group studies are distinguished from mock trials because focus groups typically do not involve live witnesses or testimony. Even then, there are different formats for such studies depending upon the goals. Focus group studies can be designed to test specific themes and specific evidence, and then phasing such themes and evidence into and out of presentations to test for receptivity. Focus groups also are used to ascertain the credibility and likeability of witnesses.

A focus group study should be conducted in or near the venue where the trial will occur. The demographics of the jury pool in the relevant forum is always an important consideration. That is why there should be a disciplined effort to recruit participants consistent with the known demographics of the trial venue. Every effort should be made to reflect the ethnic, educational, work history, and socio-economic backgrounds unique to the trial venue. This better ensures that the study yields reliable results. Clearly, what plays well in a rural Texas town is likely different from what plays well in New York City or Chicago. Equally important, a lawyer who plays well in Boston may not play well in Jackson, Mississippi, or Atlanta, Georgia. Geographic and cultural sensitivities are important considerations.

Sometimes a trial will be venued in a small town or smaller city. In those instances, there is some risk if the jury experiment is conducted within the same town or city. A focus group participant may be called to jury duty to serve on the venire panel in the actual trial. Rumors also spread more easily in smaller towns. Thus, it is important to require participants to sign confidentiality agreements to prevent disclosures and minimize any risk that opposing counsel and parties learn of the jury study. If the town or city is small, then a neighboring town or city may be selected that has similar demographic characteristics. Moving the location of the jury experiment reduces the risk of making the jury study public. Again, the jury consultant should be consulted on this type of logistical issue.

Sometimes tailoring a trial message, how the message is delivered, and who delivers the message can make the difference between winning and losing with a specific audience. Thus, demographic data is always important. Relevant data should be readily obtainable through local or regional offices of the U.S. Department of Commerce, and every large metropolitan area should have this ready resource.

Focus groups are typically conducted in one of two ways, but both formats share common features. The first phase typically involves a pre-exposure questionnaire. This is when each member of the group will respond to specific questions calculated to identify any preconceived bias or leaning; the second phase involves information exposure from the two sides of the case; the third phase involves a post-exposure questionnaire; the fourth phase may involve actual jury deliberations; and the fifth phase may involve post-deliberation interviews of the group or selected individuals.

Sometimes, two focus groups are used much like a clinical drug trial—one group receives targeted information and the other group does not. The latter group serves as a "control" group to help the consultant determine the significance of information tested in the full exposure group. In this manner, the consultant can determine if certain evidence or themes are effective or ineffective. Equally important, this method allows a more informed decision concerning what evidence is potentially harmful and how to address such evidence with a real jury.

Before a focus group study begins, the recruited participants are typically provided questionnaires drafted to identify personal pre-dispositions or backgrounds that may lead to bias. Some questions are open-ended and some more direct. The resulting answers provide data points that are cross-referenced to the individual's demographic data. This enables the consultant to draw conclusions concerning how demographic variables may potentially impact jury deliberations and ultimate trial outcomes.

Following these initial questionnaires, the focus group is typically exposed to verbal presentations by lawyers pretending to represent the different sides of the dispute. This exposure may use a format where only videotaped presentations are used. Or, the exposure can involve in-person presentations by the lawyers. The lawyers argue as advocates presenting key themes and facts. The focus group is then provided a supplemental questionnaire calculated to gauge the impact of the presentations—what was persuasive, what was not persuasive, what was helpful, and what was not helpful.

Another option involves real-time feedback. This technique involves providing each member of the focus group with a device to register his or her reactions to the lawyer's presentations as those presentations are underway. The focus group actually listens to the presentation and rates the performances in real time. Like a gameshow audience, the group participants may register their "likes" and "dislikes" on a scaled measuring system to reflect their perceptions of the strengths or weaknesses of what they hear. This data feedback is immediate, recorded, and preserved. In this manner, the jury consultant can isolate which arguments are more effective or harmful on a real-time basis. There seems to be a heightened degree of accuracy with this technique.

Following the lawyers' presentations, the focus group is typically asked to retire to deliberate a simplified verdict. These deliberations are often videotaped for future use by the consultants and the trial lawyers. One-way mirrors or real-time video may be used so the lawyer, the client, and the consultant can monitor the deliberations. Much can be gleaned from watching these deliberations.

How a "jury" acts during deliberations is both fascinating and important for the trial lawyer to understand. By observing a mock jury or a focus group in mock deliberations, the trial lawyer can better understand the importance of identifying juror candidates who are leaders. It is important to know who is aggressive, who is passive, who is talkative, and who is quiet. These personality characteristics frequently drive jury verdicts. Incredibly, some jurors, who are more reticent than others, may actually vote against their conscience to avoid disagreements with other members of a jury.

At the conclusion of deliberations, jury consultants frequently conduct group interviews to test certain assumptions relating to the mock deliberations or to seek clarification of the mock jury's answers. All responsive data is then inputted into a computer program and cross-referenced with individual group members to provide a metric for predicting decision-making trends for individual juror types based upon education and relevant background and experiences. This correlated data then becomes an invaluable resource during selection of the real jury. When armed with this information, on a venue-specific basis, the trial lawyer can focus his or her voir dire questions more efficiently. The trial lawyer also knows which questions to avoid for certain juror types to avoid the risk of contaminating the entire pool. More information, and more preparation, generally translates into a more focused voir dire and a better jury.

Another benefit of focus groups is that they provide jury consultants an opportunity to test the efficacy of specific exhibits. Demonstrative exhibits may be shown to the focus group and tested for favorable or negative reactions. Again, much like a marketing study for a consumer advertisement, jury consultants can evaluate the most effective means of marketing a trial lawyer's case. Demonstrative exhibits are like "ads," and these exhibits can be tested for impact. As a consequence, trial lawyers can make better decisions concerning preparation of effective, interesting demonstrative exhibits for trial.

Another benefit derived from focus group studies is that they allow the consultant to test witness credibility. Carefully selected excerpts from videotaped depositions of key witnesses may be shown to the focus group. Follow-up questionnaires and interviews are then conducted to determine how the individual group members react to the witness's testimony and the witness's demeanor. All jurors bring some level of bias and sympathy into the courtroom, and it is important to understand the risks of these biases and sympathies before trial begins. It is always important to know whether you have witness problems—is the witness likeable or not likeable? Is the witness believable or not believable? A properly conducted focus group study provides an opportunity to hone in on these important determinations. The lawyer's final witness selection and witness order is then better informed.

Trial lawyers sometimes go to trial in the "fog of war." They may be too close to the case after years of litigation, and this closeness may blur objective assessments. It is, therefore, useful to retain and engage independent consultants to clear this fog. Independent confirmation of the trial lawyer's perspective is useful, and certainly never harmful. What one lawyer thinks is a strong trial theme, a strong witness, or an effective exhibit may not be so. Sometimes the strongest themes are counterintuitive. Sometimes the perceived strong witness is neither credible nor appealing, so any perceived "strength" is not accurate.

Mock Trials

Another method for testing and validating a trial lawyer's assumptions about a case are mock trials. Again, a mock trial plan can be designed using either complicated or simple formats with many or few witnesses and exhibits. Similar to focus groups, a mock trial should be conducted in a venue in close proximity to the trial venue with similar cultural and demographic characteristics. Again, the goal is to identify bias or attitudes that might impact the trial. Ignoring relevant demographics may skew the reliability of the mock trial results.

A mock trial is distinguished from focus group studies because it is real time with real people. Lawyers will make opening statements and conduct abbreviated examinations and cross-examinations of key witnesses. Exhibits will be offered as evidence, and a lawyer, serving as a pretend judge, can make rulings and otherwise preside. The goal is to give a jury a taste for the drama of a trial, as well as the facts, the witnesses, and the lawyers. Both sides of the case are presented, and there may be one witness or several witnesses depending on time constraints and the objectives of the study. Abbreviated closing arguments are also typically conducted. The mock jury is then asked to retire, deliberate, and reach a verdict. Again, these deliberations are frequently videotaped for future use and analysis.

The real-time nature of this exercise provides immediate benefits. The client gets to see the lawyers in action. Both the client and the lawyers get to see the witnesses in action, and the mock jury has an opportunity to provide an assessment of all the players and the tested issues. Because feedback is immediate, witness evaluations can be confirmed, trial themes better defined, and any weaknesses in trial preparations identified.

Interpreting the Results

Regardless of whether a focus group or mock trial format is used, it is important to understand what the results mean. The client may jump to conclusions as to who won or lost a mock jury verdict. There is an immediate tendency to interpret a win or loss as a harbinger of things to come. But, that may not be the case, so it is important for the professional consultant to digest and interpret the results before conclusions are reached.

Sometimes trial lawyers use focus groups or mock trials as an opportunity to showcase their skills to their client. Some trial lawyers may even pick less skilled or experienced attorneys to represent the opposing side to "fix" the result. But, this is an expensive mistake. It is important to respect the true purpose of the jury experiment—which is not necessarily to win but to objectively evaluate specific strengths and weaknesses of the case. To do this, the presentations of the lawyers should be reasonably balanced both as to substantive content and as to the advocacy skills of those involved.

The results of a mock jury deliberation will make better sense once the jury questionnaires are cross-referenced with the relevant demographic data. It is only then that an accurate picture of the strengths and weaknesses of the case can be confirmed for the specific venue in question. This is the job of the professional consultant, and the client should be counseled that first impressions from a mock jury verdict may not tell the whole story.

TIMING OF FOCUS GROUP STUDIES OR MOCK TRIALS

A focus group study or mock trial should be timed to incorporate critical discovery, key exhibits, and important witnesses. This typically means the jury experiment should not occur until the later stages of case development. Again, the purpose of the experiment is not to win or lose, but to better gauge strengths and weaknesses for ultimate courtroom presentations. It is, therefore, important to have critical facts defined, and the most important witnesses identified, before proceeding. Otherwise, the result may yield incomplete or misleading results.

On the other hand, conducting jury experiments on the eve of trial presents different problems. If the studies reveal unexpected information concerning witnesses, trial themes or facts, it may be too late to respond in a proactive manner. Discovery may be closed and the opportunity to take new depositions or seek additional discovery may be foreclosed. Therefore, strategic timing is important.

The trial lawyer should consult with his or her client in the early stages of the case to determine whether jury consultants should be retained and, if so, the scope of their involvement. Once retained, the jury consultant can provide advice concerning both the timing and format of the study. That is, does the case require focus groups with live presentations, focus groups with videotaped presentations, or real time mock trials with all of the bells and whistles?

JURY QUESTIONNAIRES

Jury consultants are frequently used to assist trial lawyers during jury selection. Depending upon your jurisdiction, jury questionnaires can be developed to assist in the voir dire. Leave of court may be required. Typically, questionnaires reflect the joint input of all parties in the case.

Jury consultants can provide great assistance in designing preliminary questionnaires. Again, the goal is to better define the personalities, pre-conceived leanings and tendencies of individual juror types. The questionnaires can be far ranging or more limited in scope. Some of the most piercing questions are the most simple. Some examples are provided here:

- What is the last book you read?
- What is your favorite television show?
- How many hours of television do you watch daily, weekly, etc.?
- Who is your favorite hero?
- What historical figures to do admire most, and why?
- What historical figures do you admire least, and why?

The answers to these types of questions yield a wealth of information concerning the personalities, interests, and habits of prospective jurors. The consultant then uses these responses to better define the best juror type for the specific case, as well as the least preferred juror type for the case. Clearly, there is a difference between a person who reads *Readers Digest* as distinguished from the *Wall Street Journal*. Clearly, there is a difference between a juror who reads books and news periodicals as distinguished from watching hours of prime-time television or reality TV. These are helpful data points whether you are a plaintiff's attorney or a defense attorney.

Jury questionnaires also typically include questions that are case specific. Such questions can be developed to specifically identify specific past experiences or background that may cause a predisposition toward the facts of the case. A juror's prior accident history is highly relevant in personal injury cases. A juror's medical background is highly relevant in a medical malpractice, nursing home, or pharmaceutical liability case. Corporate management responsibilities and financial backgrounds may be directly relevant to a stock fraud case or an accounting malpractice case. Whether a potential juror previously served as a jury foreperson is also extremely important. A positive answer to this question suggests leadership abilities and skills of persuasion. Thus, the jury consultant should craft questions calculated to identify pre-existing leanings or other important juror characteristics. The answers are then used to ask better, more insightful follow-up questions during voir dire.

The converse is also true. Depending upon the volatility of a juror's questionnaire responses, the trial lawyer may purposefully avoid communicating with particular jurors during voir dire. Some members of the panel may yearn for an opportunity to talk in the courtroom, and they could contaminate the entire jury panel with inflammatory personal information. Their simmering anger or zeal is sometimes reflected in their questionnaire responses.

Jury questionnaires can be short and simple, or long and detailed. The substantive content is largely driven by the needs of the case. Both direct questions and open-ended questions are used for different purposes to yield different types of information. Open-ended questions seek narrative responses, and these types of questions tend to generate honest, candid answers expressing a juror's emotions or feelings. Some jurors may feel more comfortable responding to a written questionnaire with expectations of confidentiality as distinguished from providing answers publicly before a large group of strangers in the courtroom. This is particularly true if sensitive, personal information is solicited.

Direct questions are crafted to obtain specifically targeted information: age, prior jury service, prior service as a foreperson, employment status, marital status, prior involvement in suits, prior injuries, and technical background, among other information. Additional questions are tailored to meet the needs of the case and should be used to augment standard information available from the trial court. In a joint questionnaire, each side typically includes questions calculated to obtain information relevant to their decision-making process. Basic, routine information should always be requested (such as personal knowledge of the case, work history, prior jury service, accident history, a spouse's work history or accident history, etc.)

JURY SELECTION

Most jurisdictions allow a lawyer's direct participation in voir dire and the jury selection process. However, regardless of whether the court or the lawyers conduct voir dire, jury consultants are useful in evaluating a prospective juror's verbal responses. Jury consultants also are used to identify behavioral tics that may betray negative or aggressive attitudes toward one party or the other. Body language is often used to interpret a panel member's attitudes toward the court, the case, or the lawyers. It is expected that prospective jurors will form first impressions of the trial lawyers during voir dire. Jury consultants can help digest whether these reactions are favorable or unfavorable.

Some prospective jurors are vocal during voir dire. Others are reluctant speakers and will talk only if called upon. The more reticent, quiet jurors may be swing votes in the jury room, and they can frequently make the difference between victory or defeat. Indeed, it is usually the more quiet jurors who are selected to serve on the actual jury. This is because the jury selection process is really a process of jury de-selection. The more vocal jurors are typically struck because one side or the other fears the juror may be antagonistic and vocal in the jury room. If a juror remains silent during the voir dire process, any animosity toward either the trial lawyer or the client may go undetected until after the jury buzzer sounds. Trial lawyers can use jury consultants during voir dire for a more informed exercise of their peremptory strikes and strikes for cause.

SHADOW JURORS

Jury consultants also can assist in recruiting and monitoring shadow jurors. Trial lawyers in high exposure cases frequently retain shadow jurors who observe the trial as it unfolds. The jury consultant recruits the shadow jurors to sit and monitor the trial on a day by day basis. Interviews are then conducted at the end of each day to determine whether the case is going as planned or has detoured. The shadow jurors typically do not know which side retained their services. The jury consultant can thus serve as an intermediary between the shadow juror and the trial lawyer. This is important so the shadow juror provides independent, objective feedback and does not give answers that the shadow juror believes is desired. It is helpful to have more than one shadow juror to diversify feedback.

VARIATIONS ON A THEME

Although not jury trials, trial consultants also can assist in packaging themes and evidence for arbitrations. Mock arbitrations are useful in identifying weaknesses or strengths in a case much like a mock jury trial. The services of retired judges or other experienced arbitrators can be retained to serve as mock arbitrators in a dress rehearsal. Lawyers can make formal presentations to the mock tribunal, and the tribunal can deliberate and reach decisions much like an actual arbitration panel. The members of the mock tribunal are then questioned about specific aspects of the case to gauge insight into particular strengths or weaknesses. Jury consultants can assist in this process in either recruiting the members of the mock tribunal or in processing the information gleaned from the arbitration experiment.

CAVEATS AND LIMITATIONS

Jury consultants provide a variety of services to the trial lawyer both before and during trial. Trial themes can be tested; witness credibility can be evaluated; and, demonstrative exhibits can be vetted for efficacy. But, it is important to recognize the limitations of these consultations. Nothing is guaranteed and, when all is said and done, juries remain inherently unpredictable. A rogue jury is only a verdict away.

It is important to recognize that focus group studies and mock trials sometimes result in self-fulfilling prophecy. Presentations to a focus group or a mock jury may be slightly (*albeit inadvertently*) skewed to help one side versus the other. There may be a mismatch in the advocacy skills of the presenting lawyers which can skew the legitimacy of the result. Focus group participants frequently try to guess as to who is paying their per diem, and they may feel compelled to provide a certain result. That is why the skills and experience of a professional consultant are important. The end result of a jury experiment should be objective, and not the result of a suggested outcome.

Focus groups and mock trials also can lead to a client's false sense of security. Favorable results may embolden the trial lawyer and the client to proceed to trial placing themselves in harm's way. That is why a disciplined interpretation of the data from the study is crucial. The goal is to eliminate conjecture as the trial begins, and replace conjecture with realistic data points. An informed decision is always a better decision.

CHAPTER 15

The Final Screenplay

Final Trial Preparations, Witness Selection, and Exhibits

Lee M. Hollis

While this chapter is at the end of the book, work on this phase should occur throughout the entire life of the case. By now, discovery is complete, dispositive motions have been filed, and you are ready for the final ramp up for trial. This chapter will take the practitioner through the steps necessary to make sure you are ready when it is show time.

LEGAL ISSUES

As you start final preparations, go back to the beginning. Review the clams that are remaining in the lawsuit, and the applicable defenses. You should make a list of every element of the claims and defenses, and who has the burden of proof. You do this to remind yourself and your entire team what the other side has to prove and what you have to prove. Use that list as a roadmap to decide what elements your opponent must prove that you can disprove, and what elements you must prove, so that you are ready to do so.

I recommend making a chart of each element and who has the burden of proof. If your opponent has the burden of proof, note the ways in which you plan to attack. If you have the burden of proof, note the witnesses and documents you will use to carry your burden. This approach will help make sure nothing falls through the cracks in the fog of war.

DISTILL YOUR CASE THEMES

Again, your themes should have been developed from the beginning of the case and fleshed out in discovery. Now is a good time to refine them. You need to adapt your themes to whatever rulings have been made along the way, to make sure that all themes are still relevant and admissible.

Once you have refined your themes, they, along with your chart of elements of proof, become the filter through which you decide what case to put on at trial. Sometimes lawyers get so close to a case and know every detail about it through years of discovery, that they have trouble telling a story that the jury can relate to and comprehend. You can know everything about your case, but if you cannot tell a clear, understandable, and persuasive story at trial, you are hurting your chance of winning.

So, as you consider what evidence you need to present at trial, and what lines of attack to pursue, think about whether they fit with your themes. If something doesn't fit with your theme, and you do not have to prove it as an element, or knock it out as an element of your opponent, let it fall by the wayside. This is a process whereby you focus on what is most important and persuasive.

I have been involved in cases where hundreds of thousands of pages of documents have been produced, and tens of thousands of pages of deposition testimony have been taken. But, usually, most cases come down to a few key witnesses and a few key documents. Those are the ones upon which you need to focus.

TRIAL RESPONSIBILITIES

Once you have made your chart of elements of proof, and refined your themes, I recommend making a trial responsibilities chart. This chart will serve as your battle plan for trial, from beginning to end. You should list out all of the stages of the trial, the witnesses, and who is responsible for what. For example:

Pre-trial
Preparation of exhibits
Preparation of deposition excerpts
Motions to exclude or limit expert testimony
Trial brief
Pre-trial order
Proposed jury instructions
Motion for JML

Renewed motion for JML
Voir dire
Opening
Plaintiff's witnesses to cross-examine
Arguing motion for JML at the close of plaintiff's case
Defense witnesses
Arguing motion for JML at the close of all evidence
Closing

The preceding list will vary for each case, but the idea is to list out every step of the case and who is responsible for what, so everyone is prepared and singing off the same sheet of music. Again, this will minimize the risk of things falling through the cracks. Everyone will know what they are responsible for and then they can all focus on their work assignments in the days and weeks heading up to trial.

MOTIONS IN LIMINE

You should have been keeping track of evidence you would like to exclude as you have learned about such evidence through discovery. This can be in the form of documents, deposition testimony, or questions asked by opposing counsel that reveal arguments they may try to make. Many inexperienced trial lawyers file too many motions in limine that contain a lot of boilerplate evidentiary issues. Over the years, I have moved away from this approach. In many courts, motions in limine are taken up on the morning of trial when there is not much time. A laundry list of motions in limine irritates the judge and distracts the court from the important motions you really need to argue. I would not file motions in limine that are basically asking that the Rules of Evidence be followed. If the Rules are not followed, you can object or move for a mistrial at the appropriate time.

Motions in limine should be focused on truly damaging evidence that you want to keep out and you want to prevent the other side from mentioning during voir dire and opening statement. I have found that most judges will rule on the clearest cut motions in limine. However, they often will defer a final ruling until the evidence comes up at trial, so they can get a feel for the case and make a ruling in better context. However, judges will often tell the other side not to mention the evidence until the issue has been decided outside the presence of the jury. In this way, your motions in limine can educate the judge and flag issues for him or her, so the court is better prepared to make a good ruling at the time the evidence is offered. You can also accomplish the goal of limiting what your opponent can get away with during voir dire and opening statement.

Finally, you should keep a chart of all motions in limine with columns to check whether they are granted or denied with room to make detailed notes of rulings. This will make it easier for you to follow the rulings and object when your opponent does not.

PREPARE YOUR OPENING WELL IN ADVANCE

As it gets closer and closer to trial, you have more and more demands upon your time. I recommend preparing your opening statement well in advance. Your opening will summarize your case themes and evidence, and that will further inform the process of deciding exactly what points to bring out on cross-examination and what evidence to present at trial.

The opening is probably the most important part of the trial, and many practitioners do not spend enough time preparing for it. A good opening can give you two distinct advantages. First, it can give you a head start out of the blocks and force your opponent to play catch up. Studies show that jurors often begin to decide a case during the opening statements. This is when their first impressions of the lawyers and what the case is about are formed. If you can win the opening statement, jurors who are with you will tend to see the evidence in a way that supports their view of the case. Conversely, if you lose the opening statement, you will have to change jurors' minds throughout the trial. Don't make that mistake; get out to a head start in the race.

Second, a really strong and persuasive opening statement can help a case settle. Maybe your opponent has never really understood your arguments. Maybe the lawyer on the other side has not explained your arguments to his or her client before. This is your chance to show your opponent what he or she is up against. A strong, organized, and persuasive opening statement will demonstrate to the other side you are ready, and that you have a strong story to tell. After hearing your opening, if it is effective, the opposition may well reconsider its position and want to talk settlement.

It is beyond the scope of this chapter to get into the details of opening statements. But I recommend that practitioners read about the art of an effective opening statement and talk to experienced trial lawyers. To me, the key things to remember are to maintain your credibility, tell an interesting and persuasive story, and argue as much as the court will allow.

VOIR DIRE

Again, voir dire is a topic that is worthy of an entire chapter. I will touch on some of the highlights here.

You should plan your voir dire just as much as you plan your opening. I know I said earlier that the opening statement is the most important part of the trial. That is true for the jury that is in the box. But it is crucial to use voir dire effectively to make sure you do everything you can to get a jury that will see the case your way.

Voir dire is the first opportunity you will have to talk to the jury. You should be polite, organized, and efficient. This is the time the ultimate jurors will develop their first impression of you. Make it count.

The traditional view is to argue your case during voir dire. I think that can be overdone. While you certainly want to begin telling about your side of the case and developing some of your themes, if you simply argue your case and ask if anyone disagrees, you are missing a valuable opportunity to learn about your jurors so that you can make informed decisions during jury selection.

If your client has the resources, I recommend you have a jury consultant present during voir dire and jury selection. Your consultant can help identify demographics, attitudes, professions, civic organizations, and the like, that are signs of jurors who may be against you. The key is to elicit this type of information, so that you can use it when striking the jury. You should ask questions that determine whether jurors have life experiences similar to that of your opponent or hostilities towards your client or its industry. You should be looking for religious and political views that might touch on issues in your case. You should be looking for experience in any of the subject matters that will come up in the case. Generally speaking, you want to try to use your strikes to excuse jurors who are likely to relate to or sympathize with the position of your opponent, and keep jurors who are likely to relate to or sympathize with your position.

Obviously, these profiles for plaintiff-oriented or defense-oriented jurors will vary, depending on the facts of each case. A jury consultant can help come up with a list of questions to elicit the factors or traits you are looking for. And, on this topic, don't rely on stereotypes. Countless times I have seen jurors who, because of their age, gender, race, occupation, or educational level, I have assumed would either be for or against me, only to learn in jury research I was wrong. Stereotypes are terrible predictors of behavior. It is much more important to ask the types of questions that reveal biases and belief structures.

If one side or the other is likely to strike jurors along racial lines, you need to be prepared for a *Batson* challenge. As you identify potential jurors you would like to excuse, focus on them during voir dire. Ask questions that might reveal the basis of a challenge for cause, and questions that will support your striking the witness on race-neutral grounds, in the event of a *Batson* challenge. Conversely, watch your opponent's strikes, and if they are all striking jurors of a particular race, be ready to make a *Batson* challenge and require them to provide race-neutral reasons for their strikes.

Finally, look for leaders. In your questioning, look for strong personalities or people in occupations that require leadership, or that will command respect. Strong leaders can often lead deliberations in one way or another. They can also hold out, even though they are outnumbered. You want to eliminate leaders who are likely to be sympathetic to your opponent and keep leaders who are sympathetic to your own.

WITNESS SELECTION AND PREPARATION

Selecting and preparing your witnesses is crucial. Sometimes you do not have much leeway in selecting your witnesses. They are who they are. They observed the accident or were involved in the transaction, so they have to be a witness. But, sometimes, you have several witnesses to choose from, and it is important to choose wisely. You want witnesses who have credibility and who can stand up to cross-examination.

The best way to select your witnesses is to spend time with them. The more time you spend with a witness, the more you get to know them and what they are like. You can tell if they exaggerate. You can tell if they hedge the truth. You can tell if they are credible. Use your instincts. If you do not think they are credible, neither will a jury.

Prepare your witnesses for what they are going to experience. Going to court will be new to most witnesses. Take them to the courtroom and put them on the stand when no one is around. This will give them a comfort level that they are on their home turf. It will help lower their anxiety when they actually testify.

Do mock examinations. I recommend videotaping your witnesses during direct and cross-examinations. Again, this will get them used to the process and allow them to practice their answers. There is a delicate balance, however, between how much practice is enough, and how much is too much. You do not want to practice to the point that the answers sound scripted, or the witness will not sound credible. But you do want to practice enough where you can have smooth, direct examinations that get across the points you need to convey. The witness needs to understand what answers you are looking for with the question.

And practicing cross-examination is vitally important. Some witnesses crumble upon cross-examination. You should practice cross-examinations trying to imitate the style of your opponent, and you should put your witnesses through cross-examination that is much more difficult than you expect them to encounter at trial. You should ask them all the hard and uncomfortable questions you can think of and help the witness to have answers to them. Teach your witnesses to be polite to opposing counsel and not to get angry. They should use humor carefully. When it works, it can be powerful, but when it backfires, it can harm the witness. In short, your witness needs to maintain his or her credibility while sticking to his or her guns. They need to politely answer the questions, concede what they have to concede, but not be pushed around into wavering on their direct testimony.

Finally, again if your client has the resources, I recommend using a jury consultant. Most jury consultants can assist in witness preparation. I have seen absolutely terrible witnesses become star witnesses after working with a jury consultant. This is time and money well spent.

EXHIBIT SELECTION

My number one concern in exhibit selection is leaving something out. It is a terrible feeling to need an exhibit at trial and not have it on your exhibit list. To avoid this, I usually list every document in the case with a disclaimer saying that I am not waiving any objections by listing the document. This way, virtually everything in your file can be used at trial if needed. There may be tactical reasons not to take this approach, or the volume of documents may be too large, but this is a good place to start, and then you can easily delete any items you don't want to include. But at least it will be a deliberate decision on your part.

Next, I determine the documents I know I will need. I do this by referring back to my chart of burden of proof. I make sure I have every document that I need to prove a claim or defense. Then, I make sure I have every document I want to use in cross-examination. In most courts, documents used in impeachment do not have to be listed. So you may want to remove these items from your exhibit list, especially if your opponent is unaware you have them.

There will be some exhibits that you need to have in evidence for the record, but you will not use much. But there are others that will be the focal point of the trial. These key exhibits are ones you need to know inside and out and have with you. I like to make a separate set of the most important exhibits and have them with me at all times during trial. That way I have them to prepare my examinations or to review if unexpected issues arise during trial.

I am a big believer in the use of trial demonstration software. I recommend you work with someone in your office or a vendor to provide this service at trial. An experienced trial graphics person can be invaluable at trial. I load every document in the case into the trial presentation software and individually number them. Then I tell my trial presentation person which are the main exhibits I will want to use. That way he or she is prepared to put them on the screen in an instant. When you refer to exhibits during opening, you should put the important ones on the screen and draw the jury's attention to them. You should highlight and blowup key portions of exhibits during your opening, and do the same during examinations at trial. This way, the jury can read along with you and the witness each step of the way.

You should be sure to take note of the key exhibit numbers. Note them in your examinations and in your closing argument. You want jurors to remember that they need to look at certain exhibit numbers when they begin their deliberations.

Lastly, I recommend using your exhibits to bolster your case at every opportunity. Jurors can be cynical about believing what lawyers say. They also can be cynical about believing witnesses who may have an interest in the outcome of the case. But, often, words on a page or a photograph can be persuasive. This is especially true if the document in question was created well before there was a dispute. Having a photograph or writing to establish your position carries with it a certain amount of credibility that spoken words do not have. So, pick your exhibits carefully and use them throughout the trial.

One final note on exhibits: remember to offer them into evidence. I remember my first trial. As I examined each witness, I dutifully identified each exhibit I used with the witness and asked the witness about them. Each time I sat down having forgotten to offer them into evidence. Luckily, I had a very understanding judge who asked me if I wanted to offer the exhibits into evidence. To avoid this, at the end of my outline for every examination, I make a note to myself to offer the exhibits before I sit down. It is a good idea to have a chart of all exhibits for your paralegal to keep track of all exhibits and note whether they were offered or admitted. This will help make sure you have everything in evidence at the end of the trial and know what is in evidence when it comes time for closing arguments.

DEMONSTRATIVES

Demonstrative exhibits are a lot of fun. Because they are merely demonstrative and do not come into evidence, very few rules apply. So, get creative. Work with your trial graphics team and your jury consultant to develop demonstrative exhibits that help tell your story.

Juries today are visual. They are used to seeing graphs and charts and pictures on Instagram and Snapchat, so images are powerful and memorable. Use that to your advantage.

Many cases involve complex issues. Your job as the trial lawyer is to make them simple and understandable for a jury. Demonstrative exhibits can help do that. If the timing of events is important, make a timeline showing what happened when. If understanding the way a product works is important, have a diagram or animation that shows how it works. In product liability cases, I usually try to have an exemplar of the product in the courtroom so the jury can touch and feel it, and witnesses can use it to explain to the jury how it works. These types of demonstratives bring your case to life and make it understandable.

Demonstratives also can be quite effective in opening and closing as well. When I am the defendant, I often find ways to demonstrate the things the plaintiff has to prove in order to win, and then show how he has not proven them. I have seen this demonstrated in many different ways. Some lawyers use a virtual house of cards that falls when the plaintiff cannot prove a foundation of his or her case. Others use a bridge, a wall, or Jenga blocks. The point is, use an effective demonstrative to illustrate all the things your opponent has to prove and where they have fallen short.

All this is to say that demonstratives are an effective tool for helping you win your case. Get creative and use them to get your point across.

JUDGMENTS AS A MATTER OF LAW

This is a mundane but important step in the process. Of course, there are some cases where you truly believe you are entitled to judgment as a matter of law. In those cases, you will naturally focus on this and be prepared for it. But, in many cases, this step in the process is easily overlooked.

I recommend preparing your motion for judgment as a matter of law at the close of the plaintiff's case, and at the close of the evidence well in advance of trial. These should be formal, written pleadings that are filed with the court during the course of the trial. This is one where I fully endorse the kitchen sink approach. I put every conceivable ground in my motions. I list every element the other side must prove and say they have not met their burden of proof. I list every defense and say I have proven it. I list all legal shortcomings and any issue that could possibly be an issue on appeal. This way I know everything is covered when the time comes. Then at the appropriate time, I file the motion. When the court hears argument on the motions, however, I focus only on the issues that are most important. This way you are focusing the court on issues that you would like it to rule in your favor while preserving everything else for appeal.

CLOSING

Closing arguments is another one of those topics that is worthy of an entire chapter. But, here, I will touch on the highlights.

First of all, have fun. Closing argument is the most fun trial attorneys get to have. So, work hard and enjoy yourself. This is the time to bring everything together. During the course of the trial, I keep a section in my notes that is just for closing. Throughout the trial, I note anything significant that has happened that I want to use in closing. I review this list as I prepare.

The starting point for your closing is your opening. You should be hitting the same themes that you hit during opening and showing the jury that you proved what you said you would prove, and that your opponent did not. There are many nuances in a trial that may be lost on a jury. They may not have known why one piece of testimony was important. They may not have understood the importance of a letter or a document. Something may be depicted in a photograph that is in evidence that has not been brought into focus. Your job is to take all of these things and weave them together to tell a story.

You remind the jury of what people said on the witness stand. You comment on admissions in cross-examination. You call into question the credibility of witnesses where necessary. But do not overdo it. For example, I almost never come right out and say a witness is lying, unless it has been proven beyond a doubt. If you overreach and say a witness is lying when it is not clear, the jury may give the witness the benefit of the doubt. But, if you point out the inconsistencies in his or her testimony, the members of the jury can draw their own conclusions.

I believe it is important to talk about the jury charge in your closing. By the time of closing arguments, you will have had your charge conference and will know what the jury charge will be. But the jury does not know this. One way you can enhance your credibility is to predict what the judge's instruction on a particular issue will be. Then, when the judge instructs the jury just the way you "predicted," it will enhance your credibility. Along the way, I put the important jury instructions on the screen. Seeing them in black and white as the law that will be given makes it seem more important, and if the law is good for you, wrap yourself in it during your closing argument. This way, you and the judge are telling the jury the same thing and you are telling them that that means your client wins.

Freely use demonstratives during closing. Bring your closing to life with photographs, blowups, graphics, and the like. This will keep the jury engaged and focused. But, most of all, you have to make the jury want to rule in your favor. Dry charts, science, and technicalities will not do it. You have to bring to life why it matters and why your side should win.

Also remember the burden of proof. If you are the plaintiff, embrace your burden and confidently argue you have met it. In civil cases it is easy to demonstrate the preponderance of the evidence standard as one grain of sand tipping the scales of justice. Use analogies like that to help the jury understand that you win the very close case if you just barely tip the scales in your favor.

On the defense side, use the burden of proof as a shield. Build up the burden to appear as heavy as possible. I like to focus the burden of proof on each individual element. Often the plaintiff can prove many elements fairly easily. But, usually, there are one or more with which they struggle. Make the jury understand that if they fall short on any one thing they have to prove, then you win. I have found this can be a very powerful argument in cases, which is often overlooked.

These are but a few tips. I strongly recommend that you watch as many trials as possible and read books and articles on the art of closing argument. It is truly an art not a science and one that must be practiced.

PRESERVING THE RECORD

Just a quick note on preserving the record at trial. Trial lawyers often are so caught up in winning their case they forget to preserve the record for appeal. I find it helpful to have a member of your team be charged purely with protecting the record on appeal. This way they can remind you not to forget things along the way. Remember to object timely to improper evidence and argument. Preserve all issues in your Judgment as a Matter of Law motion(s). Make offers of proof if your evidence is not admitted. File written objections where appropriate, if you are concerned they are not on the record. Preserve, preserve, preserve.

INDEX

28 U.S.C. § 1404(a), venue, 41–42

A

ABA Litigation Section Conference, 140
ABA Section of Litigation, 131
accident scene inspection, informal discovery, 97
Act of State Doctrine, 40
admissibility test, 35–36
Advisory Committee Notes, 141
aerial photographs, 120–21
Age Discrimination in Employment Act, 153
agents, litigation holds, 56
Allstate Ins. Co. v. Hague (1981), 33, 34
Americans with Disabilities Act, 153
American Tort Reform Foundation (ATRF), 36
Anderson v. Liberty Lobby, Inc. (1986), 134–35, 135n28
Aristotle, 113, 114, 122
Arizona, 156
Article III, standing, 29–31
attorney's fees
    allowance and determination, 157
    costs and, 149
    costs and Rule 68, 153–54
    Texas Rule 167, 158
Auxer v. Alcoa Inc. (2011), 42

B

Banco Nacional de Cuba v. Sabbatino (1964), 40
Batson challenge, 209
BEEDOCS.com, Timeline 3D, 126
believability standard, 132
Bell Atlantic v. Twombly (2007), 35, 90
Bevill factors, corporate privilege, 10n10
Bing, informal discovery, 96
blatant contradiction, 133, 133n16
Bristol-Myers, jurisdiction, 28
burdens of production and persuasion, summary
    judgment, 135–36

C

California Supreme Court, 28–29, 30
case assessment
    costs of prosecution or defense, 106–7
    for defendant's side, 109–10
    dispute resolution, 110–11
    early investigation, 99–101
    initial interview, 101–3
    litigation strategy, 110
    for plaintiff's side, 107–9
    preparation, 103–4
    theme of case, 105
    work-up and analysis, 104–7

case management
    PowerPoint, 123–25
    timelines and chronologies, 123–28
Celotex Corp. v. Catrett (1986), 134–37, 141, 142
chronologies, case management, 123–28
civil liability, spoliation, 48–49
Class Action Fairness Act of 2005 (CAFA), 29, 31
client responsibility, litigation holds, 68
clients, determination of, 2
closing arguments, 213–14
Cloud, good information management practices, 79
common interest agreements, 17
communication, litigation holds, 53
compliance, litigation holds and, 67–68
Comprehensive Environmental Response, Compensation,
    and Liability Act (CERCLA), 80–81
confidentiality
    privilege vs., 10–11
    report of investigation, 3–4
    see also privilege
Conflicts of Laws, Restatement of, 33
cooperation credit
    mandated disclosures, 17
    voluntary waiver of privilege for, 15–17
Cordoba v. Dillard's, Inc. (2005), 139
corporate *Miranda* warnings, 9–11
corporation, *Upjohn* warnings, 9–11
costs
    attorneys' fees and, 149, 153–54, 157
    under Rule 68, 153–54
counsel
    in-house, 24
    opposing, 24
    witness access to, 14
court records, informal discovery, 97
credibility
    attacking, of experts, 164
    expert qualifications and, 170–71
    of eyewitnesses, 168–69
critical witness deposition, 161–63
    chart showing qualifications of conflicting experts,
        169–71
    checklists to reveal or impeach, 171–72
    collecting factual admissions from lay witnesses,
        168–69
    consistency in deponent portrayal, 173
    credibility of eye witness, 168–69
    definitions and credibility of experts, 164
    definitions underlying expert opinions, 165–66
    demanding definitions from lay and expert witnesses,
        163–67
    ending with a bang, 176
    experts and definition changes, 166
    fitting witness into story, 173–74
    identifying assumption by expert witness, 167–68
    making good television, 172–76
    neurological timeline, 176, 177

critical witness deposition (*continued*)
    qualifications and credibility, 170–71
    staging, 174–75
    steps for designing strategy, 162–63
    transforming definition into visual target for expert,
        166–67
    use of props and visuals, 175
    use of timeline, 176
Cuban government, 40
custodians
    identifying additional, 65, 74
    litigation holds, 54–56
    scope of preservation questions, 61–62

D

Daubert v. Merrell Dow Pharmaceuticals (1993), 35
defendant, case assessment, 109–10
demonstrative exhibits
    simplifying messages, 120–22
    trial preparation, 212–13, 214
deposition(s)
    demonstrative exhibits simplifying messages, 120–22
    discovery plans, 114–15
    every, as trial deposition, 115–16
    simplifying questions during, 117
    steps to designing strategy, 162–63
    use under Texas Rule of Civil Procedure Rule 202,
        95–96
    see also critical witness deposition
discovery, 88
    being proactive in, 85
    building a plan, 80–84
    computers and, 77–78
    creating a production plan, 83
    documents cutting off endgame, 82–83
    expedited, 89
    finding a translator, 84–85
    good information management practices, 79
    identifying offensive needs in case, 80–81
    informal, 96–97
    judges and, 86
    mediating after, 22–23
    planning, consistency, and transparency, 78–79
    points for resisting, 86–87
    pre-discovery conferences, 181
    preparing requests, 181–82
    preparing responses, 182–83
    preservation, collection, and review issues, 81–82
    pre-suit, 89
    pre-suit discovery allowable under Rule 27, 91–93
    protection orders and privilege logs, 83–84
    state rules allowing pre-suit, 93–96
    see also e-discovery; motion to compel
discovery motions, educating the court, 179–80
discovery rule, 101
discovery sanctions, for spoliation, 45–48
discovery themes
    action words in questions, 118–19
    asking "duty" and "no lose" questions, 119
    demonstrative exhibits for simplifying messages,
        120–22
    effective trial themes, 113–14
    every deposition as trial deposition, 115–16
    plans for, 114–15

simplicity for, 116–17
    simplifying questions during depositions, 117
dismissal, case, based on venue, 41–42
dispute resolution
    litigation and, 110–11
    meet and confer requirements, 184
doctrine of forum non conveniens, 41–42
document preservation, 49–50
    legal scope of, 56–58
    nuts and bolts of, 59–63
    practical scope of, 58–59
    questions for custodians, 61–62
    questions for IT and records management personnel,
        62–63
due process clause, 34–35

E

early mediation, 21–22
e-discovery, 77–78, 88
    computers and, 77–78
    cutting off endgame, 82–83
    finding a translator, 84–85
    good information management practices, 79
    judges and, 86
    planning, consistency, and transparency, 78–79
    points for resisting, 86–87
    privilege logs, 83–84
    proactive disclosure, 85
    protective orders, 83–84
    technology-assisted review (TAR), 83, 85
    see also discovery
Eighth Circuit Court, 152
electronically stored information (ESI), 46
    amended Rule 37(e) for, 47–48
    avoiding inadvertent destruction of, 65, 73
    document collection, 106
    retention of, 65, 72
Eleventh Circuit Court of Appeals, 132
ethos, 113, 114
Evidence Rule 904, case management, 124–25
exhibits
    demonstrative, 212–13, 214
    selection for trial, 211–12
expert discovery, mediating after, 23
eyewitness credibility, 168–69

F

Facebook
    e-discovery, 77, 78
    informal discovery, 96–97
facts
    material, 133–34
    mediating after discovery, 22–23
Fair Labor Standards Act (FLSA), 153, 154
Federal Judicial Center, 103, 135, 135n30, 138
Federal Rules Advisory Committee, 52
Federal Rules of Civil Procedure, 46
    case plan for discovery, 80–84
    Rule 4 for serving notice, 92
    Rule 11(a) pleading, 100
    Rule 11(b), 100, 101
    Rule 11(c), 91
    Rule 12(b), 155

Rule 16, 81
Rule 16(b), 58
Rule 26(b), 57
Rule 26(f), 55, 58–59
Rule 27, 90–93
Rule 34, 90, 187
Rule 35, 90
Rule 37, 46, 59, 82
Rule 37(a), 189
Rule 37(c), 185–86, 187
Rule 56, 103, 139, 143n55, 147–48
Rule 56(a), 147
Rule 56(b), 138, 147
Rule 56(c), 141, 147
Rule 56(d), 138, 144–45, 148
Rule 56(e), 148
Rule 56(f), 148
Rule 56(g), 148
Rule 56(h), 148
Rule 68, 150–51, 155, 157
Fegley v. Higgins (1994), 153
final trial preparation
    case themes, 206
    closing arguments, 213–14
    demonstrative exhibits, 212–13
    exhibit selection, 211–12
    judgments as matter of law, 213
    legal issues, 205
    motions in limine, 207–8
    preparing opening statement in advance, 208
    preserving the record, 215
    responsibilities, 206–7
    voir dire, 208–10
    witness selection and preparation, 210–11
Florida Supreme Court, 157
focus groups
    analysis of trial themes, 195–98
    deliberations, 196–97
    interpreting results of, 198–99
    questioning recruited participants, 196
    real-time feedback, 196
    self-fulfilling prophecy, 203
    testing witness credibility, 197
    timing of, 199
forum non conveniens, doctrine of, 41–42
forums for litigation
    factors affecting, 32–37
    moving for dismissal or transfer, 41–42
    removal for preferred forum, 37–40
    variations in judges, juries, and judicial efficiencies,
        36–37
    variations in procedural rules, 35–36
    variations in substantive law among, 33–35
Fourth Circuit Court, 152, 153
Freedom of Information Act (FOIA) requests, informal
        discovery, 97
Frye standard, 36

G

genuine dispute, summary judgment, 132–33
Google, 94, 96
Google Earth, 97
Grable & Sons Metal Prods., Inc. v. Darue Eng'g & Mfg.
    (2005), 39–40

H

Harlan, John M. (Justice), 40
hearing
    summary judgment, 145
    Texas Rule of Civil Procedure Rule 202, 95
Hippocrates, 3
How Judges Think (Posner), 141

I

informal discovery
    court records, 97
    FOIA requests, 97
    inspecting scene of accident, 97
    Internet, 96–97
    simple interviews, 97
    Westlaw/Lexis, 97
    see also discovery
information management practices, discovery and, 79
information technology (IT), scope of preservation
        questions, 62–63
inherent power, spoliation sanctions, 46
in-house counsel, mediation, 24
In re City of Dallas (2016), 94
In re Doe (2011), 94
internal investigations, 1, 17
    circulation and control of final report, 14–15
    client determination, 2
    compelling witness participation, 13
    creating transcripts, 12–13
    disclosure of report of, 15
    editing ability for report, 5
    establishing privilege, 9–11
    ethical requirements for dealing with witnesses,
        11–12
    independence of investigation team, 4–5
    intended recipients of report, 3–4
    joint defense/common interest agreements, 17
    mandate of, 2–3
    privilege implications of report, 15
    protecting notes of witness interviews, 12
    recording interviews, 12–13
    special procedures for, 5–6
    threshold issues, 2–9
    Upjohn warnings, 9–11
    voluntary waiver of privilege to earn cooperation
        credit, 15–17
    waiver of privileges, 15
    whistleblowers, 6–9
    witness access to counsel, 14
    work papers and drafts of report, 14
Internet, informal discovery, 96–97
interviews
    informal discovery, 97
    recording, 12–13
investigations. *See* internal investigations
Iqbal v. Ashcroft (2009), 35, 90

J

joint defense, 17
judgments as a matter of law, 213, 215
judicial efficiencies, 37
judicial hellholes, 36

jurisdiction
    judges favoring plaintiffs, 36–37
    judicial hellholes, 36
    personal, 28–29
    state courts, 29n10
    subject matter, 29
juror
    attention span of, 116
    demographics of jury pool, 195
    questionnaires for, 200–201
jury consultant(s)
    caveats and limitations of, 202–3
    focus groups, 195–97
    jury questionnaires, 200–201
    jury selection, 193–94, 201–2, 209
    role of, 194
    shadow jurors, 202
    variations on theme, 202
    voir dire, 209
jury selection, 193–94, 201–2, 209

L

LaPierre v. City of Lawrence (2016), 152
litigation
    dispute resolution and, 110–11
    factors affecting forum for case, 32–37
    personal jurisdiction, 28–29
    rules prescribing, 27–32
    standing, 29–31
    subject matter jurisdiction, 29
    venue, 31–32
    see also forums for litigation
litigation hold(s)
    agents, 56
    amended Rule 37(e), 47–48
    client responsibility, 68
    communicating orally and in writing, 53
    concept of, 43–44, 69
    contents of written, 64–65
    custodians, 54–56
    discovery sanctions for spoliation, 45–48
    document preservation saving clients' money,
        49–50
    identifying recipients of, 54–56
    loss of evidence helping client's claims or
        defenses, 49
    mock, memorandum, 70–75
    monitoring compliance, 67–68
    preparing to write, 50–53
    privilege and, 66–67, 73
    purpose of, 44–45
    scope of preservation, 56–63
    service providers, 56
    spoliation causes of action, 48–49
    third party consultants, 56
    timing for, 50–51
    triggering duty to preserve, 52–53
    writing, 64–67
    written, and privilege, 66–67
    see also mock litigation hold memorandum
logos, 113, 114

M

mandate, defining, in internal investigation, 2–3
Marek v. Chesny (1985), 151–52
Massachusetts, General Law Chapter 93A, 30–31
material facts, summary judgment, 133–34
Matsushita Elec. Indus. Co. v. Zenith Radio Corp.
    (1986), 134, 135, 142
mediation, 19–20, 25
    after completion of fact discovery/investigation,
        20, 22–23
    after expert discovery, 20, 23
    early, 19, 21–22
    early(ish), 20, 22
    false belief in summary judgment, 25
    in-house counsel, 24
    just prior to trial, 20, 23–24
    opposing counsel, 24
    phobias about giving away too much, 25
    pre-suit, 19, 20–21
Mississippi, state rules and statutes, 155–56
mock litigation hold memorandum, 64, 70–75
    avoiding inadvertent destruction of documents,
        65, 73
    distribution list, 65, 75
    documents and electronically stored information
        (ESI) for retention, 65, 72
    identifying additional custodians, 65, 74
    introduction, 64, 70–71
    no discussions with unauthorized persons,
        65, 73
    protecting privilege, 65, 73
    relevant documents, 64–65, 71–72
    subject matter, 64, 71
    see also litigation hold(s)
mock trials, 198
    interpreting results of, 198–99
    self-fulfilling prophecy, 203
    timing of, 199
Model Rule of Professional Conduct 1.13(f), 11
Model Rule of Professional Responsibility 4.3, 11, 13
models, delivering simple messages, 122
motion. *See* summary judgment
motion in limine, 183, 207–8
motion to compel
    arguing, 190–91
    considerations before filing, 185–86
    creating win/win scenarios, 186–87
    developing the record, 180
    establishing relevance, 183–84
    handling failures to respond, 188
    implications of ruling on, 192
    meet and confer requirements, 184
    pre-discovery conferences, 181
    preparing, 188–90
    preparing discovery requests, 181–82
    preparing discovery responses, 182–83
    salvaging victory from defeat, 191
Mullenix, Linda S. (Professor), 135–36, 141

N

neurological timeline, 176, 177

O

offer(s)
attorney's fees, 153–54, 157
balancing litigation, 149
construction and interpretation of terms, 157
costs, 153–54, 157, 159
favorability of, compared to judgment, 154
requisites and sufficiency of, 151–53
Rule 68 for offer of judgment, 150–51
state rules and statutes, 155–56
Texas Rules of Civil Procedure Rule 167, 158–59
time limitations, 156
using for judgment strategically, 155, 159
opening statement, preparing in advance, 208
opposing counsel, mediation, 24
order, Texas Rule of Civil Procedure Rule 202, 95

P

pathos, 113, 114
personal jurisdiction, litigation rules, 28–29
Phillips Petroleum Co. v. Shutts (1985), 34
phobias, 25
photographs
aerial, 121
delivering simple messages, 120–21
Piper Aircraft v. Reyno (1981), 33, 42
plaintiff, case assessment, 107–9
plausibility standard, 35
Plavix, marketing, 28
Posner, Richard (Judge), 141–42
PowerPoint, case management, 123–25
preparation. *See* final trial preparation
pre-suit mediation, 20–21
pre-trial mediation, 23–24
primary purpose test, courts applying, 10
privilege
confidentiality vs., 10–11
corporate, 10n10
implications with disclosure of report, 15
logs in discovery, 83–84
protection of, 65, 73
report of investigation, 3–4
Upjohn warnings, 9–11
voluntary waiver of, 15–17
waiver of, 15
written litigation holds and, 66–67, 73
procedural rules, variations by forum, 35–36
props, depositions, 175
protections
interviews and transcripts, 12–13
whistleblowers, 6–9
witness interview notes, 12

Q

questions
action words for, 118–19
asking "duty" and "no lose," 119
bland vs. interesting, 118
complicated vs. simple, 117
simplifying during depositions, 117

R

Radecki v. Amoco Oil Co. (1988), 152
Readers Digest (periodical), 200
reasonable and proportional, legal scope of preservation, 58
recipients, report of investigation, 3–4
records management personnel, scope of preservation questions, 62–63
relevance
establishing, 183–84
legal scope of preservation, 56–58
litigation hold, 64–65, 71–72
removal
federal jurisdiction, 38n51, 40n73
moving cases to preferred forum, 37–40
report of investigation
circulation and control of final, 14–15
confidentiality or privileged nature of, 3–4
intended recipients of, 3–4
labeling work papers and drafts of, 14
review and editing of, 5
Rogers, Will, 113
Rule(s)
Mississippi state rules and statutes, 155–56
Rules of Evidence, 207
Texas Rules of Civil Procedure, Rule 167, 158–59
Texas Rule of Civil Procedure Rule 202, 93–96
see also Federal Rules of Civil Procedure

S

Saunders v. Wire Rope Corp. (1991), 38–39
Scalia, Antonin (Justice), 132
Scheduling Conference, Rule 16(b), 58
scope of preservation
legal, 56–58
nuts and bolts of, 59–63
practical, as Rule 26(f) conference, 58–59
questions for client's IT and records management personnel, 62–63
questions for custodians, 61–62
relevant, reasonable, and proportional, 56–58
Scott v. Harris (2007), 132, 133
Sedona Conference, 52
service providers, litigation holds, 56
settlement, phobias about giving away too much, 25
Seventh Amendment, summary judgment and, 145n65
sexual assault, victims of, 5–6
shadow jurors, 202
Sinochem v. Int'l Co. v. Malay Int'l Shipping Co. (2007), 42
Sixth Circuit Court, 154
social networking, informal discovery, 96
Song-Beverly Credit Card Act, 31
Speedy Trial Act, 142
Spokeo, Inc. v. Robins (2016), 30–31
spoliation
causes of action, 48–49
definition of, 45
discovery sanctions for, 45–48
inherent power sanctions, 46
Rule 37, 45

spoliator, 49
standing, litigation rules, 29–31
state rules, allowing pre-suit discovery, 93–96
Stevens, John Paul (Justice), 34–35, 132
subject matter jurisdiction, litigation rules, 29
substantive law, variations by forum, 33–35
summary judgment
    burdens of production and persuasion on, 135–36
    cost of filing, 137–38
    decision to file, 137–38
    description of, 130–31
    false belief in, 25
    genuine dispute, 132–33
    hearing request, 145
    judges deciding, 141–43
    material facts, 133–34
    motion for partial, 143–44
    motions for, 129–30
    moving for, 139–41, 146
    opposing, 144–45
    orders establishing facts for case, 143–44
    Rule 56, 147–48
    rules governing, 36
    simplicity, 139–41
    standard, 131–34
    term, 129
    timing for filing a motion, 138–39
    trilogy of Supreme Court cases for, 134–37
Supreme Court, 34–35
    precedent on standing, 30
    Scott v. Harris (2007), 132, 133
    trilogy of decisions for summary judgment, 134–37
Susman, Steve, 140, 140n48

T

TC Heartland LLC v. Kraft Foods Group Brands LLC
    (2017), 32
technology-assisted review (TAR), e-discovery, 83, 85
Telephone Consumer Protection Act, 31
television, staging depositions, 172–76
testimony, blatant contradiction, 133, 133n16
Texas, choosing forum, 36
Texas Rule of Civil Procedure Rule 202
    hearing and order, 95
    law, 93–94
    practical approach, 94–95
    use of deposition in, 95–96
Texas Rules of Civil Procedure, Rule 167, 158–59
third party consultants, litigation holds, 56
time limitations, offers, 156
Timeline 3D from BEEDOCS.com, 126
timelines
    case management, 123–28
    neurological, for deposition, 176, 177
    PowerPoint, 123–25
    Timeline 3D from BEEDOCS.com, 126
Title 28, subject matter jurisdiction, 29
topographic models, delivering simple messages, 122

toys, delivering simple messages, 122
transcripts, creating, of interviews, 12–13
transfer, moving case based on venue, 41–42
translator, e-discovery and, 84–85
trial preparation. *See* final trial preparation
Truman, Harry S., 179
Truth in Lending Act, 31
Tulane University's School of Architecture, 175

U

Upjohn Co. v. United States (1981), 9
Upjohn warnings
    court split on former employees, 10n9
    internal investigations, 9–11
    protections, 9n8
U.S. Department of Justice (DOJ), Yates memo, 15–16

V

venue, litigation rules for, 31–32
video screen, delivering simple messages, 121–22
Virginia, choosing forum, 36–37
visuals, depositions, 175
voir dire, 113, 149, 194, 197, 200, 208–10

W

Wallace v. SMC Pneumatics, Inc. (1997), 142
Wall Street Journal (newspaper), 200
Westlaw/Lexis, informal discovery, 97
whistleblowers
    duty to cooperate, 8n5
    federal statutes, 6n3
    involvement of, 6–9
    protections, 8–9n6
    state statutes, 6–7n4
win/win scenarios, creating, 186–87
witnesses
    access to counsel, 14
    collecting factual admissions from lay, 168–69
    compelling participation, 13
    ethical requirements for dealing with, 11–12
    eyewitness credibility, 168–69
    protecting notes of interviews, 12
    selection and preparation, 210–11
    see also critical witness deposition

Y

Yahoo, informal discovery, 96
Yates memo
    cooperation credit, 16
    joint defense/common interest agreements, 17

Z

Zubulake v. UBS Warburg, LLC (2003), 81–82